JOURNEYS OF FAITH

EVANGELICALISM, EASTERN ORTHODOXY, CATHOLICISM, AND ANGLICANISM

ROBERT L. PLUMMER, GENERAL EDITOR

ZONDERVAN®

ZONDERVAN.com/
AUTHORTRACKER
follow your favorite authors

We want to hear from you. Please send your comments about this book to us in care of zreview@zondervan.com. Thank you.

ZONDERVAN

Journeys of Faith
Copyright © 2012 by Robert Plummer

This title is also available as a Zondervan ebook. Visit www.zondervan.com/ebooks.

Requests for information should be addressed to:

Zondervan, *Grand Rapids, Michigan 49530*

Library of Congress Cataloging-in-Publication Data

Journeys of faith : evangelicalism, Eastern Orthodoxy, Catholicism, and Anglicanism / Robert L. Plummer, general editor.
    p.   cm.
    Includes bibliographical references (p. 225–256).
    ISBN 978-0-310-33120-9 (softcover)
    1. Ex-church members—Protestant churches—Religious life. 2. Orthodox Eastern converts—United States. 3. Catholic converts—United States. 4. Anglican converts—United States. I. Plummer, Robert L. (Robert Lewis), 1971–
BV4930.J68   2012
248.2'4—dc23   2011038435

Cover design: Micah Kandros Design
Interior design: Sherri L. Hoffman

Printed in the United States of America

---

12 13 14 15 16 17 /DCI/ 22 21 20 19 18 17 16 15 14 13 12 11 10 9 8 7 6 5 4 3 2 1

A very important book. Members of these different traditions often badly misunderstand each other. *Journeys of Faith* illuminates differences between them that do and don't matter, fostering crucial mutual understandings in service of Christian fellowship and unity. Deserves a very wide reading.

—CHRISTIAN SMITH,
author of *The Bible Made Impossible*

This important book will address a hidden issue in many religious communities: moving between churches. Many materials available are uselessly partisan to help or hopelessly compromised on the issues that divide Christendom. This book contains charitable but firm discussion by converts who understand the issues and never avoid controversy. At the same time, these are leaders that are charitable in their public presentations. I will be using this book for years.

—JOHN MARK REYNOLDS,
Professor of Philosophy, Biola University

This book is not so much about conversion as it is about conviction. Each of the contributors speaks with candor and passion, but also with charity, about the particular pilgrimage of faith that has led them to claim a home within the body of Christ. This is ecumenism at its best!

—TIMOTHY GEORGE,
Dean and Professor of Divinity, Beeson Divinity School;
General Editor of the *Reformation Commentary on Scripture*

Religious conversions often leave the converted unable to speak objectively about what they have left behind or to recognize flaws in the religion to which they have moved. The contributors to this unusually illuminating collection are different. Its personal accounts of conversions are well-balanced, informative, and also charitable to the faith position left behind. Extra attractions in the book are comments added by critics who challenge the necessity of converting, and then helpful rejoinders from the converted. For a subject that regularly generates considerable heat, this is a book full of the best kind of light.

—MARK A. NOLL,
author of *Protestantism: A Very Short Introduction*

Too often, books about personal conversion turn into angry diatribes. *Journeys of Faith* is just the opposite. The four authors relate their stories with genuine respect for the churches they left, even as they tell us—often with touching honesty—why they moved into a new communion. If you have ever wondered, "Why in the world would someone become *that* type of Christian?" this book provides the answer.

—BRYAN M. LITFIN,
Professor of Theology, Moody Bible Institute

A frank and respectful exchange of ideas and convictions from across the Christian spectrum, *Journeys of Faith* is a mesmerizing instance of ecumenism at its finest.

—MICHAEL P. FOLEY,
Associate Professor of Patristics,
Honors College, Baylor University

*To my mother and father,
people of conviction and grace*

CONTENTS

❧

Foreword

Scot McKnight

Evangelicalism prides itself on personal testimonies, and rare it is to find an Evangelical who doesn't well up inside when someone tells a story of conversion. So proud are we of conversions into the faith—and by that we often mean the Evangelical faith, and not just the Christian faith—that we are prone to accept anyone who makes the claim. Sometimes we clap our hands for people who are hoodwinking us, and sometimes we don't pause long enough to see if the person really is a convert.

But when one of our own "converts" from Evangelicalism to Catholicism, Eastern Orthodoxy, or even the much more liturgically shaped Anglicanism, we can feel like a mother or father whose child has chosen to join another family, and we can genuinely wonder about the salvation of the other person. The pain many such converts have experienced at the hands of their former Evangelical friends—and stories of pain have been told well by many of these converts—reveals just how violently many Evangelicals can respond to such conversions. You see, we Evangelicals may not always think we've got everything right, but we do tend to think that we are the "rightest" when it comes to theology and especially the necessity of the new birth. I'm speaking now for a group, and sometimes I don't agree with the group. But the one thing we are sure of is that the necessity of personal salvation is our singular emphasis, so when someone leaves us, it disturbs us and makes us wonder more about the convert than it does about the faith we affirm.

Conversions by former Evangelicals to Catholicism, Orthodoxy, and Anglicanism are more common today than they were even twenty years ago. I sometimes watch the Catholic-based TV series *Journey Home* hosted by Marcus Grodi on EWTN. That show tells stories of people, mostly former Evangelicals, who have become Catholic, and one night when I was watching, it featured the story of one of my former students! I know of no such media coverage for the Orthodox nor for Anglicans, but I know there are many migrating from Wheaton (Evangelicalism) to Rome (Catholicism) or Canterbury (Anglicanism) or Constantinople (Orthodoxy). As a professional conversion chronicler (you can read my work in *Turning to Jesus* or *Finding Faith, Losing Faith*, coauthored with Hauna Ondrey), I can be more intrigued by these stories than I am chagrined, but I do have to confess that each time I read such a conversion away from Evangelicalism, I'm grieved that either we have failed our own or they are mistaken in the conversion. Perhaps my years of studying conversions has blunted the grief, but this book has reawakened for me the reality of how many are responding to stories of migration from Evangelicalism into churches or communions both theologically and socially other.

I am therefore happy to commend this frank, sometimes hard-hitting, and at other times proselytizing discussion between those who have migrated and those who in one way or another want to call them back to their Evangelical roots.

Is this anything to worry about? It depends. If you are worried that Evangelicalism is getting thinner theologically and that such superficiality is leading some into more robust theological traditions, then you've got something to worry about. If you are worried about numbers, they are still on the side of Evangelicals: more convert to Evangelicalism than away from it into Catholic, Orthodox, and Anglican churches. But I will tell you this story: Once a professor wrote and asked to meet with me. He asked me not to mention our meeting to my friends who taught at his school, because my name was connected to fair-minded descriptions of the stories of migrations out of Evangelicalism and not enough to apologetic warnings against those who were migrating. We met and he promptly told me that conversions to one of the three great liturgical traditions of the church had become an epidemic at his school. He asked me to help him understand what was going on. His question was this: "Is there something wrong with us?"

This book, I think, will help us better understand the surge in migrations away from Evangelicalism. It will also, I pray, help us to think more biblically and theologically about what we believe.

ACKNOWLEDGMENTS

✂

Robert L. Plummer

It has been said that it takes a village to raise a child. It certainly took many people to produce the book you hold in your hands. I want to begin by expressing appreciation to the trustees and administrators of the Southern Baptist Theological Seminary, where I am enabled to pursue my twin passions of teaching and writing about the Bible. Thanks also to my fellow elders at Sojourn Community Church who encouraged me in this project—especially Mike Cosper and Daniel Montgomery. To the contributors to this book, who gave generously of their knowledge and time, thank you. Also, thanks to Scot McKnight for his gracious words in the foreword. To the library staff at Southern Seminary, I am grateful for your consistently speedy and helpful assistance. Special thanks to Paul Roberts and Ben Gantt. Great appreciation is due the competent and gracious staff at Zondervan. I worked with too many people to name, but I would be remiss not to mention Paul Engle, David Frees, Ryan Pazdur, Jesse Hillman, Brian Phipps, Robin Schmitt, and Madison Trammel. Southern Seminary student Matt Smethurst did quite a bit of proofreading on drafts of this book, and I am amazed at his ability to detect even the smallest variation in spacing. Philip Van Steenburgh also read through a set of the proofs and corrected errors. Behind my public ministry stand my wife and children. To Chandi, Sarah Beth, Chloe, and Bella—thank you for being such a wonderful family and for encouraging me in the work to which God has called me. Finally, to my father and mother, Paul and Sonja Plummer (to whom this volume is dedicated)—you are people who model firm belief in the truth while treating others with exemplary compassion. I'm so thankful that God blessed me with you as my parents.

INTRODUCTION

✥

Robert L. Plummer

A few years ago I was working in my office when I received an unexpected email from a former student. John[1] explained that he had cheated on some quizzes in my Greek class. This admission, in itself, was no surprise. I receive about one such confession per semester. What did surprise me, however, was the motivation behind John's repentance.

"I am joining the Greek Orthodox Church," he wrote, "and part of that process is to make a lifetime confession — confessing every sin that I can consciously recall and making amends, if possible."

I promptly wrote back to John, assuring him that I forgave him and encouraging him that his expression of repentance likely indicated that the Holy Spirit was working in his life.

John and I have kept in touch intermittently. After completing studies at an Eastern Orthodox seminary, he was ordained as a deacon, and shortly thereafter as a priest. In his Facebook photo, he sports a bushy beard and flowing black garments. It's hard to believe that he is the same youthful student I recall from class.

John's story illustrates a growing phenomenon. In the last several years, I have observed several Evangelical seminary students or church members convert to Eastern Orthodoxy, Catholicism,[2] or various other Christian traditions normally viewed as quite distant from Evangelical practice and belief.[3] In responding to questions that members in my church raised about these conversions, I became aware that there were not many helpful books on this phenomenon. Gradually it became clear to me that a book was needed which would accomplish several goals:

1. To help Evangelicals understand why persons are leaving their churches for Christian traditions which are more liturgical.
2. To help Evangelical leaders in responding to questions from church members who are attracted to liturgical Christian traditions.
3. To help non-Evangelicals, such as Catholic and Orthodox Christians, in understanding why persons have departed their traditions for Evangelicalism, why some Evangelicals are now moving in the other direction, and what fundamental differences remain between Evangelical and non-Evangelical communities.

Below I will briefly elaborate on these issues and introduce the writers who will help answer them. But first we need to clarify what we mean by *Evangelical* and *liturgical*.

DEFINITIONS: *EVANGELICAL AND LITURGICAL*

In a famous 1964 Supreme Court case on pornography, Justice Potter Steward stated that though he could not technically define pornography, "I know what it is when I see it." Similarly, many persons in the broader culture may not be able to define Evangelicalism, but they are confident that they can recognize an Evangelical when they see one. As the stories in this book concern movement away from or toward Evangelicalism, however, it is essential that we not simply assume the meaning of the word *Evangelical*. British historian David Bebbington has possibly given us the best current-day understanding of the debated term. In his influential 1989 monograph *Evangelicalism in Modern Britain: A History from the 1730s to the 1980s*, Bebbington identifies four essential characteristics of Evangelicalism:

1. *Conversionism*—a belief that all persons need to experience repentance and spiritual rebirth to come into relationship with God
2. *Activism*—an expectation that all genuine Christians will be gathering together regularly and promoting their faith through word and deed
3. *Biblicism*—a high regard for the Bible's authority and trustworthiness

4. *Crucicentrism*—an emphasis on the necessity and efficacy of Jesus' death to save sinners[4]

So our main concern in this book is with Evangelicals (persons having the characteristics above) shifting ecclesiastical allegiance to Catholic, Eastern Orthodox, and Anglican Christian traditions. These traditions are distinct from one another, but they also share a common commitment to a more liturgical expression of the Christian faith. By "liturgical," I mean that the organization and practices of such churches are typically more hierarchical, formal, and self-consciously submitted to hundreds of years of postbiblical tradition. Though the term *liturgical* is potentially confusing, it is arguably the best one to express the common way these three Christian traditions differ from Evangelicalism. At this point, a few readers are surely wondering if it is appropriate to include Anglicanism alongside Eastern Orthodoxy and Catholicism—especially since Anglicanism, in some expressions, espouses a thoroughly Evangelical theology. While this observation is true, the history of prominent "free church" Evangelicals walking "the Canterbury trail" is a phenomenon which fits naturally in this conversation.[5]

I will now briefly introduce three of the main questions that this book seeks to answer.

Why Are Persons Leaving Evangelical Churches?

The Pew Forum on Religion & Public Life reports, "Americans change religion early and often. In total, about half of American adults have changed religious affiliation at least once during their lives."[6] Traditionally, Evangelicals have been on the receiving end of these conversions.[7] Catholic and mainline Protestant churches often lament losses to the Evangelical world. In a recent article of the *National Catholic Reporter*, Thomas Reese writes, "One out of every 10 Americans is an ex-Catholic. If they were a separate denomination, they would be the third-largest denomination in the United States, after Catholics and Baptists. One of three people who were raised Catholic no longer identifies as Catholic.... The Catholic church is hemorrhaging members. It needs to acknowledge this and do more to understand why. Only if we acknowledge the exodus and understand it will we be in a position to do something about it."[8] Indeed, the story of Chris Castaldo in this volume (with a response from Notre Dame professor Brad Gregory) illustrates the widely attested migration of Catholics to Evangelicalism.

A new form of spiritual migration, however, is gradually being recognized. Evangelicals are moving in the other direction — joining Catholic, Eastern Orthodox, and Anglican churches.[9] As I have discussed this book project with students at the Evangelical seminary where I teach, almost every student to whom I have spoken knows at least one person who is joining or is attracted to a more liturgical Christian tradition. Inevitably, in these short conversations, puzzled students ask, "Why are people converting?" Speculations quickly follow. Aesthetics? A desire for deeper roots in church history? Perhaps the superficiality of many Evangelical churches is driving members away?

One of the benefits of this book is that it does not present Evangelicals speculating on why persons are moving to liturgical traditions. Instead the very persons who have made such spiritual pilgrimages are allowed to explain in their own words what attracted them to their new faith commitments. These stories are meant not to be used but to be received (that is, to be listened to). C. S. Lewis famously distinguished between these two radically different ways of reading: "The first reading of some literary work is often, to the literary [that is, "careful reader"], so momentous that only experiences of love, religion, or bereavement can furnish a standard of comparison. Their whole consciousness is changed. They have become what they were not before. But there is no sign of anything like this among the other sort of readers. When they have finished the story or the novel, nothing much, or nothing at all, seems to have happened to them."[10]

We must confess that we often fail to measure up to Lewis's description of the careful reader. We are superficial listeners. We quickly apply our preconceived notions to a dilemma rather than seeking to arrive at a new, deeper, and more accurate understanding. It is my hope that persons reading this book will listen carefully to the persons who have converted to new faith traditions and will truly seek to understand the motivation behind such spiritual journeys.

Persons who recount their faith pilgrimages in this book are listed below.

Wilbur Ellsworth was active in Southern Baptist life for decades and served as pastor of First Baptist Church in Wheaton, Illinois, prior to his recent conversion to Eastern Orthodoxy. Ellsworth now ministers at the Holy Transfiguration Antiochian Orthodox Church in Warrenville, Illinois. He is also a regular speaker on Ancient Faith Radio's *Let My Prayer Arise: Meditations on the Psalms* and president of the Society for the Study of Eastern Orthodoxy and Evangelicalism.

Francis J. Beckwith is professor of philosophy and church-state studies, and resident scholar in the Institute for Studies of Religion, at Baylor University. He is a graduate of Fordham University (PhD, philosophy) and the Washington University School of Law, St. Louis (MJS). His books include *A Second Look at First Things: A Case for Conservative Politics* (St. Augustine Press, 2011), *Return to Rome: Confessions of an Evangelical Catholic* (Brazos Press, 2008), *Defending Life: A Moral and Legal Case against Abortion Choice* (Cambridge Univ. Press, 2007), *To Everyone an Answer: A Case for the Christian Worldview* (InterVarsity Press, 2004), and *The New Mormon Challenge* (Zondervan, 2002), finalist for the 2003 Gold Medallion Award in Theology and Doctrine.

Chris Castaldo, a prominent convert to Evangelicalism from the Catholic faith, has written extensively about his spiritual pilgrimage in *Holy Ground: Walking with Jesus as a Former Catholic* (Zondervan, 2009). After eight years on staff of the influential College Church in Wheaton, Illinois, Castaldo became director of the Ministry for Gospel Renewal at the Billy Graham Center, Wheaton College, in May 2011.

Lyle W. Dorsett was influenced by a number of Evangelical traditions before converting from a nondenominational affiliation to the Anglican Church. He now serves as senior pastor of Christ the King Anglican Church in Birmingham, Alabama (AMiA), alongside his duties as the Billy Graham Professor of Evangelism at Beeson Divinity School.

WHAT CAN EVANGELICALS LEARN FROM LITURGICAL TRADITIONS, AND WHAT NONNEGOTIABLES REMAIN?

After listening to and learning from persons who have left one's faith tradition, one has a responsibility to respond. We live in a day when cultural currents would tell us to smooth over our differences. I am glad that the contributors to this volume recognize genuine differences among Christian faith traditions and see the value in making biblical, logical, historical, and experiential cases for what they believe are the most compelling expressions of Christian community.

When lining up contributors to respond to the conversion stories, I (as editor) asked them to write independent essays critiquing their assigned faith tradition and then to nuance those essays in light of the particular conversion stories told in this volume. Persons who converted were allowed to have the final word, however, with a concise rejoinder.

Persons critiquing the new faith traditions of converts are:

Craig Blaising is executive vice president and provost and professor of theology at the Southwestern Baptist Theological Seminary. Blaising is a Patristics scholar and a former participant in the Society for the Study of Eastern Orthodoxy and Evangelicalism. He is the author of numerous books and a contributor to Zondervan's *Three Views on the Millennium and Beyond* (1999) and *Three Views on the Rapture* (2010). In this book, Blaising critiques Eastern Orthodoxy from an Evangelical perspective.

Gregg Allison, a former missionary to Italy, is the author of *Historical Theology* (Zondervan, 2011) and a recognized Protestant expert on Catholicism. He serves as professor of Christian theology at the Southern Baptist Theological Seminary. Allison responds to Catholicism.

Brad S. Gregory is Dorothy G. Griffin Associate Professor of Early Modern European History at the University of Notre Dame. Gregory is the author of many scholarly articles and the award-winning book *Salvation at Stake: Christian Martyrdom in Early Modern Europe* (Harvard Univ. Press, 2001). In this volume, Gregory critiques Evangelicalism from a Catholic perspective.

Robert A. Peterson is professor of systematic theology at Covenant Theological Seminary in St. Louis, Missouri. He is the author or editor of twenty books, including *Salvation Accomplished by the Son: The Work of Christ* (Crossway, 2012), *Our Secure Salvation: Preservation and Apostasy* (P&R, 2009), and *Hell Under Fire* (Zondervan, 2004), coedited with Christopher Morgan. Peterson responds to Anglicanism.

WHAT CAN LITURGICAL CHRISTIANS LEARN FROM THIS BOOK?

According to the Pew Forum on Religion & Public Life, only 45 percent of persons raised Anglican remain in that religious tradition as adults.[11] Ten percent of persons raised Anglican eventually land in an Evangelical church.[12] Eastern Orthodox and Catholic churches face similar defections.

In this book, Chris Castaldo's story illustrates the widely recognized phenomenon of persons moving from liturgical church backgrounds to Evangelicalism. Liturgical Christians must certainly see the benefit of listening to Castaldo as he recounts what he still values from his Catholic background and why he chose to leave. Of interest to liturgical Christians as well should be a deeper understanding of what is attracting a new stream of Evangelical converts, and an honest assessment by Evangelical scholars of what nonnegotiable differences remain between Evangelical and liturgical Christian traditions.

A READING STRATEGY: QUESTIONS TO KEEP IN MIND

"This book is a going to be fascinating!" I frequently said to others while working on the project. Lest someone think I was overconfident in my own writing, I would quickly add, "Not because of anything I contribute—but because of the amazing writers I've lined up!" In fact, I think the rest of this book is so interesting that I do not want to delay you from getting to the "real stuff." Allow me, however, to usher you out of this literary foyer with a few questions to keep in mind as you read:

1. For persons converting to a new faith tradition, what were the decisive factors?
2. Do you detect any commonalities in the conversion stories?

3. Are there any questions you would like to ask the persons who converted? What matters have not been handled sufficiently in their retelling of their conversions?
4. For those critiquing a different faith tradition, what are the most significant factors in leading them to discourage conversion?
5. Would you add anything to the critiques? Did the writers miss any key issues, in your opinion?

And now to the stories and critiques. I hope you find them as interesting as I did.

PART 1

EASTERN
ORTHODOXY

CHAPTER 1

A JOURNEY TO EASTERN ORTHODOXY

Wilbur Ellsworth

Who can say when a journey begins?

People, places, times, and experiences all contribute to the journey, but they soon become part of the past as the journey keeps unfolding. My Baptist heritage nourished me with wonderful hymns and spiritual songs that continue to lift my heart to this day. One such song, Fanny J. Crosby's "All the Way My Savior Leads Me," speaks of the Lord's presence that "cheers each winding path I tread." I think Crosby's phrases describe the components of the journey: "My Savior," "winding paths" that seldom give us a sense of where we are really heading, and "me," the traveler. The observable paths and people are important parts of the story, but beyond the visible parts that can be described, there is the hidden presence of God—and one wandering soul, hoping to get it right.

AN UNINTENDED PATH

For me to tell my story, I must begin by saying that I hope I've gotten this journey right, that I have discerned the guidance of the Lord, that I haven't fallen into the comfortable confidence that I have figured it all out and that others who don't see it this way are all wrong. When people ask, "How could you have done this?" I respond that I didn't set out to leave the circle of my Baptist beginnings, ending up in a world I had never thought about before. It was well after I had taken a sharp turn that the world of Orthodox faith even crossed my mind.

I had plenty of reason to stay where I began. In that world, I experienced the love of God through his people, I heard the gospel of Christ and embraced his salvation, I was taught the Scriptures, and I was given great privileges to serve in churches and institutions. What more could anyone ask for?

I look back on a secure Christian community: My parents loved God, each other, my older brother Don and me, and the Baptist church in upstate New York where my spiritual formation took place. I look back on the Christian college and seminary that taught me and gave me wonderful insight into the goodness of God. I was blessed by the faithful, loyal, and kind people who invested in my life, encouraged me, and opened doors for me that gave me forty years of fruitful ministry and support. I owe my Baptist world *a lot.*

A few months ago my wife, Jean, and I spent an evening with a woman we had taught forty years earlier at a Christian college in Southern California. She told us that when she heard we had become Orthodox, she wasn't surprised. I found in her words a hint that my journey began long before I knew I was traveling. In those intervening forty years, Jean and I had lived in California, Ohio, and Illinois and had served three Baptist churches. During those years, we had been involved with various Evangelical organizations and colleges and had felt deep fulfillment and purpose in serving them. We sent our two children to Evangelical schools and colleges. We weren't planning to go anywhere else, and yet there was always a sense that we needed to discover and grow into something more, something greater, richer, and more compelling.

FIRST BAPTIST CHURCH OF WHEATON, ILLINOIS

The journey became more evident in the thirteen years we lived in Wheaton, Illinois, and served one of Wheaton's oldest and larger churches, First Baptist. My first concern as I became pastor of this historic church was its worship life. In many Baptist churches, the worship service is shaped by a pastor, a music director, and the desires of the congregation. These various pieces don't always mesh well. In those days (the middle of the 1980s) the "seeker sensitive" movement had begun to gain national prominence, and in fact one of its founding proponents had been a leader at First Baptist Church. Wheaton's

Christian community and its churches were coming to terms with this phenomenon that had sprung up in our own back yard.

Seeker sensitive worship services were based on a desire to engage in worship and evangelism simultaneously. The Sunday morning worship service increasingly was planned with the goal of being palatable for both non-Christians and believers. This type of hybrid service was proving to be very successful numerically, with great increases in attendance. Our church was quite taken with the excitement and success of this "new way to do church," and I was willing to learn about it too. Our staff went to seminars at Willow Creek Community Church with the desire to learn their method and to discern how it could relate to the life of our church.

Before long I began to realize that when new and different ideas regarding worship confront a congregation in the Baptist heritage, there isn't a strong biblical and historic consensus by which the church can judge those ideas. For all of the emphasis on submission to the authority of Scripture, people often find they do not have much common ground upon which they can unite. Love for God and for each other may manage to hold things together. Yet the interests of people of different ages, theological convictions, and even cultural preferences create divisions that at best must be managed and at worst will eventually split the church apart.

I want to emphasize that such churches do not necessarily have bad people in them. The people I served were very good. They loved God, they were serious about their faith, they were concerned for the salvation of others, and they were generous in reaching out to human need wherever they found it. In other words, these were people who possessed Christian virtue. What then was missing?

In my early years at First Baptist, the pastoral staff and congregation worked together to create an ethos of worship that was reverent, sincere, and made use of our rich resources of music and dedication. We engaged the congregation in worship and attracted many visitors. Nevertheless, as time went on, even though the size of the congregation continued to increase and attendees had a sense of satisfaction with the worship, many felt we needed to adopt the visions and values of "a new way to do church." I developed a growing concern not so much with what people were proposing to do in worship and evangelism as with what seemed to be a lack of any theological basis for what we should be doing. Even more troublesome, there seemed to be an alarming absence of any reason why we would not consider doing certain things. I recall growing uneasy when I would hear someone say, "I just want to see people come to Christ." To use a popular phrase at the time, such a statement seemed too uncritically "market driven." I sensed little awareness that the high and holy priestly work of worship might have priorities that were not compatible with an uncritical focus on attracting unbelievers.

Things took a sharp turn during a meeting I had with a parachurch leader who was influential in our large and active youth ministry. The ministry had been led by several youth pastors trained by Sonlife Ministries, a discipleship program begun at the Moody Bible Institute in Chicago. Eventually the Sonlife principles had begun to be applied to the larger life of the church, spawning what became known as our "Growing a Healthy Church" program. During the meeting, I was strongly encouraged to bring this organization's training to our entire pastoral staff and lay leadership as a way of strengthening evangelism.

On the one hand, I appreciated the careful biblical approach to discipleship that this ministry gleaned from the Gospels. On the other hand, I saw no parallel focus on the kind of worship to which this method of discipleship would lead. In a meeting with the leader of this organization, I synthesized my concerns into one question: Does the discipleship training program necessitate a change in the worship of the church? I formed a hypothetical situation that conveyed my concern: Could a traditional Episcopal church embrace this training and not change its worship life? I was assured this was entirely possible.

With a spirit of caution, I agreed to go ahead with the training. In weeklong seminars away from the church, we listened, learned, and began to strategize about how the changes would look at our church. Very quickly our discussions turned to worship. The conversations continued in smaller leadership meetings for a year. Somewhere along the line, however, the group began to polarize. It seemed clear that there could be no turning back.

By default my journey had begun. I began to feel a profound disorientation. I knew I was part of something at First Baptist that was moving ahead and wasn't going to stop. I believed it was moving in a dangerous direction, but nothing I could say or do could change it. Success in drawing people was more pressing than wrestling with the nature of true spiritual worship, it seemed. Some others shared my concern, but the determination to press ahead would not be denied.

A TIME OF TRANSITION

From that time on, it became clear I had no place to stand, and I resigned in May 2000. Looking back, I can see that the church had no foundation that could hold. Well-intentioned leaders were passionately advancing pragmatic methods to attract unchurched people. I believed this showed a lack of due regard for the spiritual theology of Christian worship, but I could only offer in protest what Louis Bouyer called "spiritual instincts" — those personal feelings of conviction that have been cultivated without the benefit of the entire tradition of the Church's Spirit-directed wisdom to guide them.

I realized that despite my efforts to understand the magnitude of the Church's historic theology and practice of worship, my Evangelical experience was insufficient to fully respond to the cultural pragmatism of seeker sensitive worship. The "new way" too easily assumed that as Evangelicals, we could discern what the Bible directs the Church to do to fulfill its ministry of worship and its mission of evangelism. "Spiritual instincts" similar to mine are being felt increasingly today, particularly within the more historically and traditionally oriented sector of Evangelicalism, which is seeing some of its churches move in this same seeker sensitive direction.

I wish I could say I came to clear spiritual convictions that compelled me to make bold, courageous steps onto another path, but I can only claim to be a poor relative of Abraham, of whom it is written in Hebrews 11:8, "He did not know where he was going." At our parting, the First Baptist Church kindly and generously provided six months of separation income. With that I was free to continue my journey.

One of the most painful experiences during that six months was the absence of clear direction. Within a few weeks churches in different parts of the country began sending inquiries, asking about the possibility of my becoming their pastor, but I was bound by two heavy burdens: first, many of these churches were similar to the one I had just left, and second, I did not have a full vision for a way beyond this.

CHRIST CHURCH IN GLEN ELLYN

About six months after I left First Baptist, a group of fifty people in the Wheaton area approached me with an unusual invitation. Over a dinner late in 2000, they said that they were desiring more in their Christian lives than they had previously experienced and that they had heard elements of what they were yearning for in my preaching and teaching. Would I be willing to lead them, even if only for a short time, in a search for what we all were missing?

As touched as I was by their request, I knew there were some problems: I had been careful to keep from disturbing the people of First Baptist in their need to determine their future without being troubled by my activities in the community. Further, Jean was dubious about the wisdom of such a venture. She reminded me how many times we had watched signs go up for yet another "new and improved" start-up church. And Wheaton had so many churches already. Now we were considering launching another start-up. We were about to come out from a Baptist version of the church that had departed from a Reformed version that had left the Catholic Church that had split from the other half of the One Great Church of the first Christian millennium. This seemed terribly wrong to her. She really did not want to be a part of continuing this sad story. Though I agreed with her, I couldn't see an alternative. I felt that serving the desires of this group could be the Lord's provision, a chance to explore the way to the place I was looking for but did not yet know.

With a sense of excitement and some uncertainty, I accepted the group's invitation with one condition: that we would observe the Lord's Table every Sunday. I hoped this would provide a lifeline to where it was we needed to go. While not fully understanding why I had asked this, the group agreed. Within a few weeks a fellowship was formed, meetings began on Sunday evenings, and off we went. In my quest for deeper and clearer roots, I preached and taught the Reformed Protestant doctrine that had been the foundation of my training.

Within a year, the group had become Christ Church in Glen Ellyn, a city just east of Wheaton. There we were blessed to buy a lovely English-style stone chapel. People began to join the church, and the future looked promising. One of the greatest joys of Christ Church was a prevailing spirit of reverence in its worship life. With the help and encouragement of my friend Robert Webber, a Wheaton College professor and one of Evangelicalism's leading exponents of returning to the historic roots of the Church in order to find a better way to the future, we began to explore the ancient worship practices of the Church. Congregants were united and enthused by what we began to call classical Christianity.

Early on, however, I began to sense something troubling about the fruit of my scholastic Calvinistic preaching. I felt a spiritual hardness coming to us through it. Through Robert Webber's influence, I began to study and explore with our congregation the ancient theology of the Church known as Christus Victor. In this understanding, the work of Jesus Christ in salvation is less of a judicial act that pardons our guilt and its accompanying judgment and more of a rescue through his resurrection from the bondage and futility of sin and death. This emphasis is affirmed powerfully in the central Old Testament event of Israel's release from the bondage of Egypt, as the people passed through the Red Sea, an event Israel remembered in the annual Feast of Passover by the shedding of a lamb's blood and the eating of its flesh.

THE REDISCOVERY OF REVERENCE

While we were finding a new joy in the deeper and quieter reverence of our church's worship, we wondered if there was anything behind this reverence other than our own preference and taste. Looking back on our Evangelical experience, we began to remember a mix of attitudes about worship. Positively, the Evangelicals I have known were often people of deep faith, profound love for Christ, and a passionate desire to serve God and to extend his love and grace to others. That kind of spiritual authenticity carries its own innate reverence.

On the other hand, reverence — the fear and respect for the good God who loves humankind — has fast been fading in American culture, and as reverence fades in the culture, it seems to be fading in many Evangelical churches as well.

"Contemporary" and "traditional" forms of worship have sparked the tragedy of what has been called the "worship wars." In my experience, the real issue has rarely been contemporary or traditional worship. I have seen older, godly Christians participate in singing contemporary hymns and spiritual songs with great joy. I have seen young people sing great hymns of the Church's past with intense sincerity. I suggest that the heart of the issue is reverence. Reverence is a spiritual experience that comes from consciously standing in the presence of the All-Holy Triune God, the Maker of Heaven and Earth. This Presence is so great that very often in Scripture, when people became aware they were in the presence of God, the first thing they needed to be told was, "Fear not!"

Such a message seldom seems necessary today across a wide span of American Evangelicalism. People are invited to sit back and relax and enjoy the service. It would seem the service is more about us than it is about coming into the presence of the living God. In an attempt to relate to present culture, the atmosphere of the modern church service is intentionally casual, comfortable, and user friendly. The music is to soothe, comfort, invigorate, and move our emotions. The physical characteristics of the worship space are designed to be nonthreatening, so symbols of the Christian faith are largely excluded.

Some years ago I was talking with a widely known professor in one of America's most prestigious seminaries related to a major mainline denomination. While there is a great diversity of theological views at this school, the students are serious and thoughtful. One of the notable things about this seminary, the professor said, was that the vast majority of the student body attend chapel with a spirit of reverence. There is one exception: the Evangelical students. They come with bright minds and a settled theology but with little regard for humility and respect in the presence of God.

She told me this after we had just experienced an outbreak of rowdy irreverence in an Evangelical college chapel. My point is not to charge all or even most Evangelicals with irreverence. That would be untrue, unfair, and unkind. But I do believe that the very roots of reverence have been greatly weakened in Evangelical churches. This led us at Christ Church to ask another question: What is the nature of the presence of God in Christian worship?

AN INTERLUDE OF ORTHODOXY

Before going back to Christ Church, it is time for the Orthodox Church to make its first appearance in my story. At a conference at the University of Dubuque for mainline Protestant renewal leaders,

Jean and I served as musicians and leaders of worship. During one of the break times, I saw Jim Kushiner, the editor of *Touchstone*, a journal of traditional ecumenical "mere Christianity." As we talked about some of the mutual friendships we enjoy, Jim mentioned that our friends John and Tonya Maddex had recently become members of his Orthodox church.

This news hit me like a thunderbolt. Jean and I had known the Maddexes for more than twenty years, going back to the days when we had all lived in northeastern Ohio. At that time, John was the manager of the Moody Bible Institute radio station in Cleveland, and I was the pastor of Grace Baptist Church, next to the campus of Kent State University. We had become friends. I was frequently on the station, and we would get together to talk about our shared interest in the theology and preaching of the great British Christian leader Martyn Lloyd-Jones. After our Ohio years, both of our families had moved to the Chicago area, John to head all of the Moody stations in the country, and I to serve as pastor of First Baptist Church in Wheaton.

When I returned home from Dubuque, I found the one book on Orthodoxy in my library and sat down to read about the church my friends had joined. After finishing the book, Daniel Clendenin's *Eastern Orthodox Christianity*, I called John and scheduled a long lunch to hear his story.

Afterward I stopped in a bookstore and found the two further books John suggested I might read: Alexander Schmemann's *For the Life of the World* and Timothy Ware's *The Orthodox Church*. *For the Life of the World* brought me to tears, both for the joy of reading a deep and biblical theological vision of what is involved in worship and for the sorrow that I had understood it so dimly before and had been unable to communicate it to my dear flock at First Baptist Church. Lunch with John and the three books did not seal my conversion to Orthodoxy by any means, but my journey to the continuing life of the ancient church had begun, whether I knew it or not.

Not long after this, John invited Jean and me to dinner with their priest and his wife, Father Patrick and Denise Reardon, who serve All Saints Church in Chicago. Father Patrick was born into a Catholic family, spent ten years as a monk under the guidance of Thomas Merton, left monastic life and entered the Episcopal Church, and ultimately entered the Orthodox Church and the priesthood. Along the way, he studied at St. Anselm's College and the Pontifical Biblical Institute in Rome. Later he enrolled at the Southern Baptist Theological Seminary in Louisville, Kentucky, where he immersed himself in the church fathers.

When I first met him, I quickly became aware that I had encountered a man with a vast and deep knowledge of Holy Scripture as seen through the teaching of the church fathers. Through what has become now a friendship of many years and countless hours of conversation, I began to see a world of biblical understanding that far exceeded my previous efforts to grasp the enormity of God's Word.

From my youth, I had yearned to find Christ in his glory throughout Scripture. I had gravitated toward those who seemed to grasp the Christological vision of the Bible. In my conversations with Father Patrick, I found this vision in a greater dimension than I had ever known. His book *Christ in the Psalms* further enriched my understanding of the vision of Christ in the historic church and began to make me aware of the powerful way Scripture informs the worship life of the Church. This discovery was of enormous importance to me.

Though I had long loved the beauty of Scripture and was committed to its inspiration and divine authority, I sensed I lacked a fullness of the unifying presence of Christ in Scripture, even though Dr. Marchant King, a professor I had at Los Angeles Baptist Theological Seminary, had opened this door to me years earlier. Had I not experienced this brighter and larger vision of Scripture in the first Orthodox priest I met, I probably never would have considered the Orthodox Church and the Orthodox faith. But my long friendship with John and Tonya Maddex, their serious commitment to Scripture and theology, and my new friendship with the Reardons produced in me a deep conviction that, whatever else I might come to think about Orthodox Christianity, I could be confident it was a magnificent source of biblical insight, theology, and liturgical wisdom.

Later, when Evangelical friends began to attack Orthodoxy as being unfaithful to Holy Scripture, I listened to their arguments but was unmoved by them. I began to see Protestant and anti-Catholic views of tradition as a reduced view of what the Bible describes about how God reveals himself and makes himself present in the world. This newfound conviction began to find its way into my preaching at our fledgling church in Glen Ellyn.

MEANWHILE, BACK AT OUR CHURCH

The congregation's appreciation for some of the foundations of Christian worship, such as confessing the creed, giving more care to the public reading of Holy Scripture, and weekly observing the Lord's Table, led to further questions about the nature of that table. Throughout my years as a Baptist pastor, I had felt a discomfort when we observed the Lord's Table and baptism. As Baptists who deeply embraced gospel truth and grace, we accepted the importance of these biblical practices. Our grasp of their meaning, however, was severely limited.

The Baptist (and for the most part Evangelical) view has embraced the Reformed teaching of Ulrich Zwingli, who believed it is only the communicant's faith that makes Christ present in the Eucharist. His view excluded Christ's presence in the physical bread and wine. This limitation of the Lord's Table to being solely a "symbol" and a "remembering" also carried over to a view of baptism that made it an act of obedience and a witness of the faith of the one being baptized. It carries no other grace in itself. This reduced and limited understanding of these observances leaves a real void in those who embrace this view.

At Christ Church in Glen Ellyn, our founding commitment to weekly communion had at least elevated our regard for the Lord's Table. Now as I began to study the ancient teaching of the Church on this subject, I thought it should be brought to the congregation for study and discussion. This raised a new issue for our young church: How does a congregation begin a study that could entail changing important theological convictions? This is both a theological and an ethical matter.

Part of my decision to leave my Baptist pastorate was the sense not only that I had been called to preserve and teach the doctrine of that congregation as it was set forth in its doctrinal statement but also that it was folly to press too far in trying to encourage the congregation to move beyond its unspoken but longstanding assumptions about church practices. Deepening and growth are clearly important in church life. But when doctrinal roots are old, assumed, and not open for consideration, a pastor may be doing nothing but causing trouble and dissension by reconsidering them.

Ironically, the issues at the Wheaton church arose not from my attempts to change the worship style but rather from my desire to maintain what had been established over the years. The issue in Glen Ellyn was nearly the opposite: a call to examine long-assumed theological opinions. The understanding at the formation of Christ Church was that the congregation was on a journey.

A friend who later became part of the community suggested a book about the Lord's Table for the congregation to study together: *Given for You: Reclaiming Calvin's Doctrine of the Lord's Supper* by Keith Matthison of Ligonier Ministries, a Reformed parachurch organization. As I read the book, I was impressed by two significant and, to me, surprising things: John Calvin had essentially the same view of the real presence of Christ in the bread and wine of the Eucharist as did the great and undivided church of the first thousand years of church history, and second, many recent generations of Calvinists have rejected Calvin's teaching on this point.

What was particularly important in our study was the appendix titled "The Lord's Supper before the Reformation." We began our study with this concluding appendix before reading the beginning of the book. While I was convinced that history showed the early church was united in its belief that Christ is truly present in the bread and wine, I did my best to give objective guidance to the church through the study, inviting open discussion and encouraging as many questions as people could articulate.

We spent four months in the study. I frequently asked if anyone had problems with it and with the conclusions we were beginning to form. The only objection expressed was that this teaching was Roman Catholic and should be opposed for that reason. (This instinctive anti-Catholic concern presented itself more than once during Christ Church's journey.) After the study, I asked if anyone wanted more time to examine Calvin's view or to explore any other views. The response was a strong "Enough!"

The congregation agreed we would embrace the real presence of Christ in the Eucharist as taught by our Lord in Holy Scripture, but without any attempt to define the process by which this transformation took place. We would simply pray for God the Father to send down the Holy Spirit both upon the people and upon the bread and wine. We affirmed that the real presence is a mystery, not magic. Nor would we view it as a mechanical event that simply occurs at each Eucharist. Instead we'd see the mystery as a specific gracious act of the Holy Trinity in response to the prayer of the Church.

Looking back, this study of the Eucharist was a significant point in our journey. Without premeditation, the worship life of the congregation deepened with the sense of the presence of the Lord in our midst. The joy increased and there was a growing sense that we were touching the eternal in our worship. It was inevitable that, with the thought given to the Lord's Table, the same questions eventually would rise concerning baptism. Again the background of most of the congregation was firmly rooted in the Zwinglian view that baptism has no intrinsic grace other than the blessing of God for obedience and the witness of the person being baptized. Some of the same ambiguities that marked the Evangelical view on the Lord's Table were present in this issue.

Because baptism is clearly commanded in the New Testament and because the book of Acts specifically recounts the baptisms of those who converted to Christianity, the practice of baptizing believing converts is widely practiced in Evangelical churches and is done so with joy. The questions begin when we ask what baptism actually means or accomplishes and who should receive baptism. Because Christ Church had a foundational commitment to a more reflective worship and wanted deeper theological roots in its practices, the introduction of some of the classical aspects of baptism were warmly received. The church used resources from Robert Webber's eight volumes on worship and some of the Orthodox baptismal prayers from the writings of Alexander Schmemann, and baptisms became a much fuller expression of the faith and went farther in expressing the biblical imagery of water in the Old Testament.

In our study of ancient church practices, we had come to value the central place the Easter vigil has in the history and life of the Church. Ultimately, we did most of our baptisms at the Easter vigil. Many in the congregation said that this annual service was the summit of their entire worship year experience. The only complaint was that there was too much reading of Scripture and that it took too long!

Just before what proved to be our last Easter vigil, one of the church leaders objected to a phrase in a baptismal prayer that spoke of the commandment to "be baptized and wash away your sins." He did not mention that Saint Peter preached baptism "for the remission of sins" in Acts 2:38 (NKJV). The leader who objected to this phrase and wanted it removed from the prayer was one of the most experienced and theologically educated in the congregation. His own ministry experience had exposed him to years of laboring in a culture of corrupt church practices where the churchgoers, generally speaking, seemed to have little knowledge of the gospel and even less interest in the Christian life. It was understandable that this experience left in him a deep-seated negative reaction to anything that came close to that tradition.

His reaction to experiences with Catholicism was soon repeated by a former parishioner of mine who had lived in an Eastern European Orthodox country under a Communist regime. He had been exiled by the Communist government and had come to America to raise support to supply theological books for young Christian leaders when the doors of freedom would open again. I greatly appreciated this man for the strength of his confidence in the ultimate triumph of the truth of Christ over totalitarian oppression.

We were having breakfast together during one of his return visits to Wheaton, and he was sharing his thoughts on a book he was writing on the biblical vision of salvation. He was interested in my response to it. After hearing his summary, I said that I had rarely heard the gospel more clearly or fully expressed and that I embraced what he said wholeheartedly. I then added that I had recently been reading in the early fathers of the Church and that their teaching was remarkably similar to his view. He seemed displeased and I sensed I had said something terribly insulting. He explained that the "church fathers" were merely a group of men who had corrupted the gospel with pagan philosophy. He further warned me against going to them for theological instruction and said I should get past them and go back all the way to Jesus himself. Without realizing it at the time, I had just come to another turn on my path. I felt deeply stung by his words, not because they were a rebuke to me but because they grievously dishonored those who had continued the work of the apostles in their own generation and who had given to the Church the great wisdom and spiritual insight that continues to lead the Church forward today.

I knew enough to realize the church fathers were not regarded by the Church as infallible and that, though the Church embraced most of their teaching, it did lay aside some opinions that did not conform to the Holy Tradition of the Church. However, the treasury of their work created "a rule of faith" by which Scripture could be read and by which the apostolic faith would continue to be passed on to subsequent generations. That brief conversation found its way into our congregation's conversations, and for the first time the question of Orthodoxy began to rise as a major point of concern and even controversy.

During this time, the church had grown to nearly double what it had been. People were visiting and some were staying. We began to experience a new dilemma. Some who came thought we were too Evangelical in our worship. Others felt we were too Catholic. Others liked some of each and began to ask why we did one thing and not another.

For me, the answer was quite simple, although it was painfully embarrassing. As the pastor, I had received the charge to lead this congregation on a journey "to something more." As I learned and developed further ways to express various discoveries, I discussed them with the elders of the church, but the ultimate reason why we worshiped as we did was because this was how the pastor put it together. No one knew more than I that I was not an appropriate final word on how people should worship.

Yes, we had more roots than ever before, and we had deeper theological reasons for doing what we did, but the uncomfortable truth was that we were truly one of a kind. One of our founding members once called us a "boutique church," something for the particularly discerning.

A reality began to dawn on us that created great sadness. For all our exploration of the foundations of the worship life of the Church, we were just one more group trying to "do it right" on our own, according to what we thought was good and appropriate. The new people who would come in and express their preferences could, over time, change the shape of things greatly! The smooth-sailing days of Christ Church were coming to an end.

Most of the people who had begun at Christ Church had continued in their own explorations. People were reading, talking, visiting other churches when out of town, and interacting with those who visited our church. During this time, I was also developing relationships in this new world of what Robert Webber called "ancient-future faith."

My friendships with John Maddex and Father Patrick Reardon led to an invitation to join the board of the Fellowship of Saint James, the oversight ministry of both *Touchstone* and *Salvo* magazines as well as the *Daily Devotional Guide* produced by Father Reardon. In those days, the fellowship was holding conferences and evening talks that many of our people attended, and Christ Church hosted several of these events.

This circle of Christians from Protestant, Orthodox, and Catholic traditions began to have a broader influence in our congregation. We were moving from ideas we read in books and worship experiences in our own "church laboratory" to experiencing the breadth of the great tradition that had long ago flowed from the fountainhead of history and formed a living tradition that continues to offer wisdom and life for our own generation. It was becoming increasingly clear that our people were forming different responses to what we simply called classical Christianity. No one seemed to reject this completely. After all, something similar to classical Christianity was the goal we were seeking when we came together to begin Christ Church.

Some, however, were beginning to clarify their goal as remaining in the Christian world they had come from but with some corrections to more traditional and conservative ways of being the Church. They had little or no interest in looking at the deeper underpinnings of our faith and practice. Others were openly passionate to continue to discover more of this classical Christian world that few of us knew much about. They were not gullible nor easily accepting of anything that merely seemed old or "high church," but they were deeply committed to find a place to stand in what we were beginning to call the Great Tradition. Is there a place, a church, a tradition where stability, wisdom, and fullness guide the lives of those who are in that community?

APPROACHING THE ORTHODOX DOORSTEP

During this time, Father Patrick suggested to me that even with all the reading I was doing and the conversations I was having, I really needed to participate in some formal Orthodox study to know it more readily and to experience the life of Orthodoxy. The Antiochian Archdiocese of the Orthodox Church has a program called the St. Stephen's Course, a three-year distance-learning program of directed readings, essays, and an annual weeklong residency that people with different backgrounds take to learn more about the Orthodox Church.

While I was personally motivated to enter this study, I had concerns about how it might be perceived. I had not yet arrived at a final determination about Orthodoxy, either for myself or for those following my leadership at Christ Church, and without this kind of directed and intense exposure to the Orthodox Church's own teaching, I was not confident I could gain the kind of insight and perspective necessary to make such decisions. The weight of responsibility to faithfully and wisely offer guidance to the congregation that I loved was heavy indeed. I chose to pay for the course myself rather than to ask for funds from the church or to accept offers of help that had been made by Orthodox sources. I felt that in this way, there would be no question of loyalty or indebtedness, nor any perception that my entering this program meant I had made my determination. In the end, I quietly enrolled in the program.

A growing difficulty at this time was that some began saying I had made my determination that Christ Church would become Orthodox, and I was simply biding my time to make it happen. I didn't want to do anything to give credence to that view, for it wasn't true and I feared that such an idea would violate the freedom of the congregation to come to its own decision in due time.

I have come to see this issue as one of the most difficult for both a congregation and a pastor to handle. When inclinations and interests are not settled, decisions and opposing views should both be heard and be respected, but they should not shut down an exploration by a majority of interested people in the congregation. It was clear, however, that positions were forming and even hardening at Christ Church. We were becoming divided. In one sense, this could be expected. Our original realization that we all "wanted more in our spiritual lives than we had known" was hardly a clear objective. No one had signed on for anything more than what we had said.

As we moved through our journey, people began to see things from the vantage point of different life experiences. We all began to understand more about ourselves and just what it was we were seeking. We all had to deal with our own spiritual pasts and come to some conclusions. In short, we all had to decide how far from the familiar we were willing to go.

What became clear as we headed toward a decision was that we would not all be choosing the same course for our future. In several stages, we began to attempt a good resolution for what had become our six-year journey together. The church met and agreed by a nearly unanimous vote to have various teachers come to enlighten us about the Orthodox Church. During that time, Father Patrick Reardon and Father Peter Gillquist introduced our people to the Orthodox faith. Increasingly, some became more attracted to Orthodoxy, while others did not attend the meetings. The journey had now taken two different paths. In October 2006, a meeting was called by those opposed to exploring the Orthodox faith. It soon became evident that the congregation had come to something close to an even division. Those who were favorable to Orthodoxy concluded that with many being so opposed to any further study of Orthodoxy, our journey together had come to an end. At the final meeting, those of us who desired to pursue the Orthodox faith, having heard the opposition, said that we would leave the congregation to pursue our journey. This was a profoundly sad time, but it was also a liberating time. There were overtures from those who remained at Christ Church, asking the Orthodox group to reconsider and to return for further discussions, but it seemed clear there was nothing to be gained by that. Our journey to the Orthodox faith was to take a big and decisive step forward.

On Wednesday evening, October 25, 2006, twenty-five of us drove into Chicago to attend the midweek vespers service at All Saints Antiochian Orthodox Church. It was an unforgettable night. The All Saints people came out in force and had prepared a wonderful meal to welcome us after the service. During the previous several years, Father Reardon and his congregation had prayed for us and had offered every encouragement possible. Now we were there together with them to actually experience worship in the Orthodox Church.

The fervent spirit of the All Saints parish, the reverent leadership from the altar, and the deep and Christological preaching of Holy Scripture had an instant and powerful effect. While a few of us needed to be in this atmosphere a little longer, most were won over very quickly and simply wanted some time to learn more about this wonderful and yet unfamiliar church. I was struck, both for myself and for this new Orthodox seekers group, by how much we needed to learn and to understand. All of us had been seriously involved in the Christian life and church for many years, some of us all our lives, and yet we all felt like newborn babies needing to be taught the most elementary ways of Orthodox Church life.

The forty-minute journey into Chicago became a part of our weekly pattern. Some of us went together in a van. Soon the van was sharing in a mobile version of the orthros, or matins, service of the Church. We each had our own book for the service, and we each took our turn, from the front of the van to the back, praying the prayers and singing the hymns of the service.

When we arrived at All Saints for the Divine Liturgy, we were ready. Those early weeks were like a wonderful courtship. The reverence in God's presence was palpable. Even though it took us some time to become oriented to the shape of the liturgy, we immediately experienced deep communion and adoration before the goodness of our triune God.

The phrase "the beauty of holiness" was no longer just a lovely spiritual phrase; it was a wonderful reality. Father Patrick's preaching also had a profound effect on our people. All of us had been committed students of the Bible, and no one was willing to trim, ignore, or twist anything that the Bible taught. And no one ever had to! To a person, we all sensed we were gaining a fuller understanding, a deeper meaning, and a more coherent vision of the truth of God's Word than we had ever known. We were struck both by how the All Saints people showed great love for us as newcomers and by how they felt a complete freedom not to change the liturgy or the practices of the church to accommodate us — or anyone else.

At All Saints, the Holy Tradition of the Church consists of receiving, maintaining, and passing on the apostolic faith. There was no other determining factor to the church's worship. While no effort was too great for the people of All Saints to make in meeting our legitimate needs, the other reality was that we were welcomed to "come and see" and become a part of this great stable tradition. This was most attractive to all of us.

The Divine Liturgy (the primary service of the Church that involves both the liturgy of the Word and the liturgy of the Eucharist) is, for many people, both magnetic and overwhelming. Even in an American-oriented parish, the music has a somewhat different sound to American ears.

What struck us in the early days of our Orthodox experience was that in the liturgy (literally, "the work of the people"), the energy of the people was indeed evident. The members of the congregation were in no way mere spectators. They sang from their hearts; their bodies conveyed attention and involvement. There was a deep sense of faith and love toward God in the worship of the people. The priest and the deacon were not the sole actors; rather they were taking their place with the people in offering the great priestly act of worship to God.

There was also the sense of mystery. Beyond what was said, sung, or proclaimed, there was the greatness of God that no human being can really comprehend. The combination of the simple unaccompanied singing and the rich poetic truth of the liturgical hymnody recalled to my mind the statement a thousand years ago by the emissaries of Prince Vladimir of Russia, who said of the Orthodox liturgy, "We knew not whether we were in heaven or on earth."

We became aware of the practical disciplines of the Orthodox spiritual life, particularly prayer and fasting. We began to sense that the spirit of the Orthodox faith was to give specific but not legalistic guidance in how to build these practices into our lives. We spent six months in this blessed parish, where we began to be formed in the actual experience of Orthodox life. Father Patrick came out to Chicago's western suburbs one evening a week to provide additional catechetical instruction and to answer our questions.

He finally determined that because of the studies we had participated in while still at Christ Church, and our intense, ongoing participation in worship, he would receive our group into the Orthodox Church by chrismation on the first Sunday of February 2007. That Sunday dawned bright and was filled with great joy as each of us was anointed with the oil of chrismation, an oil that had been provided by the Patriarch of Antioch. This oil, the seal of the gift of the Holy Spirit, was applied to the various parts of the body in a manner reminiscent of the ordination of Levitical priests of the Old Testament and of the apostolic laying on of hands following baptism in the New Testament. This ancient and rich liturgical act followed our confessing the Nicene Creed, our public embracing of the Orthodox faith that brought us into the historic expression of the "one, holy, catholic, and apostolic church" whose roots extend back to the city of Antioch, to the apostles Peter and Paul, and to the great martyr Bishop Ignatius. We knew that we were home. Our debt of love and gratitude to the priest and people of All Saints Orthodox Church will never end.

BECOMING ORTHODOX

The next great question was, What comes next? While our days in Chicago were blessed beyond description, we knew we needed to be rooted in our own community. Through the guidance of His Eminence Metropolitan Philip and the counsel of Father Peter Gillquist, the director of the Missions and Evangelism Department of the archdiocese, arrangements were made for us to return to our home in Chicago's western suburbs, where I would become the pastor of Holy Transfiguration Church, a parish that had been established some twenty years earlier, at a time when more than two thousand American Evangelicals had converted to Orthodoxy. The founding priest, Father William Caldaroni, and his family had done rigorous and patient work to establish this mission in the heart of Wheaton, Illinois, an American center of Evangelical Christianity.

The parish had later moved a short distance to the neighboring community of Warrenville, where it had bought an old Lutheran country church and converted it into an Orthodox temple. Father Caldaroni and his wife had previously suggested to the bishop that they believed their time at Holy Transfiguration Church was coming to an end, and they were hoping for a reassignment to the western part of the country. Since our people lived in this area, and I had served pastorates in this community, it was decided that I would be ordained to the Orthodox priesthood, and, following Easter in 2007, I would become the pastor of this parish. As is customary in the Orthodox Church, I was first ordained to the deaconate, on March 1, and then to the priesthood, on March 3, 2007. On March 4, 2007, I stood at the altar and for the first time celebrated the Orthodox Divine

Liturgy. A few weeks later, on April 18, I began my priesthood in Warrenville at the weekly vespers service.

As I look back over the years since leaving the Baptist Church in Wheaton, through the important years of learning and discovery at Christ Church in Glen Ellyn, and now being in the Orthodox priesthood at Holy Transfiguration Church, the time seems both to have crept by and flown away. There were days of profound uncertainty. There was no plan, only the need, as I had said at the beginning, "to find a place to stand." When unforeseen and seemingly coincidental encounters began to form a sense of direction, there were many questions, fears, and even opposition. Friends and loved ones were variously surprised, shocked, horrified, and saddened, but many were also extremely kind and charitable. They were genuinely interested in understanding why I had followed this path.

The sense of time flying by comes primarily from the learning curve that a Baptist-bred and Baptist-trained pastor must go through to enter into Orthodox pastoral life, which, while in many ways similar to what I had known, has a significantly different theological vision and practice. Four years later I am still learning, and the people of our parish are most kind and patient.

One of the privileges I have had during these years has been the opportunity to talk about the Orthodox Church to many from my own Evangelical background, both in private conversation and in speaking engagements around the country. I always endeavor to express my love and respect for the Christian movement that brought me to the knowledge of the gospel of Christ. All my life, I have known great Christian people who are Evangelicals, both Christian leaders and laypeople in the churches. My respect for their Christian character, their evangelistic passion, and their commitment to Holy Scripture is unbounded. I continue to regard them as beloved brothers and sisters in the Lord, and I give thanks for their labors for the kingdom of God throughout the world.

The differences that now exist between us in our understanding of the Church and the faith do not lessen my desire to honor them before the Lord for the evidence of God's grace in their lives. I am always concerned that in telling about my journey, I do not convey a spirit of alienation from or disrespect for the people and the ministries that formed my world for so many years. I yearn for the day when we will know the full unity of the faith and the regathering of the Church.

THE CHURCH AND THE BIBLE

What reasons, then, can I respectfully offer for being where I have come to and for why I have believed it necessary to make this journey? One significant reason is that the history of the Church has convinced me of the place of the Orthodox Church in the world. While a two-thousand-year history offers enormous varieties of ways of interpreting what has happened in the Church, the great events of the postapostolic world are fairly clear. The early church began to live out its new life in Christ even before the New Testament was completed. It extended its witness out into the world long before the Church identified the canon of the New Testament. It is in the Church, under the direction of the Holy Spirit, that the texts and the books of the New Testament began to be identified and affirmed. The second-century church fathers spoke of "the rule of faith" as the outline of the essential contents of the Christian faith to serve as guides in the interpretation of Scripture, which is essentially the gospel of Christ in distinction from the heresies already rising up. Contrary to the thinking of many, there is no conflict or struggle in the Orthodox Church for primacy between Holy Scripture and Tradition. The common reality that binds both together in peace is the Holy Spirit. One of the great evidences of the Church's relationship to the Bible is the effort of the early church fathers to carry on the work both of the Lord and of his apostles in interpreting the Old Testament Scriptures as "the very Scriptures that testify about me" (John 5:39).

One of the greatest contributions of the Tradition of the Church is to establish the Christological framework of the Old Testament, a framework that unifies the two testaments and makes Jesus Christ the Lord of them both. It is from this approach that the essence of the Holy Tradition finds it real roots.

I believe that many of the discussions and controversies between Orthodox and Evangelical Christians about either the authority of Scripture or being faithful to Scripture are rooted in a lack of understanding of how the early church interpreted Scripture.

I recall many years ago hearing a well-respected Evangelical seminary professor make this astounding statement: "While we must accept the way the apostles interpreted the Old Testament in their New Testament writings because they were inspired by the Holy Spirit and therefore have divine authority, we may not follow their hermeneutical methods because they are not correct." I find that amazing and hasten to say that since then, the level of Evangelical hermeneutics has greatly matured and that few would make a statement like that today. Yet there is a common view among Evangelicals that causes them to look at the Orthodox Church and say that our practices and beliefs are unbiblical.

I suggest that the question we should ask is this: Is the Bible merely making prescriptive statements that should not be extended beyond what they are precisely affirming, or is the presence and work of God a reality that flows through the words of the biblical text in a descriptive, expansive, and all-encompassing way that gives us a vision of the way God makes his presence real in his creation, which he sent his Son to redeem?

Father Peter Gillquist has a saying that I think expresses this well: "The difference between the Orthodox and the Evangelicals is in the verses they underline." For instance, it is a fairly common assumption among Evangelicals that liturgical worship is either extrabiblical or actually unbiblical. The highest and most effectual prayer, they feel, should be spontaneous, from the heart, yet the prayers of our Lord on the cross are primarily prayers from the Psalter.

The first recorded prayer of the early church is in Acts 4, and it is rooted in Psalm 2. It seems clear that the often cited description of the life of the early church from Acts 2:42 has a deeper meaning than what is usual in our modern translations: "They devoted themselves to the apostles' teaching and fellowship, to the breaking of bread [referring to the Eucharist] and the prayers" (ESV). The way this verse is translated and understood is strongly dependent on how the history and practice of the early church is understood or accepted.

Acts 13:2 describes the church setting where the Holy Spirit calls Barnabas and Saul for the work of missionary evangelism: "as they ministered to the Lord" (NKJV). The verb translated "ministered" (*leitourgeô*, from which we derive the English word *liturgy*) connotes a religious service led by people of honored position that has with it significant acts of worth and dignity. The rather common disapproval of liturgical worship, which is not untypical among Evangelicals today, is not in keeping with historic Christian church practice. This word *liturgy*, rooted in the book of Acts, continues to be used in Orthodox and other classical Christian communities for the worship service of the Church.

THE CHURCH AND HER HISTORY

It is at this point that a crucial component of the Orthodox Church became compelling to me and to those who entered the Church from our journey together. With no desire to exclude any person who confesses the gospel of Christ as being a child of God, it is an observable fact of history that the Church had a definitive beginning from the life, death, and resurrection of Jesus Christ and his pouring out the Holy Spirit upon his people at Pentecost.

The history of the Church has been marked by apostles who ordained elders and bishops and charged them with receiving, preserving, and handing down the treasury of the faith. In this Spirit-guided earthly journey, the Church has borne witness to the world that the All-Holy Triune God of Abraham, Isaac, and Jacob — and our Lord, God, and Savior Jesus Christ — has acted to bring salvation to all who will freely receive his life-giving and transformational grace.

The fullness of the Trinity, in the persons of the Father and the Son and the Holy Spirit, who are an essential unity, creates a body of those who receive this grace in repentance and faith. The Church expresses the life of the Trinity in her essential oneness and diverse fullness. As the Trinity is revealed to us in Christ through the Holy Scripture, the Church confesses we are standing before mystery itself. This mystery continues to flow through the eras of human history.

The questions of the history of Christianity are many and serious: How today are we to understand the Church with its division between East and West in the twelfth century and the Western division between Catholics and Protestants in the sixteenth-century Reformation? How does any Christian regard himself or herself in relation to this history? Do the worship practices of the Church from its beginning have any significance for worship practices today?

An ancient and usually unnoticed phrase that occurs in the Divine Liturgy soon after the reading and preaching of God's Word shines light on the contemporary relationship of evangelism and worship. There is a call that goes out in the liturgy which seems almost elitist: "The doors! The doors!" This means it is time for all the non-Orthodox to leave for further instruction while the Church enters into the holy intimacy of the Eucharist. The Church prays, "I will not speak of Thy Mystery to Thine enemies." In other words, as the holy priestly work of our High Priest in heaven unites with the priestly work of his body on earth, reverence, faith, and love are the essential energies to be found in the nave, which is the ark of salvation.

The proclamation of the gospel has gone forth. Now the Church retires to intimate communion with her Lord. Attracting those who are *outside* is no longer the concern. The Church now lifts up her heart to the Lord to give thanks. There is now no other person we seek. Our eyes look only to our God. It is in this intensity of the communion of love before the presence of the living God that the Church finds her true identity, her food, and her hope.

I believe that the historical development of the text and canon of the Scripture must inform how we are to understand the divine authority of the Bible today and that the history of the Church's tradition of interpretation must help us in our comprehension of what the Scripture teaches and what that teaching means.

REPLAYING THE JOURNEY

One of my strongest impressions in my journey from the Baptist vision of the Christian faith to Orthodoxy is how little the actual life of the Church during its two-thousand-year history really marks present-day thinking in the Evangelical church. In my student days, I recall that when church history was taught, it often seemed to be from the perspective of undermining classical Christian views and practices in favor of what American Evangelical Christians have come in these recent years to embrace. Much of the Church's worship practice which I experienced in my own early years was not necessarily theologically or spiritually determined but was in harmony with the more stable and traditionally rooted culture of the midtwentieth century in America. It is most significant to me that the church in upstate New York where I first encountered the faith and life of Christ, while still committed to the gospel and wanting to be faithful to the Bible, has changed radically in its worship practice and ethos. I know that my experience is not exceptional. In my later years as an Evangelical pastor, I was involved in reading and discussions about what came to be called "the worship wars."

It is ironic for me to hear my Evangelical friends express their distress over their sense of loss of church life and worship they have known for a lifetime. They also realize they can either be quiet and accept the changes or simply leave their church and look for another. Their further distress is that when they try to find a church that offers them a life of worship they have always known and loved, they cannot find it. What many of my Evangelical friends seem rarely to consider is that the more "traditional" ways they have known and loved are really very recent adaptations of earlier societal norms where evangelistic methods became the assumed framework to which the Church's worship life submitted.

I rarely talk with any Evangelical observer who doesn't think the worship life of the Church will continue to change often and significantly for the foreseeable future. The concerns of those advocating an allegiance to a more reverent and conservative type of worship will be pushed aside by those who feel that the first and most important goal is to adapt what we do to reach those who are outside the Church. As I survey the Evangelical landscape, it is inconceivable to me that the future Evangelical church will look much like what it is today, and I think it is impossible to envision what it will look like.

For years, I have heard Evangelical friends tell me that while the message of the Church doesn't change, its methods and approach must change. This usually conveys the assumption that the methods can be changed while the message remains untouched. Looking back over my more than fifty years in the Evangelical church, I believe the methods have changed the message in significant ways. The gospel has become simpler. Faith in Jesus Christ seems to have a more narrow vision, in which grace helps us to become better people and in which, whatever else is true of us, we can be certain without reservation that we will be in heaven after death. This is a radically reduced view of the gospel that was held by the ancient church of the apostles.

THE VISION OF THE CHURCH

The Orthodox world vision is full of wonder and mystery because Orthodox Christians believe that God is very present in his creation and is at work in giving and manifesting his presence to his people. While the Orthodox may use the word *sacrament*, that word is more a Western term with connotations that are not as expressive as the more biblical word for the gracious outpourings of God's uncreated energy in the Church and the world, which is *mystery*. Mystery is not magic. Mystery is the gracious movement of the Holy Spirit, often in response to the believing prayers of the people of God, to bring the presence and power of the Victorious Christ into the life of the Church. Simply stated, the Orthodox believe this is the kind of world the Bible describes. Both Evangelical and Orthodox Christians believe God reveals his presence as fire burning in a desert bush before an amazed Moses. God comes to be present to an uncertain Gideon by filling a fleece with the moisture of the dew. Orthodox Christians believe God hears the prayers of his people and sends down the Holy Spirit to come upon bread and wine and make it to be what our Lord Jesus himself says it is, his body and blood.

We Orthodox Christians also believe that because the Holy Spirit has come down and joined the Son of God, one of the Holy Trinity, with human flesh, he is also able and willing to bring the blessing of his presence upon the Holy Icons of the Church, where believing and prayerful Christians encounter the presence of grace in what is represented in the icon. The Orthodox faith also believes in the communion of the saints.

Many of our journey companions struggled with their long-held disagreement with the honor given to the Virgin Mary, the *Theotokos*, or "God-bearer," a term that comes from the conciliar definitions of the postapostolic church, wrestling with the profound and stunning implications of the Son of God's true identity and union with man. We came to understand the Church's clear and warmhearted insight into the spiritual power of the Theotokos's uniting of her will to God's, and, in this act of obedient trust, saying yes to being the gate by which the Word of God became the Man to save us, his lost brothers and sisters. Such union with the will of God is the key to her spiritual strength. This humble Jewish maiden, in her courage of faith, leads the way by which all people come to the God who seeks the admission of his only begotten Son into their lives. Mary is indeed the true prototypical Christian, for she fully received Jesus not only into her heart but also into her womb and thus gave him birth into his creation. Why? So that he might save it.

The warm love and devotion to Mary in the Orthodox Church is first of all amazement and thanks for her being our access to her Son. It hardly seems strange, and certainly is the least we could do, to honor the mother of our Lord. The Bible records her saying, "All generations will call me blessed" (Luke 1:48). We found that this relationship to Mary, so coldly received outside the Orthodox or Catholic churches, is natural and appropriate in the ways that God has made known to us.

These confessions have been the faith-rooted assumptions of Orthodox Christians for two thousand years. These things we assume because they are the kinds of things that happen in the world which the Bible describes. It has been said, "The Bible is not so much a book of facts to be learned as it is a world described that is to be experienced." Facts *are* important, but they are always in the service of the greater picture of what kind of world God created and how he acts within it.

The message of the Orthodox Church is that the world God created really is full of his glory, that he is actively present in it, and that his presence brings grace and salvation. This world, and every human person in it, is full of mystery because everything comes from the goodness and love of the personal God who has made humanity to love and know him. The Church is not merely an earthly institution of a religious nature; it is a mystery, an incarnate revelation of the All-Holy Trinity.

To be sure, the Church has this treasure of the mystery in clay vessels, but the clay doesn't diminish the treasured glory, and without that hidden mystery, the message itself becomes a mere idea to be discussed, embraced, or rejected. The Psalter confesses, "There is a river whose streams make glad the city of God" (Ps. 46:4); that river is the presence of the Christ-bearing Spirit of the Father. This life-giving stream brings the water of life to people perishing with thirst.

I experienced so much of that life-giving, thirst-quenching River of Life in the Evangelical church. It was also true, sadly, that I encountered rejection of the ways in which Holy Scripture has described, and the Church's great tradition has experienced, the gracious presence of God throughout the centuries. We do well when we prize both the gospel and the mystery it brings to us.

It is understandable and yet troubling when I see Evangelicals reacting negatively to the Divine Liturgy of the Orthodox Church because it is both "too different" and "too much." Where differences come from the cultures that carried Orthodox faith to America, the American Orthodox Church needs to do the patient work to make this Holy Tradition accessible to the language and culture of America. Where it is too much, the fullness of the Church requires wisdom both in teaching the fullness of the faith that has come to be rejected by Evangelicals and in presenting it in digestible portions for a society with a diminishing attention span.

For those of us who journeyed together into the Orthodox Church, we found the River of Life in fuller measure. We saw those beloved brothers and sisters who chose not to come with us return to churches that essentially deny or at least distrust the "something more" that we all set out to find.

Now that we are Orthodox Christians, we encounter a great mercy and a great glory. But we also face a great responsibility. Every Sunday, both at the beginning and at the end of the Divine Liturgy, we pray, "Preserve the fullness of Thy Church."

Our entering the Orthodox Church has been a gift, not an achievement. It is the gift of Christ, who proclaimed before his crucifixion, "I will build my church and the gates of Hades will not prevail against it" (Matt. 16:18). The vocation now is to receive what the Holy Spirit has given us and to faithfully seek to preserve it in its fullness before passing it on to the next generation.

Our danger is that we will see ourselves as the privileged, the correct, and not as the blessed who must humbly hold forth this precious treasure of the fullness of the faith and the fullness of the Church to any who hunger and thirst for more.

Others journeyed before us and welcomed us on our journey. For all of us, this journey is possible only because we have come to believe in the Christ who said, "I am the way" (John 14:6). His way is the gospel, poured out through his life. Keeping this gospel central, clear, and compelling in the richness of the faith which "was once for all delivered to the saints" (Jude 3 ESV) is the way forward on this journey until we stand in the full beauty of his glory.

✐

CHAPTER 2

A RESPONSE TO
EASTERN ORTHODOXY

Craig Blaising

A t the outset, let me express my appreciation to the editor and publisher for an opportunity to respond to Wilbur Ellsworth's essay promoting the Orthodox Church. I accepted this invitation without knowing either who the author would be or what approach he would take. Imagine my surprise to find the author was Wilbur Ellsworth, the former pastor of First Baptist Church, Wheaton, Illinois. I think this surprise may be shared by many readers of this book as well. I was intrigued by Ellsworth's narrative of his spiritual journey from Baptist pastor to Orthodox priest but pleased that he chose to share his story and appreciative of the gracious, humble, and engaging manner in which he presents it. I was also pleased to see that Ellsworth is truly appreciative of his Baptist and Evangelical heritage while candid about the concerns that led him to search for "something more." His testimony leads naturally to the question of how to evaluate the move theologically, and so, toward the end of his narrative, Ellsworth provides a brief, gentle apology for some obvious differences between Orthodox and Evangelical belief and practice. I do hope that my reply will carry the same spirit of sincerity and grace in which Ellsworth has shared his journey. Truly, that should be the case for all of us who seek to serve Christ, since the authority to which we appeal is not in ourselves but in Christ. As servants of Christ, we humbly defer this matter to him and to his Word, which is "profitable for teaching, for reproof, for correction, and for training in righteousness" so that we might be "competent, equipped for every good work" (2 Tim. 3:16–17 ESV).

Let me begin at the point of Ellsworth's appreciation for his Baptist background, in which he heard the gospel and was first nurtured in Christ. It is very important to note that Ellsworth acknowledges that the gospel is preached by Baptists, that he himself heard it, received it, was saved thereby, and as a Baptist pastor, preached that gospel to others. Furthermore, he acknowledges that there are many in Baptist churches who are sincere and godly believers. It is very important to understand what is being said here. Ellsworth is not simply saying that there are nice, sincere, pious, or even religious people in the Baptist and Evangelical churches with which he was associated. Rather he is saying that the gospel is preached and believed there. Faith in the gospel is foundational to Christian identity, and Ellsworth, as a former Baptist and Evangelical, knows that. There is only one gospel (Gal 1:6–9), and it is the power of God for salvation (Rom 1:16). Traditionally, Evangelicals are very jealous for the gospel and distinguish between those churches that clearly preach it and those that do not. Ellsworth's estimation of his early Christian and ministerial background is typically Evangelical, and it is noteworthy that he still speaks of the churches he was formerly affiliated with as truly churches.

Furthermore, the freedom with which Ellsworth sought out "something more" and then went on to embrace, profess, and practice it is itself a Baptist principle — the principle of religious freedom. Ellsworth is certainly free to be or not to be Baptist or Orthodox, and I, as a Baptist, completely uphold his right in this matter. However, not all of the Orthodox see it this way.

This may be surprising to the American Evangelical who is looking at the Orthodox Church as a "possible alternative" among a variety of Evangelical communions. That perspective, and the alternative it seems to offer, is particularly Western, and even in the West, it may be more apparent outside an Orthodox church than inside it. Moving beyond Western democracies, in traditional Orthodox countries, the freedom of Baptist and Evangelical ministries is often significantly restricted and many times politically harassed by the Orthodox Church working through the state.[1] If this is simply a matter of misunderstanding, then it is incumbent upon Orthodox priests like Ellsworth and others in Orthodox churches in the United States who know that Baptists and Evangelicals are preaching the true gospel to set the record straight and bring the harassment to an end. For, as every Evangelical and in fact as every true Christian knows, the first priority is the proclamation of the gospel. The apostolic position on this matter is one of indifference as to who is preaching it or even what their motive is as long as the true gospel is preached (Phil. 1:15–18). The eternal destinies of many are at stake here. The Orthodox harassment of ministries preaching the gospel, however, raises the question of how widely the perspective held by Ellsworth on Baptists, Evangelicals, and even the gospel itself is actually shared in Orthodox circles.

As appreciative as he is of his Baptist heritage, Ellsworth highlights a problem which caused him to look for "something more"—a deeper, richer, more reverential form of worship. For Ellsworth, the problem of a seemingly shallow worship was exacerbated by the impact of the seeker sensitive movement on the church with which he was affiliated. The seeker movement, drawing upon market-driven methodologies, recast the church service so as to be suitable to an assembly of seekers rather than a congregation of believers. This is one aspect of the "worship wars" troubling Evangelical churches, and Ellsworth is right to complain about it. On the one hand, given the Evangelical concern for the gospel and the cruciality of personal faith, it is understandable that churches would and should do everything they can to make the gospel clear within their gatherings. On the other hand, this practice of turning the primary gathering of the church into a seeker service constitutes a challenge to the traditional Baptist doctrine of a believers' church.[2] A believers' church, at the very least, is a gathering of believers to worship God and grow together in grace and the knowledge of God's Word. Even Willow Creek has admitted failure in their church's ministry responsibility to believers.[3] Ellsworth is a pastor who has struggled with this issue, and it constitutes an overarching theme in his essay from beginning to end. While many have sought and are seeking to correct the problem, Ellsworth's own quest for a solution led him to Orthodoxy, which by the very meaning of the word is a literal claim to "right worship."

In response, I wish to neither understate nor overstate the problem, nor is it possible in the scope of this reply even to begin to deal with the many aspects of true and proper worship (something on which many books and articles have been written). I do think that there are

Baptist and Evangelical church services that deeply reverence God, and there are those that seem like shallow performances. Any one person's experience is anecdotal and context specific. However, I think it would be a mistake to assume that a scripted liturgy in itself solves the problem. Has there never been an Orthodox service in which the liturgy seemed a rote performance or from which congregants left having repeated familiar, even memorized, lines without the truth touching their hearts in a deep way? I have seen this happen on occasion with the singing of profoundly theological and biblically rich hymns in an Evangelical service. If it can happen there, I rather think it could and probably does happen sometimes with the performance of liturgy in an Orthodox service. The issue here is not simply a matter of finding the right "worship program." Ellsworth is certainly right that worship requires a deep reverence for God. Worship also expresses a deep gratitude and joy for the grace of God in Christ and manifests itself in faith, hope, and love. Pastors have a responsibility to instruct and lead their churches in true worship and guard against the mere rote performance of a program, whether that be new or old.

Ellsworth's quest for a deeper, truer form of worship, however, did not lead merely to an adjustment in the form of the service but led him to convert to the Orthodox Church, and that inevitably raises the issue of theological differences between Baptists and Orthodox. In concluding the account of his journey, Ellsworth admits "a significantly different theological vision and practice" between his beginning and end points, and he addresses some of the key issues, albeit rather lightly, at the end of his essay.

The first issue has to do with the authority of Scripture in relation to the Tradition of the Church and is addressed by Ellsworth in his sections "The Church and the Bible" and "The Church and Her History." The concern that Baptists and other Evangelicals have here is that the Orthodox extend the locus of divine inspiration and authority beyond the Scripture to the Church itself, specifically to the decisions of the ecumenical councils, but more generally and on a practical level to the entirety of Orthodox tradition.[4] For all practical purposes, this means that church tradition is not correctible by Scripture. Rather Scripture is ruled by Tradition, which defines its message and application.[5]

The Orthodox usually defend their view by arguing the primacy of the Church over the Scripture: the Church existed prior to the New Testament Scripture and was itself the source of Scripture. As it was the source of Scripture, so it was the source of the Tradition that integrates and applies Scripture.[6] This typical Orthodox argument is, I think, what Ellsworth is alluding to when he says, "I believe that the historical development of the text and canon of the Scripture must inform how we are to understand the divine authority of the Bible today ..." The Orthodox believe that the actual history of the canon and the beliefs and practices of the early church support this view. However, I do not believe that this reading of early church history is correct.

The problem is that the Orthodox blur the New Testament and early patristic distinction between apostolic and episcopal authority. Ephesians 2:20 says that the Church is founded on "the apostles and prophets, Christ Jesus himself being the cornerstone" (ESV). This is said in a letter in which an apostle directs the church to his writings in order to understand the mystery of Christ, a matter revealed to apostles and prophets (Eph. 3:3–4). This same apostle stipulated that bishops must hold to the faith as he taught it, and warned that the time was coming when some would depart from that faith. In fact, both Paul and Peter warned that heresy would arise *within the church* and directed the bishops and teachers to Scripture (Acts 20:28–32; 2 Tim. 3:1–4:8; 2 Peter 1:12–2:3; 3:1–18)—which those apostles saw as inclusive of their own writings (1 Cor. 2:6–13; Eph. 3:1–4; 2 Peter 1:12–21; 3:1–2, 14–16)—in fulfilling their charge of guarding and proclaiming the faith. The early Christian episcopal writings express this same sense of dependency and obligatory faithfulness in their regard for and use of Scripture, and this was especially evident in the Church's early response to heresy.[7]

The Orthodox are particularly concerned about the problem of heretics misusing Scripture, and so they appeal to Tradition as a guard against such distortion. The problem is, however, that Scripture-twisting heresies normally arise not outside but rather inside the Church. The New Testament warns of *the problem of discovering heresy present within* the episcopal and teaching structures of the Church, a problem that would have to be dealt with not by appealing to one set of episcopal authorities over against another but by appealing to Scripture.[8] This is a problem of which Evangelicalism, by virtue of its Reformation heritage, is well aware.[9]

The Arian controversy, which is viewed as pivotal by present-day Orthodox and Evangelicals alike (as well as Roman Catholics), is a case in point. Arius claimed to be doing nothing more than passing along the Tradition that he had been taught.[10] The Arian heresy was discovered *existing within* the teaching structure of the fourth-century Alexandrian church and was then found to be favored by bishops and teachers in other churches as well. The controversy was formally settled (though Arianism continued an historical presence) on the basis of biblical authority through an intensive debate over the meaning of Scripture. All the documents bear witness to this.[11] The Nicene Creed was drafted as a concise statement of what Scripture taught on this issue. As Athanasius makes clear in his *Defense of the Nicene Creed* and his *Letter to the African Bishops*, it was the objective of the council *to use the acknowledged language of Scripture*.[12] This carried over into the actual construction of the statement, which is a remarkable composition of biblical words, phrases, and allusions collated into the structure of 1 Corinthians 8:6.[13] Athanasius also makes clear that the council's regard for the authority of Scripture led it to address the matter in this way. When they did use the nonbiblical word *homoousios* and the phrase *ek tes ousias tou patros*, the referential meaning of those words was explicitly tied to a collection of biblical texts, so that the meaning of the phrases, and thus of the creed as a whole, would be, in a derivative sense, exactly the meaning of the Scripture.[14] The creed functioned in the same way as expressions of the rule of faith in earlier patristic writings. The rule of faith was not the *imposition* of a doctrinal rule upon Scripture but the *exposition* of a rule inherent within Scripture.[15]

Between the fourth and eighth centuries, however, a not-so-subtle shift of authority took place within the Church, a shift that is starkly evident when one compares the language of the First Council of Nicaea (325) with that of the second (787).[16] The Second Council of Nicaea addressed the doctrinal issue of venerating icons in Orthodox life and liturgy, a practice that had developed within the Church to the point that it was regarded as a problem, was challenged, and was even proscribed by some on the basis of biblical prohibitions against idolatry.[17] Whereas the First Council of Nicaea dealt with its controversy solely upon biblical authority, the second council spoke solely on the basis of episcopal and popular tradition, a tradition that is found neither in the New Testament nor in the earliest days of the Church.[18] It was *a practice that developed within* the Church. Not only did the council authorize this practice solely upon its own tradition, but it went on to declare Tradition itself as a Holy Spirit–given, sufficient basis for any doctrine and practice and anathematized "anyone who rejects any written or unwritten tradition of the church."[19] By that act and with that express teaching, the Second Council of Nicaea formalized a departure from the tradition of sole biblical authority in doctrinal matters that was evidenced by its earlier namesake. Contrary to apostolic teaching and early episcopal practice, it legislated for the Church a new conception of Tradition, one that is, in principle, immune from biblical correction.

The issue is not the existence of Tradition per se. We all have traditions. Not only are they unavoidable; they are quite necessary. At their best, they offer familiar and accepted ways of expressing faith and obedience to Christ. In fact, we expect that in the Church's life and worship, there will be traditional ways of speaking and acting that reflect the constancy and continuity of the unchanging gospel and the abiding canon of Scripture. Scripture gives instruction on the unchanging faith and unchanging character of life in Christ Jesus, who is the same, yesterday, today, and always. So we should be able to see in and through our traditional practices continuity with the New Testament church.

Developments do take place in traditional practices.[20] This is true even in Orthodox liturgy. Certainly the liturgy is old, but Orthodox liturgy in its current form was not performed by the earliest church. Nor has it been practiced in exactly the same way among various Orthodox churches past or present. Differences have developed in time and in different regional contexts, not to mention certain doctrinal differences, as seen for example between Eastern and Oriental Orthodox.[21] New Testament uses of *leitourgeo* and *leitourgia* do not refer to a performance of liturgy like that of the Orthodox today. The New Testament usage is quite interesting and clarified by Paul in his epistles. The apostolic work of proclaiming the gospel, conversion, and then the growth of the Church into maturity in Christ was seen as a *leitourgia* or "priestly service" in which the Church is offered up to Christ as a holy, living sacrifice. It was not the offering up of a sacrifice on behalf of the Church (as in the Catholic performance of the Mass) or the performance of a scripted service (as in Orthodoxy) but evangelism, conversion, and edification in godliness through apostolic teaching directed toward the formation of a holy communion that presents itself to Christ now and at his coming.[22]

Developing Tradition is not a problem in itself unless it is found to act as a hindrance to a fully formed biblical faith and wholehearted obedience to God's Word. This is something Jesus found in the Judaisms of his day. The only way to guard against this is to focus first and foremost on Scripture, submitting our traditions to the Word of God either for reaffirmation, renewal, or reformation.

This is not to say that Orthodox tradition generally and the liturgy specifically are lacking in biblical content. On the contrary, the liturgy is richly endowed with biblical citations and allusions. It manifests a biblical depth that is richly rewarding to the participant who carefully considers its content in itself and intertextually with the canon of Scripture.[23] The liturgy is a carefully constructed framework by which one can not only learn and be reminded of basic theological truth but also contemplate deeper matters of the faith. Consequently, it is not surprising that Ellsworth and many others who have longed for deeper biblical and theological worship have been greatly blessed by participation in Orthodox liturgy. In spite of various developments, the high value the Orthodox have placed on Tradition has for the most part preserved this collection of Scripture texts and biblically informed prayers and admonitions for the guidance and instruction of generations of worshipers. However, Evangelicals in continuity with the Reformation sincerely believe that side by side with these are some practices and theological expressions that are in tension with if not actually contrary to the intent and teaching of Scripture. Along with the matter of the unique authority of the Word of God, these are other features of what Ellsworth calls a significantly different theological vision.

Take the matter of the use of icons in worship. We need to note that Scripture clearly teaches that the focus of worship is on God alone. It is not focused upon ourselves, either as individuals or as a church, but upon God. Candidly, one of the issues we as Evangelicals sometimes struggle with is the danger of a worship service becoming focused on ourselves or on a performer rather than on Christ. We know that this is a temptation in the Church, and we need to be continually reminded of Paul's instruction in 1 Corinthians 1–4: we preach not ourselves but Christ. But just as surely as we are not to focus on ourselves as the living Church today, neither are we to focus our worship on dead saints. The dead in Christ are with Christ. Their examples and testimonies may be cited in the service (particularly in preaching, as illustrations of faith and obedience) along with the examples and testimonies of living believers today. But they should not become the point of focus in the worship service.

The problem for the Orthodox, however, seems greater than a shift in focus. Orthodox liturgy requires the *veneration* of icons. Scripture gives absolutely no basis for lighting candles or incense for dead saints and clearly forbids the use of images in worship, avoiding even the temptation to idolatry.

It is true that the Orthodox offer a distinction between the honor given to icons on the one hand and idolatrous worship on the other. The Second Council of Nicaea argues such a distinction.[24] However, the concern here is the same as that articulated by the Reformers against the Church of Rome: the supposed distinction may sometimes be too subtle for actual practice.[25] I grant that a well-trained and well-educated clergy and laity may comprehend and maintain the distinction. I think that Ellsworth maintains it, as do many Orthodox that I know personally. But is this always the case? In the New Testament, Paul taught that he would rather go without meat than by eating meat offered to idols cause a weak brother to stumble back into idolatry—the weaker brother not being able to comprehend or maintain the distinction that prevents idolatry-like behavior from being actual idolatry. Why then would the Church authorize a practice in Christian worship *that might in any way* cause someone to stumble into idolatry?

The problem of iconology extends to Mariology in Orthodox practice. The fact that Mary said that all generations would call her blessed does not authorize forms of veneration that are practically indistinguishable from worship. Evangelicals consider Mary blessed and expect to see her with all the saints when we are together with the Lord. But we expect that she would be just as appalled as were Paul and Barnabas at Lystra, or as was the angel in John's vision in Revelation, when actions directed toward her even look like worship.[26] Her words in Scripture were, "Do whatever *he* tells you" (John 2:5, italics added). She is honored when multitudes do as she advised by listening to and submitting themselves to her Son.

Of course, one might attempt to excuse practices of veneration by arguing that these are forms of honor and respect that belong to ancient culture, and while they may seem strange to modern sensibilities, they were acceptable then. The problem with this is that it ignores the fact that this veneration did provoke a strong reaction in the eighth century by many in the Church concerned about the sin of idolatry. Icon veneration was actually proscribed for a while precisely because of this fear. Consequently, even in ancient times there was concern that a line might be or was being crossed. A practical solution to the problem now would be simply to dispense with these practices which are no longer culturally relevant and were even then religiously suspect and replace them with activities that are better understood and not problematic. However, this is where we run into the problem of Tradition once again. Tradition has fixed the practice on its own presumed divine authority so that it is alterable neither by practical considerations nor out of regard for biblical instruction.

Another significantly different theological perspective mentioned by Ellsworth has to do with the Eucharist and baptism. The Eucharist especially plays a prominent role in Orthodox liturgy, and the liturgy clearly advocates (by invocation and proclamation) a real change of the bread and wine into the actual body and blood of Christ.[27] Ellsworth candidly admits that this doctrine was not easily accepted by him or by those from Christ Church who joined him, but came to be accepted through extended study. It is not necessary for me to rehearse here the arguments of Baptists and other Evangelicals who dissent from the real presence interpretation of the Lord's Supper. These are well known and can be easily accessed. But it may be helpful to recall what the issue is in the different views. The issue, once again, is faithfulness to the Lord's command and to apostolic instruction. Historically,

Baptists have reacted to sacramental views of grace which they argue are not biblical. Baptists believe that Zwingli was basically correct in seeing a metaphorical intent in the Lord's remarks at the Last Supper. However, the deeper issue has to do with how grace is transmitted and received. Baptists see no justification in Scripture for connecting grace to anything other than the direct gift of God to personal faith directed to his Word of promise. There is no doubt that a sacramental view of the Eucharist did develop through the early centuries of the Church so that a real presence view *came to be found within* church teaching. But Baptists do not believe this was in fact the view of the New Testament churches. In fact, Baptists have even criticized Zwingli for inconsistency in not recognizing that this deeper theological issue extends also to the understanding of baptism. Accordingly, Baptists affirm believer's baptism, which is taught consistently in the New Testament. Baptism is a proclamation and testimony by a believer of a grace received from God through faith promised to the believer by God in his Word.

Having said all this, I think it is fair for Ellsworth to raise the question to Baptists whether there is something legitimately more than mere memory in a communion service and whether baptism is more than the mere obedience to the Lord's explicit command. In fact, Baptists have theological resources that are deeper and richer than those conveyed in some contemporary practices. It is, after all, not mere memory but a living remembrance of faith, hope, and love that is called for, the content of which is informed by the theologically rich divine Word of promise. However, many Baptists have reacted so strongly against sacramentalism that they have neglected to develop and expand the rich depth of the theology they profess. This is a responsibility that rests squarely on the shoulders of pastors and teachers who are tasked with faithfully preaching and teaching the Word of God for the edification of the Church. They must not be deterred in that task by traditions of neglect, whether those be formal or informal traditions.

Pastors and teachers must be careful not to neglect declaring to the Church "the whole counsel of God" (Acts 20:27 ESV). The doctrine of the atonement is central to that counsel and is presented in Scripture through several images, metaphors, and direct instruction. Unfortunately, much of the current debate on the atonement tends to be reductionist, highlighting one or another of the images to the neglect of the whole. While I agree with Ellsworth that the notions of victory, release, and redemption should powerfully inform our understanding of the work of Christ, I don't see any reason to neglect the equally powerful and rich New Testament teaching on the penal and judicial meaning of the cross. We may differ on which may be better suited as a unifying image theologically, but as long as we include the whole counsel, we will not differ much on this issue in the long run.

There are other things that could be highlighted among the theological differences between Baptists and Evangelicals on the one hand and the Orthodox on the other. However, I would like to close this response with a word of appreciation and a challenge that I think both of us can appreciate. Talk about differences must be balanced by noting what we share in common, chief among which is a Trinitarian theology revealed in Scripture and faithfully expounded by pastor-theologians in the early centuries of the Church. This is a theological heritage that is bequeathed to both Eastern and Western Churches. Theologians on both sides have reflected on this common orthodoxy, but interaction among them has been limited because of the historic separation of the churches. The immigration of Orthodox Christians to the West at the beginning of the last century brought renewed contact between Eastern and Western theologians and has made the work of Eastern theologians more accessible to the West. Important contributions have been made, and we would be remiss not to acknowledge that fact. The contact between East and West has also sparked a renewed interest in and recovery of patristic sources. New critical editions and modern-language translations of a number of patristic texts have been published in the last century, bringing a renewed interest in and more developed knowledge of the theology of the early church among Catholic, Orthodox, and Protestant theologians. In the last quarter of the century, Evangelical theology began to benefit from this greater engagement with patristic thought as well.

Many benefits can be cited, but a particularly relevant aspect of this *ressourcement* is the focus that has been brought to bear on patristic biblical interpretation with critical editions and translations of numerous homiletical and expositional works, many of which received little attention in the past.[28] This has brought into view more clearly than ever before both the great value the Fathers placed on Scripture and the wealth of insight and wisdom they drew from it for the edification of the Church. The challenge for us today, as I see it, is to recover that biblically enriched mindset in Christian ministry—a ministerial mind that is immersed in Scripture. For surely, the one who knows the Scripture deeply is the one who is able to draw out its riches—not for mere curiosity's sake but for the nurture and edification of the Church. In the early church, the focal point of the service in which this took place was the sermon. But this was no short homily tacked onto the liturgy, or some friendly religious talk addressed to "felt needs." Perhaps it is just my opinion, but maybe both sides can yet learn something from those who went before us. Maybe if the churches recover a deep love for, a deep knowledge of, and a deep obedience to God's Word, then we'll have a better perspective from which to address those debates about worship that are troubling the Church today. For the issue ultimately is a matter not of a program per se but of a deep abiding of the whole Word of God—living and written (which are bound together)—in the heart, mind, and soul of the Church so that what is done and what is said is a pleasing and fragrant offering to God.

CHAPTER 3

EASTERN ORTHODOXY REJOINDER

Wilbur Ellsworth

I am grateful to Dr. Blaising for the warm and gracious spirit in his response to my account of our journey to the Orthodox Church. It should surprise no one that two brothers in Christ who both have lived decades of their lives in the vitality of American Evangelical Christianity share deep common values. Moreover, both of us identify some weaknesses in this Christian movement and also see shortcomings of some sort within the Orthodox Christian Church.

Dr. Blaising and I share a high regard for Holy Scripture. We both affirm the centrality of preaching the gospel. We both uphold the necessity throughout Christendom to respect the moral freedom of every person to come to faith in Christ without coercion. We both value the importance of a reverent spirit in the Church's life of worship.

Yet we have significant differences across the Evangelical-Orthodox divide. In this last part of our conversation, I will seek to identify the roots of these differences and offer an Orthodox witness for the beliefs that I and so many others hold.

1. IS THE GOSPEL CENTRAL AND CLEAR IN THE ORTHODOX CHURCH?

Dr. Blaising writes that "Evangelicals are very jealous for the gospel and distinguish between those churches that clearly preach it and those that do not." While Dr. Blaising does not overtly charge that the gospel is not clearly preached by the Orthodox Church, he does raise the question. Having observed both worlds, I suggest that the clarity of gospel preaching is a matter for continual, humble, prayerful, and historic sensitivity on both sides of this divide. I vigorously affirm that both Evangelicals and the Orthodox embrace and proclaim what Saint Paul called the core of the gospel, as stated in 1 Corinthians 15:1–4: Christ's saving death for our sins, burial, and resurrection in accordance with the (Old Testament) Scriptures. But in this same text, the apostle Paul raises another issue, that it is possible to believe "in vain." That is, a person may fail to stand in this faith. Saint Paul contends that his life gives evidence that God's grace toward him was not in vain (v. 10) and is an example of a life of salvation. The strength of Evangelical preaching is its directness in preaching what is sometimes called "the simple gospel." All Christians should rejoice in the countless lives transformed by that proclamation.

The Orthodox Church preaches the gospel of Christ, but not so simply, believing that Holy Scripture says much more about salvation and what it means than is usually contained in "the simple gospel." For example, Evangelicals often begin with Romans 3:23: "All have sinned and fall short of [or lack] the glory of God." Orthodox tradition does not see this as merely a statement about being guilty of failing to attain to the standard of God's holiness; rather it is a reflection on the tragic loss of the fullness of God's likeness caused by man's sin.

The Orthodox proclamation of the gospel is about the recovery of what the Father purposed in sending his Son: to bring "many sons and daughters to glory" (Heb. 2:10). The nature of this glory is the participation in the revealed life of the Holy Trinity, in grace, love, and communion. This transformational salvation is rooted in and dependent on the work of Christ and the Holy Spirit as the Christian strives (not meritoriously but dependently on God's grace) to put off sin that continues to rob us of glory and perpetuate death. This is a major theme of Orthodox teaching, for the very word *orthodox* means "right glory."

Sadly, this view of salvation is often regarded by Evangelicals as "salvation by works" and antithetical to the gospel. As an Orthodox priest, I recognize the pastoral importance of keeping the gospel clear, central, and compelling while constantly encouraging God's people in their life in Christ. Evangelicals are mistaken to confuse such exhortation with obscuring or even abandoning the gospel.

2. DOES ORTHODOXY ABUSE THE SPIRITUAL FREEDOM OF OTHERS?

Dr. Blaising raises the difficulties that Evangelicals have experienced when the Orthodox Church, working through a secular government, hinders their work. I cannot defend the Orthodox Church when it uses political force to hinder the Christian work of others. However, to understand the problem, we should be aware of the historical, cultural, and political realities involved, even though these are not excuses. Uncharitable actions of some Orthodox toward Evangelicals reflect the hurt caused by the Orthodox perception that the Evangelicals regard them as ungodly pagans, this after many of them have suffered for years under oppressive governments. For example, if an Orthodox priest were to appear on an Evangelical campus in full liturgical vestments and tell students, "You need to be truly saved!" he would be asked to leave, and rightly so. It is not difficult, then, to imagine how an Orthodox Christian in Russia reacts to an Evangelical missionary who tells her she needs to become a Christian.

The theology of the Orthodox Church is deeply committed to the moral freedom of every human to make decisions regarding faith, without coercion of any sort. When any Orthodox depend on political force to protect or advance Orthodoxy, or fail to recognize the core of Christian belief in non-Orthodox Christians, they need to seek better understanding and to repent. In such cases, we Orthodox in our failings need to pray the words of our liturgy, "Preserve the fullness of Thy Church."

3. DOES ORTHODOX TRADITION OPPOSE THE AUTHORITY OF SCRIPTURE?

Orthodox theologian Georges Florovsky wrote, "The Scriptures are indeed one Holy Scripture, one Holy Writ. There is one main theme and one main message through the whole story ... There is a beginning and an end, which is also a goal ... Every particular moment [in Scripture] is a process going on between these two terminal points. And this process has a definite direction ... No moment can be understood except in the whole context and perspective."[1]

In his preface to the *Brazos Theological Commentary on the Bible*, R. R. Reno recalls the second-century apologist Irenaeus, who in his

Against the Heresies likened Scripture to a great mosaic whose many pieces form the portrait of a handsome king. He imagines the pieces of that mosaic being packaged for transporting. Upon arrival the various tiles need to be put into their proper order and relationship to one another in accordance with the artist's intention. In his story, the lack of the master plan produces a picture not of the king but of a dog! The difficulty is that Scripture comes to us in its individual pieces, but the order and sequence are not obvious. While there are important guiding statements within the pieces, the mosaic must still be arranged under a larger vision than each piece provides. This is the work of biblical interpretation, and the role of the Church's life, guided by the Holy Spirit, is to form the Tradition — or, to use the New Testament word, *paradidomi*, it is "the handing down" of Tradition. In keeping with Irenaeus's story, we must remember that the purpose of the mosaic is accomplished only when the portrait of the handsome king emerges from the arranging of the pieces. If the image of the king is not clearly seen, the perspective and context of the entire effort has failed.

The Lord's words in John 5:39–40 create a foundational understanding of biblical interpretation that became Holy Tradition in the life of the Church. In speaking to his religious opponents, he said, "You search the Scriptures because in them you think that you have eternal life, and it is they that bear witness to Me, yet you refuse to come to Me that you may have eternal life" (my translation). I wonder if the translators of the King James Version of this verse weakened Western Christian understanding of the Lord's teaching by translating the verb *search* as an imperative, "search the Scriptures." The correct meaning of the passage is that searching the (Old Testament) Scriptures *apart from Christ* is a mistaken quest that will not bring eternal life. The words "you think" clearly indicate that the pursuit of Jesus' religious opponents was misguided or inadequate. He then brings the corrective needed for a life-giving reading of Holy Scripture: "it is they that bear witness about Me, yet you refuse to come to Me that you may have eternal life."

The Lord is hardly giving license here to disregard the truth of Scripture or freedom to revise it to conform to changing human opinion. Rather he is saying that the Scriptures, given through men by the inspiration of the Holy Spirit, find their true and ultimate authority in faithfully and redemptively revealing him. He is saying it is a mistake to make Scripture the ultimate source of life, because that source is Christ himself. The value and authority of Scripture (which is truly great!) lies in its witness to Christ, who alone is the one sent from God to bring life and light. Orthodox theologian Bradley Nassif has written that the Orthodox understanding of the Bible is "personalist in its emphasis." He further states, "The question, 'What is the authority of Scripture?' is resolved in the prior answer to 'Who is truth?'"[2]

Luke 24 tells of the Lord's conversation with two disciples returning from Jerusalem to Emmaus on the day of his resurrection. The two were confused and discouraged by the events of the past few days. Later he appeared to his disciples. In both of these meetings, the Lord interpreted to them "in all the Scriptures the things concerning himself" (v. 27 NKJV). The scope of his biblical teaching came from "Moses and all the Prophets ... and the Psalms" (vv. 27, 44) — in other words, the entire Old Testament. The Lord centered his hermeneutical approach on himself. This became the apostolic pattern and was followed by the fathers of the Church. It lies at the heart of the Church's tradition. It is, above all else, a personal vision of Christ that fills the Old Testament Scriptures. While the Old Testament shone its light forward to prepare the way for the coming of Christ, the apostolic writers of the New Testament wrote through the Holy Spirit to shine the light of Christ back into the Old Testament Scriptures, illuminating their incomplete light by what can be fully seen only in Christ.

There is a growing sensitivity among Evangelical hermeneutical scholars to the living vision of the Tradition's Christological view of Scripture, yet I believe that much of Evangelicalism today remains bound in an unhistoric and reductionist view of the Bible. Some years ago I attended a lecture given by a prominent Evangelical theologian who taught at one of America's most respected Evangelical seminaries. In essence he said that we must not criticize the way the apostles interpreted the Old Testament because they were inspired by the Holy Spirit, but we must not imitate their hermeneutical method because it is wrong!

Admittedly, this was one man speaking, and many, perhaps even most, Evangelical hermeneutical scholars would not identify with that statement. But I have heard the same view expressed more than once by prominent Evangelical preachers who continue to shape the understanding of the popular Evangelical movement. I believe that such a view causes Evangelicals to prejudge Orthodoxy as unfaithful to Scripture, at least according to how Evangelicals interpret it. I hear such an understanding expressed often and find it profoundly ironic. I suggest that those who wish to better grasp what the Orthodox hold regarding the authority of Scripture consult *Christ in the Psalms* by Patrick Henry Reardon. This book was instrumental in my coming to see the greater Christological vision of the interpretive view of both the Lord and his apostles. It faithfully expresses the view of the Orthodox Church.

Dr. Blaising charges the Orthodox with blurring the distinction between apostolic and episcopal authority. As a participant in decades of Evangelical theological debates, I find this charge less than compelling. Also, in the areas in which Dr. Blaising raises objections to specific teaching or practices established by Orthodox tradition, the history and the context of the Church's teaching are passed over quickly. I believe that the Orthodox Church can rightly object, "Not so fast!"

I remember my earlier skepticism, as an Evangelical, for various historic Christian beliefs and practices. It came from an unsympathetic understanding of the nature of the Church's life, an understanding that either disregarded or ignored the context of the development of the Tradition. In my Evangelical training, sixteenth-century reactions to various corruptions in the Western Church were often used to reject and discard valuable spiritual wisdom that was deeply responsive and submissive to Scripture.

The better action would have been to unstop the wells that had become clogged by corruption, rather than rejecting the wells themselves. I believe that such rejection has done great damage to Christianity and has produced a tragically diminished vision of the fullness of the gospel and the salvation that Christ brings to fallen humanity. The rejection of the Tradition's faithfulness to Christological biblical interpretation has been popularly embraced among Evangelicals in response to Catholicism. Orthodoxy often gets the overflow of that same reaction.

4. Is the Orthodox Church Idolatrous in Its Use of Material Things in Worship?

The Lord's use of soil mixed with his saliva to bring sight to a blind man is a graphic example of the Lord's use of the material creation as an instrument of his grace (John 9:6–7). Acts 19:12 tells of handkerchiefs and aprons that had touched Paul's skin being used to heal the sick and to exorcize the oppressed. Clearly, the New Testament does not reflect a gnostic view of the world. The accusation that the veneration of icons is either intrinsically idolatrous or a dangerous seduction toward idolatry reflects a gnostic view of creation, as well as a Protestant tendency to reject biblically rooted devotional practices rather than adopting the original vision of the Tradition. It is this type of biblical interpretation that the Orthodox Church encountered and rejected in the fourteenth century in the controversy between Barlaam of Calabria and Gregory Palamas. Barlaam's rejection of certain Orthodox practices was rooted not so much in faithfulness to the tradition of biblical interpretation as in the philosophical nominalism of William of Ockham, which, as Orthodox theologian John Meyendorff described it, viewed the Bible as "a source of quotations and references, and not as a means of living communion with the spirit of God."[3]

Whether it is icons or the real presence of Christ in the bread and the wine of the Eucharist, the same questions come to us: How did the Lord and his disciples view the material creation? Does God bring his divine power and presence into the world in a material and concrete way? I have repeatedly encountered earnest Christian people passing over these foundational questions in their passion to lament abuses they have experienced (or have heard about) related to ancient church practices. For them, the burden of proof is on those who see in the Bible a depiction of creation not as a place of magic but as a theater of the divine mystery of God's love and mercy manifesting itself in and through the physical world. This divine mystery, of course, rises to its greatest height in the incarnation of our Lord.

When Dr. Blaising accuses later church councils of abandoning Scripture for the raw power of ecclesiastical authority, citing particularly the Seventh Ecumenical Council's vindication of the veneration of icons, I am perplexed by his passing over the historical context of that council, where political forces were trying to protect the empire from Islamic opposition to icons and from some who were condemning icons as idolatrous. One of the giants of this era was John of Damascus, who just a few years earlier had written, "Of old God the incorporeal and uncircumscribed was not depicted at all. But now that God has appeared in the flesh and lived among humans, I make an image of the God who can be seen. I do not worship matter but I worship the Creator of matter, who for my sake became material and deigned to dwell in matter, who through matter effected my salvation. I will not cease from worshipping the matter through which my salvation has been effected."[4]

As councils returned to controversial matters, such as the Christological understandings articulated at the Council of Chalcedon in 451 and the Second Council of Nicaea in 787, they did not shrink from asserting their wisdom in choosing between contradictory claims of various interests and between conflicting views of biblical support for various positions. The Tradition of the Church is a living Tradition. It does not deal with merely interesting or even significant abstractions. It remembers that great problems deal with life and salvation. As Baptist theologian D. H. Williams pointed out in *Retrieving the Tradition and Renewing Evangelicalism*, "There is no way one can remain faithful to the gospel without learning how the Fathers defended it, without sharing in their struggles to formulate it."[5]

There are times when it is appropriate and good in spiritual discussions to begin by standing clearly in the Tradition of the Church. A practical example of this, and one that most Evangelicals have experienced, is the unexpected visit at the door by members of the Jehovah's Witnesses, a contemporary expression of the ancient Arian heresy. As a Christian and a pastor, I always want to be faithful in my witness to the mystery of Christ's person. Yet I have become weary and frustrated "chasing" my front door guests all over the Bible in an attempt to prove Christ's full divinity and humanity. Many people in congregations I have served have asked me how to be faithful to the gospel in such discussions while at the same time not putting the day's responsibilities on hold indefinitely.

It was in becoming Orthodox that I began to find my way. Without any desire to be manipulative or controlling, but in simply looking for a clear place to stand, I can now say, "I am an Orthodox Christian, and I believe in the full deity and humanity of the Lord Jesus Christ as taught by the councils of the Church in faithfulness to Holy Scripture." I never use that kind of statement to end conversation; rather I use it to base the conversation on something more than merely what I think the Bible says. In every case, this confession of faith has focused the conversation, clarified historic Christian belief, and made it clear that this understanding, rooted in the Church's long, careful, and faithful exploration of Scripture and of the life of Christ in which the Church lives, has settled the matter for me. There are times when appealing to the Holy Tradition of the Church is better than appealing to personal reasoning that will only perpetuate an unending and unanchored discussion.

5. Is There Any Relationship between Worship on Earth and Worship in Heaven?

This question is fairly modest, but it represents the reason I began my journey toward Orthodoxy in the first place. Is there *any* relationship between worship in heaven and worship on earth? I am willing to accept a fairly wide range of what and how extensive that relationship might be. History is clear that even in the Orthodox liturgy there have been developmental changes through the centuries. Liturgical architecture, vestments, and details in rubrics have changed. On the other hand, I cannot recall any extensive Evangelical discussions on conforming our worship on earth to worship in heaven. Concern for evangelism often seems to have overcome all other considerations, including the relationship between heavenly and earthly worship.

Hebrews 8 states that the Christian Church has a high priest in heaven, a "minister" — or, in Greek, *leitourgos*, which can also be translated "liturgist." While the alternate translation "liturgist" should not be pressed too far to claim a complete vindication of liturgical worship, it should give pause to the Evangelical tendency to reject liturgical worship out of hand. Furthermore, Hebrews 8:5 quotes Exodus 25:40, where God tells Moses to fashion the tabernacle and its instruments "according to the *pattern* shown you" (emphasis added). Hebrews makes it clear that Christ's offering has fulfilled old covenant worship, rendering it obsolete and ready to vanish. However, Christ is still in heaven, the *leiturgos* ministering in the "holies" (*tôn hagiôn*) on the basis of his perfect offering. The eschatological ramifications of all this are hinted at in Hebrews 10:25, where Christians are exhorted not to neglect meeting together but to encourage one another, and "all the more as you see the Day approaching."

In the early chapters of Revelation, we find the apostle John standing in worship on the Lord's Day when he experiences a vision of the Lord present and walking among the churches. I recently took our parish through the early scenes of this mystical book, and those present—many of whom were new to Orthodox worship—were astounded at the obvious parallels between the descriptions of John's experience and what is seen and done in the Orthodox Divine Liturgy. Orthodox teacher Thomas Hopko asserts that one cannot fully grasp John's vision apart from familiarity with the patterns of Orthodox worship. Are the parallels exact in every detail? No. But the relationship between the vision of heaven, Christ's presence in the Church on earth, and contemporary Orthodox worship is profound and dramatic.

I am grateful that Dr. Blaising does not stand alone among Evangelicals in recognizing the need for reverence and clarity of the gospel in churches' worship lives. In identifying the older Baptist view of a "believers' church," he touches on the current tensions between worship and evangelism that have so deeply divided Evangelicals. From my own experience in Evangelical discussions about worship, I have not seen concern for reverence and gospel clarity leading churches to a form of worship that is guided by the early Tradition of the Church. In fact, the distinction between "traditional" and "contemporary" worship that has swept through America's religious scene implies that traditional worship is at best merely one option of preference. I do not think it is unfair to say that the traditional-contemporary bifurcation is usually seen by "worship planners" this way: traditional worship is a necessary and temporary concession to older and less-in-touch people, while contemporary worship is a missional, progressive, and realistic way to move churches into future fruitfulness.

Willow Creek Community Church's admission of its failures, mentioned by Dr. Blaising, is sometimes cited as a reason for hope for the future of Evangelical worship in America. Though I have not followed Willow Creek's ongoing process of rethinking their ministry, their early statements gave me little hope, for there is one thing they did not say they were going to do that I believe is crucial. Dr. Blaising seems to omit this crucial aspect as well. Neither gives any attention to the great Tradition of the nearly two-thousand-year history of the Church or to the historic roots of Israel's worship as any kind of guide.

Dr. Robert Webber's call toward an "ancient-future faith," with its invitation to explore the broad tradition of how early Christians worshiped, the elements of their services, and what was central in the structure of them, is starkly absent. Even when Evangelicals consider such things, they seem to see them as options rather than a pattern, as interesting pieces from which to pick and choose.

I believe this perspective reveals an unfounded confidence that it is possible today, armed only with our Bibles and a sensitivity to the prevailing culture, to craft, usually with an emphasis on creativity, a model of worship that will fulfill the Church's call. Today's Evangelical methods are drawing many people, and for this I am thankful. Yet it is becoming increasingly evident that the gospel is being reduced from what the Scriptures and the history of the Church hold forth.

It is true, I did look for "something more," but it wasn't a vague vision of what would work to most easily attract people. The "something more" asked questions: How does the Church's historical worship reflect the worship lives of our Lord and the first generation of Christians? Why is such historical reflection often ignored? Can the wisdom of the Church's historical Tradition be regained when that Tradition has been rejected by Christians who are culturally alienated from their roots?

Looking back, I see that so many fervent Christians I served for many years, while they may have been pleased with the worship our church provided, found worship to be more a matter of personal preference or treasured memories than a confidence that the Holy Tradition of the Church gives us a pattern of worship as a place to stand, an anchor for the Church when the surrounding culture is demanding an ever-changing "worship style." The question becomes, Must the Church turn from its rich and venerable heritage in order to attract and reach people outside the faith?

Dr. Blaising's comment that many in the Evangelical world "have sought and are seeking to correct the problem" raises a serious question for people who have done what I have done. Should I have remained where I was and joined in their efforts? I have wrestled with that question repeatedly and earnestly. I did not take lightly this journey from the world I had known and loved all my life to a world that was then unknown to me. To borrow Dr. Blaising's words, I came to recognize that "the issue here is not simply a matter of finding the right 'worship program.'" I had been attempting that for years. It simply wasn't enough. The ground continued to shift. The questions were much larger.

I agree with Dr. Blaising that it is wrong to "assume that a scripted liturgy in itself solves the problem." However, his phrases "scripted liturgy" and "an adjustment in the form of the service" are revealing expressions of what I have come to see as the unavoidable problem: we cannot tweak our way to the deep roots of the Church and its faith. There is a great difference between scripted worship and inscripturated worship. There is a great difference between free-form worship that may even add a few liturgical touches and a worship that is rooted in the depths of Israel's worship, transformed by the reality of the incarnation and resurrection of Christ, moving in a quiet and responsive way to the various contexts in which the Church lives. Current innovations are too little and too late, and they have little hope of enduring.

Orthodox worship grants no exemption from spiritual earnestness, prayerful preparation, and close attention to the participation of the people of God in worship. It does, however, provide a place to stand in the Liturgy of the Word and the Liturgy of the Eucharist, in hearing the Word and then receiving the Word in the present person of Christ.

Sadly, I left my beloved Evangelical world because in it I found I really didn't have a place to stand. With deep gratitude to the Lord, in the Orthodox Church I do.

PART 2

CATHOLICISM

CHAPTER 4

A Journey to Catholicism

Francis J. Beckwith

I was baptized in the Catholic Church as an infant, several weeks after I was born on November 3, 1960. In January 1967, our family moved to Las Vegas, Nevada, where I received First Holy Communion (May 1968) and the Sacrament of Confirmation (May 1973).

It was soon after my confirmation that I became intensely interested in the person and work of Christ. I had come across a copy of the *Good News for Modern Man* version of the New Testament that a family friend, Frank Strabala, had left on our kitchen table after he talked with my parents one evening about his renewed Catholic faith. Not knowing at first that it was the New Testament, I began reading it. I was drawn to the Jesus of the Gospels. I really did not know what to do. So I called up Mr. Strabala and asked him some questions. He invited me to a weekday service at a local "Jesus people" church, Maranatha House. It was there for the first time that I came in contact with Christians from a variety of Protestant denominations. They, along with the Catholics on hand, were part of the burgeoning "charismatic movement," a renewal movement that emphasized the baptism of the Holy Spirit and spiritual gifts. There were none of the accoutrements of Catholic liturgy at these worship services. Rather there was Scripture reading, expository preaching, and contemporary and expressive worship. For a young Catholic interested in following Jesus more deeply and authentically, this was profoundly attractive.

Although there were Catholics who worshiped at Maranatha House, the ecclesial ambience was Evangelical Protestant. The authors and speakers whose books and tapes I devoured, and the sermons

I heard, were virtually all Protestant. Thus, it seemed to me — in comparison with my experience as a young Catholic — that Protestants, at least the ones I knew, were far more serious about their faith. Although I considered myself Catholic through my high school years, I had assimilated much of Protestant thinking on salvation, Scripture, ecclesial authority, and worship. Nevertheless, it was only after high school that I began to think of myself as an Evangelical Protestant.

I. INTELLECTUAL AND SPIRITUAL FORMATION

Although I had attended Catholic schools from first through twelfth grades, my knowledge of Catholic thought was grossly superficial. Everything that I would come to believe substantively about Catholicism during my years of intellectual and spiritual formation as an Evangelical would come from Protestant authors, some of whom were deeply hostile to Catholicism (for example, Loraine Boettner[1]), while others were critical though appreciative (for example, Norman L. Geisler[2]).

After graduating in 1983 from the University of Nevada, Las Vegas (UNLV), I went on to earn a master of arts degree in Christian apologetics at Simon Greenleaf University in Southern California (which eventually merged with Trinity International University in 1997). It was founded in 1980 by the Lutheran theologian and legal scholar John Warwick Montgomery. While there, I studied church history, biblical criticism, the history of apologetics, world religions, and New Testament Greek. Although I received an excellent Protestant education, I was also brought into contact with several Catholic thinkers that Montgomery thought were worth studying. These included Saint Augustine of Hippo (though a towering presence in all Western Christianity, including Protestantism), John Henry Cardinal Newman, G. K. Chesterton, and Avery Dulles, S.J.

When I graduated from Greenleaf at the age of twenty-three, I was a firmly committed Protestant, a fairly standard low-church, nonsacramental, American Evangelical who believed in biblical inerrancy, justification by faith alone *(sola fide)* through grace alone *(sola gratia)*, *sola scriptura*, the Trinity, the priesthood of all believers, and the deity of Christ, while denying infant baptism, apostolic succession, the real presence of Christ in the Eucharist, and an ordained priesthood. The churches I attended during this time held Sunday services that consisted almost exclusively of corporate worship and a sermon. With two exceptions, these churches embraced and practiced the charismatic gifts.

Between my teens and my early twenties, I read countless books by many Evangelical Protestant theologians, philosophers, and popular writers. I was also drawn to several non-Evangelical authors who were Thomists, followers of the Catholic philosopher Saint Thomas Aquinas (AD 1225–74). With that influence, coupled with the influence of some Evangelical thinkers sympathetic to Aquinas, I had begun to consider myself a Thomist by the time I entered the PhD program in philosophy at Fordham University in 1984.

It was at Fordham, a Jesuit institution, that I first encountered intellectually serious Catholics in my academic life. Among my professors was W. Norris Clarke, S.J., from whom I took a course on Thomas Aquinas. In Father Clarke's course I became convinced that Saint Thomas's account of reality and view of the human person made the most sense and were the most consistent with the picture of creation and the nature of man found in Scripture. My experience at Fordham was formative in changing my perspective on Catholicism. I began to think of the Catholic Church as a Christian body that had preserved and protected the core of Christian orthodoxy (that is, the inspiration of Scripture, deity of Christ, Trinity, etc.) but had drifted away in other areas (that is, rejecting justification by faith, incorporating unbiblical practices such as penance, etc.) that could be remedied if the Church would embrace the insights of the Protestant Reformers.

During my time at Fordham, I also began to see the importance of the early church in the formation and formulation of the Christian orthodoxy that I had accepted as an Evangelical Protestant. As a believer in *sola scriptura*, I believed that this orthodoxy could be derived from the Bible. But to do so involves hard and sustained work, since even the great heresies in church history, such as Arianism and Nestorianism, were offered by their advocates as "biblical." So I began to increasingly appreciate and understand the decisive role that Church councils played in protecting the Christian Church from false teachings. By the time I left Fordham in 1987, I had come to the conclusion that the ecumenical councils (and a few nonecumenical ones) of the first six centuries had done the Church a great service in setting a benchmark by which to "test the spirits." These councils included the First Council of Nicaea (AD 325; affirmed the deity of Christ and God's triune nature), the Council of Chalcedon (AD 451; affirmed the two natures, two wills, and one personhood of Christ), and the Second Council of Orange (AD 529; rejected the Pelagian and semi-Pelagian heresies and affirmed *sola gratia*).

II. SLOUCHING TOWARD THE TIBER

On July 11, 1987, I married the former Frankie Rozelle Dickerson. After completing my PhD in November 1988, I began a full-time faculty appointment in the philosophy department at UNLV. Although UNLV hired me as a philosopher of religion, I began teaching courses in ethical theory, applied ethics, and politics.

Because of these changing interests, I was drawn more to Catholic authors who seemed to have a better grasp of the underlying philosophical issues that percolated beneath many contemporary moral debates. I found myself continually moved by the case Catholic authors made for their Church's philosophy of the human person and what that told us about a variety of contested subjects, including the nature of marriage, the unborn, homosexual conduct, religious liberty, and the free market.

Although Protestant authors could cite Scripture in defense of their views on all these subjects, their cases lacked the elegance and intellectual richness of the Catholic authors. Moreover, the Catholic Church could locate its moral beliefs deep in Christian history, connecting its moral theology to its predecessors, from the earliest Christians to the present day, while at the same time accounting for genuine development in these beliefs consistent with its earlier teachings. Protestantism, on the other hand, seemed easily influenced by cultural fads and secular movements in the formation of its moral theology. So, for example, after the Anglican Church discarded its ban on artificial contraception in 1930,[3] it took only one generation for conservative American Evangelicals to make a case for contraception and nonconjugal sex as being consistent with biblical Christianity.[4]

In retrospect, it is clear to me now that I had, by gravitating to and eventually embracing the Catholic Church's teachings on these matters, begun to see the Catholic Church as a "truth-telling institution," as my friend Hadley Arkes puts it.[5] So as an Evangelical, I found myself, like Hadley, often looking to this Church, its leaders, and its great authors for insight on moral and philosophical questions, though I sometimes found theological wisdom as well. Consider, for example, John Paul II's 1998 encyclical *Fides et Ratio*.[6]

As a Christian philosopher, I have always had a keen interest in how faith and reason interact with each other and what that means for both the life of the mind and our walk with Christ. Although I had read many books and articles on these matters, authored by both Catholics and Protestants, the ones that seemed the most sensible to me were those that I would later learn were more Catholic than Protestant in their spirit and approach.

After reading *Fides et Ratio*, I concluded that the most important lesson that Evangelicals can learn from this document is the pope's insights on how certain philosophies will, because of their own internal logic, undermine confidence in the truth of the gospel message.

John Paul II was interested in saving souls, and he understood that bad philosophy, if not challenged by good philosophy, would make his Church's mission of soul saving more difficult. Although he notes that there is no one correct Christian philosophy, there are limits to the extent to which a philosophy can be employed to illuminate Christian truth. For example, a Christian scholar cannot incorporate scientific materialism, deconstructionism, or moral relativism into Christian theology without distorting fundamental truths about the order and nature of things taught in Scripture and church history. That is to say, biblical scholars and systematic theologians who think they can extract doctrine from Scripture unaided by the resources of philosophical analysis are kidding themselves and are not doing a service to the Church.

This is why, for John Paul, an interpreter of Scripture must be conscientious in ensuring that he is approaching the text with sound philosophical principles. As he notes, "Those who devote themselves to the study of Sacred Scripture should always remember that the various hermeneutical approaches have their own philosophical underpinnings, which need to be carefully evaluated before they are applied to the sacred texts."[7]

As an Evangelical Protestant who embraced *sola scriptura*, I found myself not entirely comfortable with the pope's critique of "biblicism," which he defined as a perspective "which tends to make the reading and exegesis of Sacred Scripture the sole criterion of truth."[8] Although my discomfort was the result of the late pontiff's appeal to the Church's magisterium as the authoritative interpreter of Scripture,[9] I concluded that he was correct that Scripture could not by itself be the source of theological knowledge without the assistance of philosophical reflection.

It became obvious to me that every major doctrinal dispute in the first six centuries of the Church could not have been resolved by mere citation of Bible verses. Rather it required an elegant and rationally defensible interaction between the text of Scripture and certain philosophical categories. So, for example, when the First Council of Nicaea (AD 325) asserts that the Church believes in "one Lord Jesus Christ, the only begotten of the Father, that is, of the substance [*ek tēs ousias*] of the Father,"[10] and when the Council of Chalcedon (AD 451) affirms that Jesus Christ is "the same perfect in divinity and perfect in humanity, the same truly God and truly man, of a rational soul and a body; consubstantial with the Father as regards his divinity, and the same consubstantial with us as regards his humanity" and that "at no point was the difference between the natures taken away through the union, but rather the property of both natures is preserved and comes together into a single person and a single subsistent being,"[11] both councils are in fact employing philosophical terms of art — such as "substance," "rational soul," "consubstantial," "nature," "subsistent," and "perfect" — that provide a conceptual framework by which we may better understand the depiction of Christ in Scripture.

Just as the rules of grammar are essential to reading Scripture even though these rules are not derived from Scripture, the philosophical categories integral to the creeds are essential for deriving theology from Scripture even though they are not themselves contained in Scripture.

Although the Church employed both Scripture and philosophy in its settlement of the disputes at Nicaea and Chalcedon, they were only finalized ecclesiastically when a Church council affirmed one side as orthodox and the other as heretical. For this reason, the Catholic Church sees these judgments as the result of the Church's magisterium, in its service as interpreter of Scripture, acting in its role as the authoritative arbiter on doctrinal matters. That was not a perspective that I had seriously entertained, until late February 2006, when it was brought to my attention at a Boston College conference on the thought of John Paul II.

In the paper I delivered at that conference, I offered a critique of anticreedal Protestantism. I argued that those Christians who deny the necessity of creeds implicitly affirm creeds, because they in fact hold to certain nonnegotiable beliefs (like "no creed but Christ," "the Bible is God's Word," "God is a Trinity," or "Jesus is God"). Although these beliefs are not easily derived from a reading of the Bible or a mere appeal to the words of Christ (as I noted in my comments about Nicaea and Chalcedon), they were universally embraced by the Church in both the East and the West. And yet these beliefs — embraced by even anticreedalists as normative — are embedded in creeds that anticreedalists claim carry no normative weight. Thus, the anticreedalist fails to appreciate the role that the creeds played in the first six centuries of the Christian Church in the formulation of the theological beliefs he takes for granted.

After I finished my presentation, several members of the audience asked questions. The first query came from Laura Garcia, a Boston College philosophy professor. Laura grew up as an Evangelical Protestant but converted to Catholicism in the mid-1980s while in graduate school. She asked, "Your paper seems to imply the necessity of creeds in the first centuries of the Church. But that assumes the necessity of a magisterium that has the authority to issue such creeds and declare them normative for all Christians. So why aren't you a Catholic?" Although I answered the question — rather lamely, as I recall[12] — I was not satisfied with my answer. It was at that point that I began to take seriously, for the first time in my adult life, the possibility that I might have to consider returning to the Church of my youth. At the time, I thought that I would in fact never return, for I was confident that I would be able to adequately provide an account of the creeds that would allow me to keep Catholicism at arm's length. I was wrong.

III. RE-BECOMING CATHOLIC

Because of personal and professional responsibilities, it was not until after I became president of the Evangelical Theological Society on November 17, 2006, that I revisited the question raised by Laura. I thought the best way to answer it was to examine the four doctrinal issues over which Protestants (with a few exceptions) and Catholics disagree that were also the issues that seemed like insurmountable obstacles preventing me from returning to Catholicism: (1) justification, (2) the real presence of Christ in the Eucharist, (3) the sacrament of penance, and (4) apostolic succession. These four doctrines are inexorably tied to the belief in a visible and apostolic Church as essential to Christian life and practice, which Laura in her question maintained that I had to address. What follows is a summation of my internal deliberations about these doctrines, including the reasons and inferences that I found so compelling.

I have used the term *sacrament* several times, and I employ it often in the text that follows. But some Christians do not know what a sacrament is. In the Catholic Church, as in Eastern Orthodoxy, there are seven sacraments: baptism, penance, communion, confirmation, marriage, holy orders, and last rites. According to the *Catechism of the Catholic Church*, they "are efficacious signs of grace, instituted by Christ and entrusted to the Church, by which divine life is dispensed to us. The visible rites by which the sacraments are celebrated signify and make present the graces proper to each sacrament. They bear fruit in those who receive them with the required dispositions."[13] In many American Evangelical churches, only two are acknowledged—baptism and communion—but they are often called "ordinances," since they are not considered means of grace. Rather they are believed to be activities that we should perform out of obedience to the commands of Christ.

A. The Doctrine of Justification

Justification concerns how one is made right with God in order to be saved, acquire eternal life, and go to heaven. Because this is the disputed doctrine over which the Reformation was launched, my discussion of it will be considerably longer than my discussions of the other three.

1. Protestantism and Justification

There is not just one Protestant doctrine of justification. In fact, if one includes the Radical Reformation,[14] there is a wide spectrum of views. But for me, the only Protestant views I took seriously were those that were affirmed in the confessions of the Lutheran and Reformed traditions as well as their contemporary supporters and offshoots (including Methodism and other types of Arminianism). But even excluding the Radical Reformation, there are several Protestant views on justification, as Alister McGrath points out in his encyclopedic book on the doctrine.[15] McGrath, however, argues that these differing views share three essential characteristics: (1) "Justification is defined as the forensic *declaration* that believers are righteous, rather than the process by which they are *made* righteous, involving a change in their *status* rather than in their *nature*"; (2) "a deliberate and systematic distinction is made between *justification* ... and *sanctification* or *regeneration*"; and (3) "Justifying righteousness ... [is] the alien righteousness of Christ, external to humans and imputed to them."[16]

This is how the doctrine of justification is understood by most Evangelical Protestants. One's coming to Christ is the result of an act of faith alone *(sola fide)*, which is itself a consequence of grace alone *(sola gratia)*. The believer is saved by his faith, which is the result of God moving the will of the sinner. Because Christ died for our sins in our stead, taking the punishment we deserve, when we act in faith, God imputes Christ's righteousness to us. And it is at that moment that we are justified. God reckons us righteous rather than making us righteous. (He *imputes* but does not *infuse* Christ's righteousness.) At the same time, the Holy Spirit is poured into the believer's heart so that he may walk with Christ and grow in sanctification.[17] The believer's good works that follow from his conversion do not contribute to his justification, which happened at the moment of conversion and is entirely the work of God. Rather, good works are evidence of the believer's justification and may contribute to his sanctification. Although justification and sanctification are separate events, they are inexorably linked. For this reason, it is wrong for Catholics to think that Protestantism leads to a type of antinomianism (lawlessness) that says the believer can do anything he wants after conversion since he is now justified and has a "free ticket" to heaven. According to the Protestant, a conversion experience without evidence of justification means that the "believer" may in fact not be justified. So works, though they are not necessary for justification chronologically prior to the reception of God's grace at conversion, are necessary for the justified synchronically. To put it another way: the believer, though not saved by good works, performs good works if in fact he is saved.

The Protestant view has been ably defended as biblical by some of the finest scholars and writers in Christian history. So I do not think it is an unreasonable position. Rather, once I understood the Catholic view, it seemed to do two things that the Protestant view could not do as well: (1) account for the biblical data, and (2) show itself to be consistent with pre-Reformation Christianity.

2. Catholicism and Justification[18]

For the Catholic, saving faith, entirely the consequence of God's grace, begins with one's initial conversion, which incorporates one into the family of God. As the *Catechism* states,

> The grace of the Holy Spirit has the power to justify us, that is, to cleanse us from our sins and to communicate to us "the righteousness of God through faith in Jesus Christ" and through Baptism....
>
> Through the power of the Holy Spirit we take part in Christ's Passion by dying to sin, and in his Resurrection by being born to a new life; we are members of his Body which is the Church, branches grafted onto the vine which is himself....
>
> The first work of the grace of the Holy Spirit is conversion, effecting justification in accordance with Jesus' proclamation at the beginning of the Gospel: "Repent, for the kingdom of heaven is at hand." Moved by grace, man turns toward God and away from sin, thus accepting forgiveness and righteousness from on high.[19]

But at that point the journey is just beginning. For one then exercises one's faith, itself a gift of God's grace, in acts of charity, the spiritual disciplines, and prayer as well as in the partaking of the sacraments—all this in order to commune with God and so receive his unmerited grace to conform one into the image of Christ. For the Catholic, justification refers not only to the Christian's initial entrance into the family of God at baptism—which is administered for the remission of sins—but also to the intrinsic work of both the infusion of that grace at baptism and all the subsequent graces that work in concert to transform the Christian from the inside out.[20]

It is in and through this ongoing transformation that one is made *justified*, in the same sense of being made righteous or rightly ordered, and thus gifted to share in the divine life of Christ. Consequently, justification and sanctification are not different events, one extrinsic and the other intrinsic, as the Reformers taught. Rather sanctification is the ongoing intrinsic work of justifying, or making rightly ordered, the Christian by means of God's grace, the same grace that intrinsically changed the believer at the moment of her initial justification (that is, at baptism) into an adopted child of the Father. So although the Catholic Church teaches that the believer may act in ways for which he will be rewarded (which, as we shall see, the Bible teaches as well), that merit is not something earned, as if God owed us anything.[21] As the *Catechism* teaches, "The merit of man before God in the Christian life arises from the fact that *God has freely chosen to associate man with the work of his grace.* The fatherly action of God is first on his own initiative, and then follows man's free acting through his collaboration, so that the merit of good works is to be attributed in the first place to the grace of God, then to the faithful. *Man's merit, moreover, itself is due to God, for his good actions proceed in Christ*, from the predispositions and assistance given by the Holy Spirit."[22]

Justification, for the Catholic, is not only a matter of your getting into heaven but also, and more important, a matter of getting heaven into you.[23] Because both views admit the necessity of good works in the economy of salvation (as cooperation for the Catholic; as consequence for the Protestant), it seemed to me that the chief distinction between the Catholic view of justification on the one hand and the Protestant on the other rests on whether Christ's grace is *infused* or merely *imputed* at the moment one becomes a Christian at baptism and/or conversion. Nevertheless, the Catholic Church does not deny that there is a forensic element to justification, that it involves a legal transaction initiated by God. Rather it denies that it is *exclusively* forensic.[24]

a. The Biblical Case

Romans 4:1–8 is often cited by Protestant authors as the definitive verse establishing the forensic doctrine of justification. According to this interpretation, Saint Paul is teaching that Christ's righteousness is imputed to us because of our faith in Christ, just as God reckoned Abraham righteous (or imputed righteousness to him) because of his faith in God. However, as I studied this passage as well as some commentaries on it, I ceased to be convinced that the Protestant view was indisputable.

It seemed to me that Abraham was reckoned righteous precisely because he acted in faith and thus *became* righteous as a consequence. After all, Romans 4 does not say whether this is a once-and-for-all forensic imputation of righteousness, a theological inference that the text may support but clearly does not entail. Consider verse 3: "Abraham believed God, and it was reckoned to him as righteousness" (RSV). It is from Genesis 15:6, which tells us that Abraham believed God after the Lord promised him numerous descendants. Yet James 2:21–24 states that Abraham's faith justified him years after that incident when he obeyed God and attempted to offer his son Isaac as a sacrifice (Gen. 22:1–19). The text claims that when Abraham performed this work, "the scripture was fulfilled which says, 'Abraham believed God, and it was reckoned to him as righteousness'; and he was called the friend of God" (James 2:23 RSV). However, Hebrews teaches that Abraham was a man of faith chronologically prior to the incidents referenced in Romans (Gen. 15) and James (Gen. 22): "By faith Abraham obeyed when he was called to go out to a place which he was to receive as an inheritance; and he went out, not knowing where he was to go" (Heb. 11:8 RSV).

So, then, the real question is whether Saint Paul and the other New Testament authors teach that *the entirety of justification is mere imputed righteousness that occurs once and for all.* The answer at which I arrived was no. The following is a brief encapsulation of my reasoning.

At the Last Judgment the difference between the sheep and the goats is between what they did and did not *do* (Matt. 25:31–46). There is no indication that Jesus is thinking of the sheep's "works" as "evidence of justification." But rather these works serve in some way as the *basis on which* his judgment of their eternal fate is made. Jesus tells his disciples in Matthew 16:27, "The Son of man is to come with his angels in the glory of his Father, *and then he will repay every man for what he has done*" (RSV). In Revelation 22:11–12, John quotes Jesus as saying, "Let the evildoer still do evil, and the filthy still be filthy, and the righteous still do right, and the holy still be holy. Behold, I am coming soon, *bringing my recompense, to repay every one for what he has done*" (RSV). In Matthew 19, Jesus connects the possession of eternal life (or salvation) with keeping the commandments, selling everything one owns (as he applied it to his questioner), and leaving everything, including one's family if necessary.[25]

Couple these with Matthew 5, and the richness of Jesus' teachings on salvation comes out even clearer: it is the bearing of fruit, the hearing and *acting on* Christ's words, the *doing the will of his Father* that constitute the life of faith, a life likened by Jesus to a house that *could fall* if not adequately constructed to withstand severe adversity. In John 14, Jesus tells his followers a bit of what it will mean when he says, "Because I live, you will live also" (v. 19 RSV). He states, "In that day you will know that I am in my Father, and you in me, and I in you. *He who has my commandments and keeps them, he it is who loves me*; and he who loves me will be loved by my Father, and I will love him and manifest myself to him" (vv. 20–21 RSV). The gospel of Mark recounts these words of Christ: "If any man would come after me, *let him deny himself and take up his cross and follow me*. For whoever would save his life will lose it; and whoever loses his life for my sake and the gospel's will save it" (8:34–35 RSV). In Mark 4, Jesus explains the parable of the seeds, in which he tells his listeners of those who receive the word "with joy," but "they have no root," and thus "they fall away" immediately "when tribulation or persecution arises" (vv. 16–17 RSV). He also tells of "those that were sown upon the good soil"; they "*hear the word and accept it and bear fruit*, thirtyfold and sixtyfold and a hundredfold" (v. 20 RSV).[26]

What one finds in Jesus' teachings is an active faith by which God's grace gives us new life (not just new status), though there is a responsibility of obedience on our part to remain faithful, bear fruit, practice charity, and persevere. It is only later, in the Pauline and non-Pauline epistles — as the Church's doctrines begin to develop — that the people of God receive clarification on the role of God's grace in the life of Christian obedience.

In Romans 5:19 Saint Paul writes, "As by one man's disobedience many were *made sinners*, so by one man's obedience many will be *made righteous*" (RSV). If Adam's sin had real ontological consequences for human nature—"many were made sinners"—as this passage clearly indicates, then Jesus' death and resurrection has real ontological consequences as well—"many will be made righteous." It seems, then, that original sin and infused grace are a package deal. This is why Saint Paul can sternly reject the value of works for justification apart from one becoming a "new creation": "In Christ Jesus *you are all sons of God*, through faith. For as many of you as were baptized into Christ have put on Christ" (Gal. 3:26–27 RSV). "In Christ Jesus neither circumcision nor uncircumcision is of any avail, *but faith working through love*" (Gal. 5:6 RSV). "Neither circumcision counts for anything, nor uncircumcision, but *a new creation*" (Gal. 6:15 RSV).[27]

Although Saint Paul certainly refers to justification as a past event (Rom. 5:1–2; 5:9; 8:24; 1 Cor. 6:11), he also presents it as a continuing process (1 Cor. 1:18; 15:2; 2 Cor. 2:15), as well as one that has not been fully achieved (Rom. 2:13; Gal. 5:5; 1 Cor. 3:15; 5:5; 1 Tim. 2:15; 2 Tim. 4:8, 18).

Moreover, works done in faith by God's grace contribute to our inward transformation and eventual justification. Saint Paul writes to fellow Christians in Rome, "[God] *will render to every man according to his works: to those who by patience in well-doing seek for glory and honor and immortality, he will give eternal life*; but for those who are factious and do not obey the truth, but obey wickedness, there will be wrath and fury.... For it is not the hearers of the law who are righteous before God, but the doers of the law who will be justified" (Rom. 2:6–8, 13 RSV). Saint Paul writes to the Colossians that Christ "has now reconciled [them] in his body of flesh by his death, in order to present [them] holy and blameless and irreproachable before him, *provided that [they] continue in the faith, stable and steadfast*, not shifting from the hope of the gospel which [they] heard, which has been preached to every creature under heaven, and of which I, Paul, became a minister" (Col. 1:22–23 RSV). Saint Paul tells the Philippians to "*work out your own salvation* with fear and trembling; *for God is at work in you*, both to will and to work for his good pleasure" (Phil. 2:12–13 RSV). He teaches the Galatians that "he who sows to his own flesh will from the flesh reap corruption; but *he who sows to the Spirit will from the Spirit reap eternal life*" (Gal. 6:8 RSV). In his second letter to Saint Timothy, Saint Paul writes that "I have fought the good fight, I have finished the race, *I have kept the faith*," and consequently, "*there is laid up for me the crown of righteousness*, which the Lord, the righteous judge, *will award to me* on that Day, and not only to me *but also to all who have loved his appearing*" (2 Tim. 4:7–8 RSV). In this passage, final justification is awarded for keeping the faith and persevering, but these are connected to a certain sort of inward change, the love for Christ's appearing.[28]

Thus, one does not find in Saint Paul the sharp distinction between justification and sanctification that one finds among Protestant writers. For the passages we have covered seem to indicate that justification *includes* sanctification. There are others that do so as well, including 2 Thessalonians 2:13; Romans 6:19–23; Romans 8:3–4; and Titus 3:5–8. And there are many non-Pauline passages that offer a similar understanding (for example, Acts 26:15–18; Heb. 10:10–14; 13:12; James 1:12; 2:14, 22–24; 2 Peter 1:1–4). In fact, James 2:17 ("Faith by itself, if it has no works, is dead" [RSV]), often cited by Catholics in support of their view, fits seamlessly with Saint Paul's explicit rejection of faith alone. Remember, for Saint Paul, if one has faith without love, then one is nothing (1 Cor. 13:2), for "faith, hope, love abide, these three; but the greatest of these is love" (1 Cor. 13:13 RSV; cf. Gal. 5:6). This, as we have seen, is also the teaching of the *Catechism*: "Justification establishes *cooperation between God's grace and man's freedom*. On man's part it is expressed by *the assent of faith* to the Word of God, which invites him to conversion, and in *the cooperation of charity* [or love] with the prompting of the Holy Spirit who precedes and preserves his assent."[29]

b. The Historical Case

It did not take me long to discover that the Catholic view of justification is rooted deep in Christian history. Not surprisingly, McGrath writes that the Protestant distinction between justification and regeneration (or sanctification) introduced "a fundamental discontinuity ... into the western theological tradition where none had ever existed, or ever been contemplated, before. The Reformation understanding of the *nature* of justification—as opposed to its *mode*—must therefore be regarded as a genuine theological *novum*."[30]

I discovered that the view of the Second Council of Orange (AD 529) regarding justification is nearly indistinguishable from what is found in the Council of Trent (AD 1545–63) and the *Catechism of the Catholic Church* (1994). For me, this was telling, since the Council of Trent was convened in the sixteenth century to respond to the Reformation, and the *Catechism* was produced in the twentieth century to give a clear presentation of Catholic doctrine for the contemporary world, but the sixth-century Council of Orange, influenced by Saint Augustine of Hippo (AD 354–430; highly regarded by both Protestants and Catholics), is considered by most Evangelical Protestant writers as an affirmation of orthodox Christian belief.[31]

Orange rejected Pelagianism and semi-Pelagianism as heretical doctrines. The first, having its origin in the Catholic monk Pelagius (AD ca. 354–ca. 420/440), affirms that human beings do not inherit Adam's sin (and thus denies the doctrine of original sin) and by their free will may achieve salvation without God's grace. On the other hand, semi-Pelagianism maintains that a human being, though weakened by original sin, may make the initial act of the will toward achieving salvation prior to receiving the necessary assistance of God's grace. Orange, in contrast,[32] affirmed that Adam's original sin is inherited by his progeny and can be removed only by the sacrament of baptism. By the means of baptism, God's unmerited grace is infused for the remission of sins.[33] According to Orange, "The freedom of will that was destroyed in the first man can be restored only by the grace of baptism."[34] As with Trent[35] and the *Catechism*,[36] Orange presents baptism as the instrumental cause of justification.

According to Orange, justification is not the consequence of our initiative and then God assisting us by extending his mercy.[37] Rather "God himself," writes the council, "first inspires in us both faith in him and love for him without any previous good works of our own that deserve reward, so that we may both faithfully seek the sacrament of Baptism, and after Baptism be able by his help to do what is pleasing to him."[38] Thus, the Christian's inner transformation continues throughout his lifetime, entirely the work of the infusion of grace with which the Christian cooperates. So if a free Adam can reject God, and if our liberty by means of baptism has been restored to be like Adam's, then it makes sense for Orange to declare, "According to the catholic faith we also believe that after grace has been received through Baptism, all baptized persons have the ability and responsibility, *if they desire to labor faithfully, to perform with the aid and cooperation of Christ what is of essential importance in regard to the salvation of their soul.*"[39] For the Christian "does nothing good for which God is not responsible, so as to let him do it."[40] And yet the council proclaims, "... for as often as we do good, God is at work in us and with us, in order that we may do so."[41] And like Trent,[42] Orange employs the language of infusion to describe how grace works in baptism and in the subsequent life of the believer, including his cooperation.[43]

The Catholic Church frequently makes use of the word *cooperating* or *cooperation* in its account of justification. It is derived from the distinction between operating and cooperating grace. According to Catholic theology, infused grace is required not only for the Christian's entry into the family of God at baptism but also for her subsequent movement toward being conformed to the image of Christ. Consider, for example, Saint Thomas Aquinas's explanation of sanctifying grace as "habitual grace." It has, writes the Angelic Doctor, "a double effect of grace, even as of every other form; the first of which is 'being,' and the second, 'operation.'" For example, "the work of heat is to make its subject hot, and to give heat outwardly. And thus habitual grace, inasmuch as it heals and justifies the soul, or makes it pleasing to God, is called operating grace; but inasmuch as it is the principle of meritorious works, which spring from the free-will, it is called cooperating grace."[44] Because God is the sole mover in the infusion of habitual grace, it is entirely attributable to him. This is called operating grace. But if habitual grace is supposed to heal and justify the soul, and the soul has by nature certain powers to think and act, then this healing and justification must manifest itself in the activities of the soul. Thus, these acts allow us to cooperate with God for our inward transformation. This is cooperating grace, since any meritorious acts performed by a soul infused with habitual grace by God would lack merit without that grace and thus without God's cooperation. Writes Saint Thomas, "God does not justify us without ourselves, because whilst we are being justified we consent to God's justification [*justitiae*] by a movement of our free-will. Nevertheless this movement is not the cause of grace, but the effect; hence the whole operation pertains to grace."[45] Although Aquinas is writing in the midthirteenth century, Saint Augustine, writing in the early fifth century, is his primary source for this distinction: "Augustine says (De Gratia et Lib. Arbit. xvii): 'God by cooperating with us, perfects what He began by operating in us, since He who perfects by cooperation with such as are willing, beings by operating that they may will.' But the operations of God whereby He moves us to good pertain to grace. Therefore grace is fittingly divided into operating and cooperating."[46]

Both Orange and Trent employ Jesus' vine and branches account of his relationship to his Church (John 15:1 – 17) in order to explain the relationship between operating and cooperating grace and the role of faith and works in a believer's salvation. The Council of Orange writes, "Concerning the branches of the vine. The branches on the vine do not give life to the vine, but receive life from it; thus the vine is related to its branches in such a way that it supplies them with what they need to live, and does not take this from them. Thus it is to the advantage of the disciples, not Christ, both to have Christ abiding in them and to abide in Christ. For if the vine is cut down, another can shoot up from the live root; but one who is cut off from the vine cannot live without the root (John 15:5ff)." And given that grace, as I have already noted, we "have the ability and responsibility, if [we] desire to labor faithfully, to perform with the aid and cooperation of Christ what is of essential importance in regard to the salvation of [our] soul."[47] Over a millennium after Orange, the Church affirmed at Trent, "For since Christ Jesus Himself, as the head into the members and the vine into the branches, continually infuses strength into those justified, which strength always precedes, accompanies and follows their good works, and without which they could not in any manner be pleasing and meritorious before God, we must believe that nothing further is wanting to those justified to prevent them from being considered to have, by those very works which have been done in God, fully satisfied the divine law according to the state of this life and to have truly merited eternal life, to be obtained in its [due] time, provided they depart [this life] in grace...."[48]

The *Catechism* offers an understanding of justification that is consistent with both Orange and Trent. Like the two councils, the *Catechism* affirms the absolute gratuitousness of God's movement of the human will: "The first work of the grace of the Holy Spirit is *conversion*, effecting justification in accordance with Jesus' proclamation at the beginning of the Gospel: 'Repent, for the kingdom of heaven is at hand' [Matt. 4:17]. Moved by grace, man turns toward God and away from sin, thus accepting forgiveness and righteousness from on high."[49] And like Orange and Trent, the *Catechism* uses the language of cooperating grace in its account of human merit and the role it plays in justification: "The merit of man before God in the Christian life arises from the fact that *God has freely chosen to associate man with the work of his grace.* The fatherly action of God is first on his own initiative, and then follows man's free acting through his collaboration, so that the merit of good works is to be attributed in the first place to the grace of God, then to the faithful. Man's merit, moreover, itself is due to God, for his good actions proceed in Christ, from the predispositions and assistance given by the Holy Spirit."[50]

Sanctifying grace allows us to participate in the divine life.[51] Thus, when we act in charity, we do not contribute to our justification, as if it were merely a case of God adding up our deeds on a cosmic balance sheet. This is why the *Catechism* teaches, "The merits of our good works are gifts of the divine goodness."[52] (That does not sound like "grace *plus* good works," a caricature of Catholic soteriology.) Consequently, one's cooperation does not take away from the fact that justification is a work of God, just as Christ's human nature does not take away from the fact that he is fully divine, and just as the Bible's being authored by human beings does not diminish its status as God's Word.

I concluded that the Catholic account of justification had both scriptural and historical warrant, and thus I could no longer dismiss it as a sub-Christian and unbiblical view.

B. The Real Presence of Christ in the Eucharist

Protestants hold a range of views about what happens to the bread and wine at communion. Some believe that it is not sacramental but merely an ordinance that commemorates Christ's death. For these Christians, communion is symbolic. This seems to be the dominant view among American Evangelicals, most of whom are members of ecclesial communions that do not have a history of sacramental theology.

During most of my life as a Protestant, I held the symbolic view. But in the late 1990s, when my wife and I began attending Episcopalian churches, I moved closer to the Catholic view without fully embracing it. For this reason, the Catholic doctrine of the Eucharist was the least difficult doctrine (of the four) for me to find plausible and within the bounds of orthodoxy.

The Catholic view is that the bread and wine literally become the body and blood of Christ when they are consecrated by the priest celebrating the Mass. According to the *Catechism*, "The essential signs of the Eucharistic sacrament are wheat bread and grape wine, on which the blessing of the Holy Spirit is invoked and the priest pronounces the words of consecration spoken by Jesus during the Last Supper: 'This is my body which will be given up for you.... This is the cup of my blood....' [Luke 22:17–20]."[53]

Oftentimes non-Catholics get hung up on the term *transubstantiation*, the philosophical theory that the Church maintains best accounts for the change of the bread and wine at consecration. The way the Church explains transubstantiation was influenced by Aristotle's distinction between substance and accident. Aristotle (384–322 BC), like many of his ancient contemporaries, wanted to account for how things change and yet remain the same. So, for example, a substance like an oak tree remains the same while undergoing accidental changes. It begins as an acorn and eventually develops roots, a trunk, branches, and leaves. During all these changes, the oak tree remains identical to itself. Its leaves change from green to red and then to brown and eventually fall off. But these accidental changes occur while the substance of the tree remains. On the other hand, if we chopped down the tree and turned it into a desk, that would be a substantial change, since the tree would literally cease to be, and its parts would be turned into something else, a desk. According to the Church, when the bread and wine become the body and blood of Christ, the accidents of the bread and wine do not change, but the substance of each changes. So it looks, tastes, feels, and smells like bread and wine, but it literally has been changed into the body and blood of Christ. That's transubstantiation.

There are several reasons why it would be a mistake to dismiss the Catholic view of the Eucharist simply because of Aristotle's influence on its formulation. First, Eastern churches in communion with the Catholic Church rarely employ the Aristotelian language of transubstantiation, and yet the Catholic Church considers their celebration of the Eucharist perfectly valid. Second, the Catholic Church maintains that the Divine Liturgies celebrated in Eastern churches not in communion with Rome (commonly called "Eastern Orthodoxy") are perfectly valid as well,[54] even though their theologians very rarely employ the term *transubstantiation*. Third, the belief that the bread and wine are literally transformed into Christ's body and blood predates Aristotle's influence by over a thousand years. For it was not until the thirteenth century, and the ascendancy of Saint Thomas Aquinas's thought, that Aristotle's categories were employed by the Church in its account of the Eucharist. In fact, when the Fourth Lateran Council employed the language of substantial change in AD 1215, Saint Thomas had not even been born!

It was that third point which I found so compelling and which convinced me that the Catholic view of the Eucharist was a legitimate Christian perspective. It did not take long for me to see that eucharistic realism (as I like to call it) had been uncontroversially embraced deep in Christian history. This is why Protestant historian J. N. D. Kelly writes, "Eucharistic teaching, it should be understood at the outset, was in general unquestioningly realist, that is, the consecrated bread and wine were taken to be, and were treated and designated as, the Savior's body and blood."[55] Here are a few quotes from several church fathers and early Christian documents that make it clear what the Church has always believed about Holy Communion:

> I have no taste for corruptible food nor for the pleasures of this life. I desire the bread of God, which is the flesh of Jesus Christ, who was of the seed of David; and for drink I desire his blood, which is love incorruptible.
>
> — Saint Ignatius of Antioch, AD 110[56]

> Take note of those who hold heterodox opinions on the grace of Jesus Christ which has come to us, and see how contrary their opinions are to the mind of God.... They abstain from the Eucharist and from prayer because they do not confess that the Eucharist is the flesh of our Savior Jesus Christ, flesh which suffered for our sins and which that Father, in his goodness, raised up again. They who deny the gift of God are perishing in their disputes.
>
> — Saint Ignatius of Antioch, AD 110[57]

We call this food Eucharist, and no one else is permitted to partake of it, except one who believes our teaching to be true and who has been washed in the washing which is for the remission of sins and for regeneration [that is, has received baptism] and is thereby living as Christ enjoined. For not as common bread nor common drink do we receive these; but since Jesus Christ our Savior was made incarnate by the word of God and had both flesh and blood for our salvation, so too, as we have been taught, the food which has been made into the Eucharist by the Eucharistic prayer set down by him, and by the change of which our blood and flesh is nurtured, is both the flesh and the blood of that incarnated Jesus.

—Saint Justin Martyr, AD 151[58]

He [Paul] threatens, moreover, the stubborn and forward, and denounces them, saying, "Whosoever eats the bread or drinks the cup of the Lord unworthily, is guilty of the body and blood of the Lord" [1 Cor. 11:27]. All these warnings being scorned and condemned — [lapsed Christians will often take communion] before their sin is expiated, before confession has been made of their crime, before their conscience has been purged by sacrifice and by the hand of the priest, before the offense of an angry and threatening Lord has been appeased, [and so] violence is done to his body and blood; and they sin now against their Lord more with their hand and mouth than when they denied their Lord.

—Saint Cyprian of Carthage, AD 251[59]

These are, of course, not the only early church writings that address the nature of the Eucharist,[60] though they are representative. They should, however, not surprise us, given what the Bible says about communion. When Jesus celebrated the Last Supper with his disciples (Matt. 26:17–30; Mark 14:12–25; Luke 22:7–23), which we commemorate at communion, he referred to it as a Passover meal. He called the bread and wine his body and blood. In several places, Jesus is called the Lamb of God (John 1:29, 36; 1 Peter 1:19; Rev. 5:12). Remember, when the lamb is killed for Passover, the meal participants ingest the lamb. Consequently, Saint Paul's severe warnings about partaking in Holy Communion unworthily make sense only in light of eucharistic realism (1 Cor. 10:14–22; 11:17–34). He writes, "The cup of blessing which we bless, is it not a participation in the blood of Christ? The bread which we break, is it not a participation in the body of Christ?... Whoever, therefore, eats the bread or drinks the cup of the Lord in an unworthy manner will be guilty of profaning the body and blood of the Lord" (1 Cor. 10:16; 11:27 RSV).

Moreover, when one combines all these passages with the fact that Jesus called himself the Bread of Life (John 6:41–51) and that he said his followers must "eat the flesh of the Son of man and drink his blood" (John 6:53 RSV), the eucharistic realism of the early church, the Eastern churches (both in and out of communion with Rome), and the pre-Reformation medieval Church (fifth to sixteenth centuries) seems almost unremarkable.

C. The Sacrament of Penance

Evangelical Protestants are familiar with the backslidden Christian who rededicates his life to Christ at an altar call (for example, at a Billy Graham Crusade) or in counsel with his pastor. This public or private confession is an act of reconciliation in which the repentant prodigal returns into the welcoming arms of his Father. In the Catholic Church (as well as in Eastern Orthodoxy) there is a sacramental means by which this reconciliation may be appropriated. It is called penance, though sometimes it is referred to as reconciliation or confession.

When I was a Protestant, the main thing that troubled me about penance is that it involves the believer confessing his sins to a priest who then gives the confessor absolution and requires that the confessor "do penance." The penance may be the recitation of several prayers, acts of spiritual discipline, and/or good deeds. As an Evangelical Protestant, I thought that this took away from Christ's sufficiency to forgive all our sins, past, present, and future. If I have to do something in order to acquire forgiveness—such as confess to a priest or do penance—does not that diminish the scope of Christ's atonement?

But once I better understood the biblical, historical, and pastoral reasons for the sacrament of penance, I could no longer believe that it was unbiblical or sub-Christian. Here is how I thought it through. First, as I noted above, even Evangelical Protestants have a means by which to deal with postbaptismal sin: rededication. In some cases, the backslider, given his postconversion sloth, rededicates his life to Christ thinking that his initial "conversion" may not have been authentic. In fact, given the Protestant understanding of justification and sanctification—that good works and good living follow from being truly saved—the backslider's own experience may lead him to believe that his first profession of faith was a sham. So he confesses again. Others, not believing they have left the faith, nevertheless sense a real need to "walk the aisle" and come clean after days, weeks, or years of living in less-than-holy ways. Thus, it became clear to me that Christianity—whether Protestant, Catholic, or Orthodox—required some way to deal with postbaptismal sin, especially of the seven deadly sort (Prov. 6:16–19).

Second, postbaptismal sin is a reality acknowledged in the New Testament in many places. In the Lord's Prayer, Jesus mentions the need for ongoing repentance in the believer's life: "Forgive us our debts, as we also have forgiven our debtors" (Matt. 6:12 RSV). Saint John writes to baptized Christians, "If we say we have no sin, we deceive ourselves, and the truth is not in us. If we confess our sins, he is faithful and just, and will forgive our sins and cleanse us from all unrighteousness" (1 John 1:8–9 RSV). Moreover, Saint Paul (1 Cor. 6:9–10; Gal. 5:19–21; Eph. 5:3–15; Col. 3:5–10), Saint John (1 John 5:16–17), and the author of Hebrews (Heb. 13:4–5) warn believers of sins that are mortal—that is, if the Christian commits them, he risks losing what Catholics call "sanctifying grace." Hence, it is no wonder that, with the exception of Reformed Christianity beginning in the sixteenth century, no other theological school of thought—including Orthodoxy, Lutheranism, and Methodism—denies the possibility of a Christian losing sanctifying grace. But even the Reformed, as I noted above, need to account for how the backslider is reconciled. Thus, Christianity by its very nature requires a ministry of reconciliation (2 Cor. 5:14–20).

Third, "doing penance" is not a work the Church requires in order to guarantee forgiveness. For Christ's death is "the ransom that would free men from the slavery of sin."[61] And when one confesses and receives absolution in the sacrament, one's sins are forgiven by God, for "only God forgives sins."[62] "But," as the *Catechism* puts it, "it does not remedy all the disorders sin has caused."[63] So, for example, if a man confesses to a priest that he has stolen five hundred dollars from his neighbor, the man will receive absolution. Although he is forgiven for his offense, for penance the man must at least return his neighbor's property. But all sins (including theft) diminish, and sometimes rob us of, our spiritual health. For this reason, acts of penance "help configure us to Christ, who alone expiated our sins once and for all. They allow us to become co-heirs with the risen Christ, 'provided we suffer with him' [Rom. 8:17; 3:25; 1 John 2:1–2]."[64] And given the Church's understanding of operating and cooperating grace, even the merit we acquire from our penance is a work of God's grace.[65]

Fourth, given the reality of postbaptismal sin and its eradication in the pursuit of holiness, it is unsurprising that the New Testament speaks of fasting, prayer, and spiritual discipline as means by which one may become better equipped and more disposed to holiness in one's Christian journey (Matt. 6:1–8, 16–18; Acts 13:2–3; 14:23; 1 Cor. 9:25–27; 2 Cor. 1:4–6; Col. 4:2; Eph. 6:18; 1 Thess. 4:4–8; 1 Tim. 4:7–8; 2 Tim. 1:7; James 4:8–10; 1 Peter 4:7). In fact, the author of Hebrews writes of the reality of God's fatherly discipline of us, his sons, in the formation of our souls (Heb. 12:5–13).

Fifth, and finally, although the Catholic Church teaches that God may remit a believer's sins without the believer's partaking in the sacrament,[66] reconciliation is a ministry of the Church. Thus, it encourages its members to participate frequently in the sacrament,[67] even for the confession of venial sins (those that are not serious[68]). Given the Church's view of justification (as we have already covered), this all seemed to make sense to me. But also, given the Church's understanding of itself, including its own power and authority, as well as the importance it places on the quality and degree of a Christian's communion with the Church — whether he or she is fully reconciled with it — the sacrament of penance, as presently practiced, seemed to me like a natural development of what one finds in Scripture and church history. Let me explain.

It became clear to me from my reading of Scripture that the Church and its leadership are integral to the ministry of reconciliation. Christ came to earth to forgive sins (Matt. 9:6), and after his resurrection he imparted to his followers that same power: "Jesus said to them again, 'Peace be with you. As the Father has sent me, even so I send you.' And when he had said this, he breathed on them, and said to them, 'Receive the Holy Spirit. If you forgive the sins of any, they are forgiven; if you retain the sins of any, they are retained'" (John 20:21–23 RSV). In Matthew 18, in the context of the administration of church discipline, Jesus said to his disciples, "Truly, I say to you, whatever you bind on earth shall be bound in heaven, and whatever you loose on earth shall be loosed in heaven" (v. 18 RSV). James encouraged the sick to seek out the Church's presbyters so that they might "pray over him, anointing him with oil in the name of the Lord; and the prayer of faith will save the sick man, and the Lord will raise him up; and *if he has committed sins, he will be forgiven.* Therefore *confess your sins to one another, and pray for one another, that you may be healed.* The prayer of a righteous man has great power in its effects" (5:14–16 RSV, emphasis added).

Once I grasped its biblical foundation, I was not surprised to learn that the sacrament begins to develop early in Christian history. According to Kelly, "With the dawn of the third century the rough outlines of a recognized penitential discipline were beginning to take shape,... [though] there are still no signs of private penance (i.e., confession to a priest, followed by absolution and the imposition of penance)."[69] Nevertheless, the ecclesial and theological elements on which private confession is based—that the penitent confesses to the Church that it has not only the power to absolve him of his sins but also the power to impose penance on the penitent—is already in place. Writes Kelly, "The system which seems to have existed in the Church at this time, and for centuries afterwards, was wholly public, involving confession, a period of penance and exclusion from communion, and formal absolution and restoration—the whole process being called *exomologesis.* The last of these was normally bestowed by the bishop, as Hippolytus's prayer of episcopal consecration implies, but in his absence might be delegated to a priest. There is plenty of evidence that sinners were encouraged to open their hearts privately to a priest, but nothing to show that this led up to anything more than ghostly counsel."[70]

Here it was, very early in church history, and fully in place: penance, without a hint of controversy. In fact, the biggest controversy swung the other way: there were some Christians who thought that certain sins, such as denying Christ to avoid martyrdom, were unforgiveable![71] And there is no shortage of passages from the church fathers that clearly show that penance was an integral and uncontroversial part of the sacramental infrastructure of the Christian life.[72] Consider just these four examples:

> For as many as are of God and of Jesus Christ are also with the bishop. And as many as shall, in the exercise of penance, return into the unity of the Church, these, too, shall belong to God, that they may live according to Jesus Christ.... For where there is division and wrath, God does not dwell. To all them that repent, the Lord grants forgiveness, if they turn in penitence to the unity of God, and to communion with the bishop.
>
> —Ignatius of Antioch, AD 110[73]

> Sinners may do penance for a set time, and according to the rules of discipline come to public confession, and by imposition of the hand of the bishop and clergy receive the right of Communion. [But now some] with their time [of penance] still unfulfilled ... they are admitted to Communion, and their name is presented; and while the penitence is not yet performed, confession is not yet made, the hands of the bishop and clergy are not yet laid upon them, the Eucharist is given to them; although it is written, "Whosoever shall eat the bread and drink the cup of the Lord unworthily, shall be guilty of the body and blood of the Lord" [1 Cor. 11:27].
>
> —Saint Cyprian of Carthage, AD 250[74]

> Priests have received a power which God has given neither to angels nor to archangels. It was said to them: "Whatsoever you shall bind on earth shall be bound in heaven; and whatsoever you shall loose, shall be loosed" [Matt. 18:18]. Temporal rulers have indeed the power of binding; but they can only bind the body. Priests, in contrast, can bind with a bond which pertains to the soul itself and transcends the very heavens. Did [God] not give them all the powers of heaven? "Whose sins you shall forgive," he says, "they are forgiven them; whose sins you shall retain, they are retained" [John 20:23]. What greater power is there than this? The Father has given all judgment to the Son. And now I see the Son placing all this power in the hands of men [Matt. 10:40; John 20:21 – 23]. They are raised to this dignity as if they were already gathered up to heaven.
>
> —Saint John Chrysostom, AD 388[75]

For those whom you have seen doing penance, have committed heinous things, either adulteries or some enormous crimes: for these they do penance. Because if theirs had been light sins, daily prayer would suffice to blot these out.... In three ways then are sins remitted in the Church; by Baptism, by prayer, by the greater humility of penance.

—Saint Augustine of Hippo, c. AD 395[76]

Given the biblical basis for penance, the development of the sacrament is not surprising at all. And the fact that Western and Eastern Rite Catholics as well as the Eastern Orthodox practiced it without controversy until the time of the Reformation made it impossible for me to think that it was not at least a legitimate Christian practice consistent with biblical theology.

D. Apostolic Succession

Catholicism holds that if a Church claims to be Christian, then it must be able to show that its leaders—its bishops and its presbyters (or priests)—are successors of the apostles. That is why the Catholic Church accepts Eastern Orthodox ordinations and sacraments as valid, even though Eastern Orthodoxy is not in full communion with Rome.

What amazed me is how uncontroversial apostolic succession was in the early church.[77] I expected to find factions of Christians, including respected church fathers, who resisted episcopal ecclesiology. There aren't any. In fact, in the early church, a leading argument against heretics was their lack of episcopal lineage and continuity and thus their absence of communion with the visible and universal Church. In his famous apologetic treatise *Against Heresies* (AD 182–88), Saint Irenaeus (c. AD 140–202) makes that very point in several places.[78] Tertullian offers the same sort of apologetic as well.[79]

Of course, the very early Christians did not have the elaborate hierarchy and canon law of today's Catholic Church. But they also lacked a secure and officially closed New Testament canon, conciliar creeds, detailed and sophisticated articulations of the Trinity, the incarnation, and justification, and a global church with a global reach. An infant Church is like a human infant. In its earliest stages, it possesses in its essence properties that when fully mature are exemplified differently but are nevertheless rooted in the nature of the being itself. So the same human being who says, "Mama, me pooh-pooh" may someday practice internal medicine. Thus, as the Church grows and develops, its intrinsic properties mature in order to accommodate its increasing membership as well as meet new theological, political, geographic, and pastoral challenges unanticipated by its younger incarnation. For example, because of the challenge of Arianism, the First Council of Nicaea (AD 325) convened and produced a creed that all members of the Church were required to embrace. Such conciliar resolutions make sense only if such bodies have real authority. And, as I came to learn, the only authority recognized in the early church for settling doctrinal disputes was apostolic, whether original or received.

By the time the earliest church fathers are writing their epistles, an ecclesial infrastructure is already and uncontroversially in place, albeit in primitive form. Although we can see clues of this in the New Testament, suggesting a particular pattern of leadership and authority, they remain only clues when isolated from how the early readers of Scripture, including the apostles' disciples and their successors, understood them.

First, it is clear that the New Testament church was an apostolic church. Its leadership consisted of the apostles, who were given this authority by our Lord, including the powers to bind and loose (Matt. 16:19; 18:18), forgive sins (John 20:21–23), baptize (Matt. 28:18–20), and make disciples (Matt. 28:18–20). We see this kind of leadership exhibited in numerous ways throughout the New Testament, including the instruction that the Church is built on Christ and his apostles (Eph. 2:19–22), the deliberation and pronouncement within an episcopal structure about a theological controversy (Acts 15:1–30), the proclamation of what constitutes an appropriate reception of true doctrine (1 Cor. 15:3–11), the rebuke and excommunication of members (Acts 5:1–11; 8:14–24; 1 Cor 5; 1 Tim. 5:17–22; 2 Tim. 4:2; Titus 1:10–11), the judgment of the adequacy of a believer's penance or penitent state (2 Cor. 2:5–11; 1 Cor. 11:27–32), the ordination and appointment of ministers (Acts 14:23; 1 Tim. 4:14), the choice of successors (Acts 1:20–26), and the entrustment of the apostolic tradition to the next generation (2 Thess. 2:15; 2 Tim. 2:2). The Catholic properties were all in place, albeit in embryonic form.

Second, the full meaning of these "clues" found in the practices of the nascent Church is unambiguously answered by the second generation of Christians and their successors. In addition to the testimonies of Saint Irenaeus and Tertullian, as noted above, there are others.[80] Here are just a few:

> And thus preaching through countries and cities, they appointed the first-fruits [of their labors], having first proved them by the Spirit, to be bishops and deacons of those who should afterwards believe. Nor was this any new thing, since indeed many ages before it was written concerning bishops and deacons.... Our apostles also knew, through our Lord Jesus Christ, that there would be strife on account of the office of the episcopate. For this reason, therefore, inasmuch as they had obtained a perfect fore-knowledge of this, they appointed those [ministers] already mentioned, and afterwards gave instructions, that when these should fall asleep, other approved men should succeed them in their ministry.
>
> — Saint Clement of Rome, c. AD 70
> (possibly as late as AD 98)[81]

> [T]he Church is one, and as she is one, cannot be both within and without. For if she is with [the heretic] Novatian, she was not with Cornelius. But if she was with Cornelius, who succeeded the bishop Fabian, by lawful ordination, and whom, beside the honor of the priesthood the Lord glorified also with martyrdom, Novatian is not in the Church; nor can he be reckoned as a bishop, who, succeeding to no one, and despising the evangelical and apostolic tradition, sprang from himself. For he who has not been ordained in the Church can neither have nor hold to the Church in any way.
>
> — Saint Cyprian of Carthage, AD 254[82]

> And again, in the Gospel, when Christ breathed on the apostles alone, saying, "Receive the Holy Ghost: whose soever sins you remit they are remitted unto them, and whose soever sins you retain they are retained." Therefore the power of remitting sins was given to the apostles, and to the churches which they, sent by Christ, established, and to the bishops who succeeded to them by vicarious ordination.
>
> — Firmilian, Bishop of Caesarea in Cappadocia, AD 256[83]

The consent of peoples and nations keeps me in the Church; so does her authority, inaugurated by miracles, nourished by hope, enlarged by love, established by age. The succession of priests keeps me, beginning from the very seat of the Apostle Peter, to whom the Lord, after His resurrection, gave it in charge to feed His sheep, down to the present episcopate …

—Saint Augustine of Hippo, AD 397[84]

For if the lineal succession of bishops is to be taken into account, with how much more certainty and benefit to the Church do we reckon back till we reach Peter himself, to whom, as bearing in a figure the whole Church, the Lord said: "Upon this rock will I build my Church, and the gates of hell shall not prevail against it!" The successor of Peter was Linus, and his successors in unbroken continuity were these: Clement, Anacletus, Evaristus, Alexander…. In this order of succession no Donatist bishop is found. But, reversing the natural course of things, the Donatists sent to Rome from Africa an ordained bishop, who, putting himself at the head of a few Africans in the great metropolis, gave some notoriety to the name of "mountain men," or Cutzupits, by which they were known.

—Saint Augustine of Hippo, c. AD 400[85]

The Catholic Church also embraces the primacy of the bishop of Rome and the doctrine of papal infallibility. I do not have room to address that aspect of apostolic succession. Suffice it to say, once I had found apostolic succession to be a legitimate Christian doctrine both historically and biblically, Petrine primacy seemed to fall into place. There are two reasons for this: (1) While a Protestant Christian who was baptized and confirmed in the Catholic Church as a youngster, I was in schism with the Catholic Church, not the Eastern Orthodox Church. Thus, Eastern Orthodoxy (which is really the only alternative if you accept apostolic succession, the seven sacraments, and reject the Western papacy) did not seem to be the appropriate place for me to reestablish full communion with the one, holy, catholic, and apostolic church. (2) However, I discovered that the case for Petrine primacy was pretty strong,[86] so much so that even the Orthodox who reject the modern papacy nevertheless maintain that Rome has some sort of ecclesial primacy.[87] (Some say more modestly, "a primacy of honor.") So, given both of these reasons—as well as the Catholic Church's public positions on the moral and philosophical issues that I mentioned in part II—Eastern Orthodoxy was never really a live option for me.

Nevertheless, apostolic succession was, for most of Christian history, uncontroversially embraced by the churches of the East and the West, at least until the Reformation. Although I thought it certainly possible that apostolic succession is a mistaken view, I also concluded that it was at least a legitimate position within the confines of acceptable Christian belief.

IV. Coming Full Circle

I concluded that the four Catholic doctrines on justification, communion, penance, and apostolic succession were defensible Christian beliefs and practices that not only could be supported scripturally but also were uncontroversially believed and practiced by the church universal during the times in which the most important early creeds and canons were penned and promulgated (for example, Nicaea, Chalcedon, Orange). It became clear to me that the same Church that shepherded Christianity through the tumult of doctrinal conflict over issues concerning the Trinity, Christ's nature, and original sin was Catholic in its ecclesiology as well as in its liturgical and sacramental practices. And during the Church's first three centuries, when the canon of the New Testament had not yet been fixed by that Church, it understood itself as apostolic (in the sense of apostolic succession) and delivered to its people, without controversy as to their gracious efficacy and status as legitimate Christian practices, the sacraments of penance and the Eucharist for the sake of the believer's justification.[88] So I could not legitimately isolate and insulate my Protestant reading of the New Testament from the practices of the Church that fixed the canon of that New Testament without suggesting the counterintuitive notion that the Church had enough of the Holy Spirit to know what books belong in Scripture but not enough of the Holy Spirit to know what practices and ecclesiology are consistent with, or legitimate derivations from, that Scripture. For if I remained Protestant, I had to bear the burden of explaining why I could not read the Scripture along with the Church that fixed the

Scripture's canon. Because it was clear to me I was not wiser than that Church, I had to seriously consider returning to it.

At this point, I thought, "If I reject the Catholic Church, there is good reason for me to believe I am rejecting the Church that Christ himself established." That's not a risk I was willing to take. After all, I figured, "If I return to the Church and participate in the sacraments, I lose nothing, since I will still be a follower of Jesus and believe everything that the early creeds teach, as I have always believed. But if the Church is right about itself and the sacraments, I will acquire graces I would not otherwise receive." Thus, the burden was on me, and not on the Catholic Church, to show why I should remain in schism with the Church in which my parents baptized me, even as I could think of no incorrigible reason to remain in schism.

Although it was only five months after I became president of the Evangelical Theological Society that my wife and I would decide to seek full communion with the Catholic Church, I had been instinctively thinking like a Catholic for well over a decade (perhaps longer). My intellectual and spiritual development while I was an Evangelical Protestant had been, at crucial points, shaped by an understanding of Christian doctrine and the nature of the human person that has ancient roots predating, and often contrary to, the intuitions formed by the reflexes of the ecclesial communions that developed out of the Reformation. It is only in retrospect that I now fully appreciate how far I had moved toward Catholicism when I finally came to understand, and eventually embrace, the four doctrines that seemed like insurmountable obstacles to my reversion.

Nevertheless, as an Evangelical Protestant, I had received a wonderful gift, something that few Catholics have had the opportunity to experience. I had seen, firsthand, the practical consequences of a tradition that puts a premium on individual conversion, the public sharing of one's faith, and the reliance on the authority of Scripture as the only written Word of God. These virtues—that are often found in abundance in the best of Evangelical churches—are often diminished by, and thus significantly lacking among, even observant Catholics. This is, sadly, one of the consequences of a divided Western Christianity. We Catholics lose something of ourselves and the grandeur of our common faith when we mistakenly come to believe that some of the beliefs and practices of our separated brethren are entirely alien to the Catholic faith, when in fact they are rooted in traditions as ancient as the Church itself. The necessity of conversion by grace alone,[89] the call to evangelism,[90] and the inspiration and authority of the Bible[91] are Catholic beliefs, which are sometimes better expressed and taught by our separated brethren. I have had the privilege to study under, and I remain friends with, many of these fine Evangelical Protestants, whose work has left an indelible mark on both my character and my Christian walk. My return to the Catholic Church would not have been possible if not for these brethren who assisted me, with all their God-given graces and talents, in fulfilling the promise of my baptism.

✄

CHAPTER 5

A Response to Catholicism

Gregg Allison

I am by conviction and without shame a Protestant and an Evangelical who has a fascination with Catholic theology and practice. That being the case, the twofold purpose with which I have been tasked is (1) to highlight the similarities and differences between Protestantism and Catholicism so that readers of this book will understand better and more clearly their commonalities and their divergences, and (2) to present a critical assessment of Catholicism so that, if any readers are contemplating a journey toward the Catholic Church, they will be persuaded that they are moving not from lesser faithfulness to greater faithfulness but from greater faithfulness to lesser faithfulness, a journey they must reconsider and abandon. In the unfolding of my task, my preference would be to present first an Evangelical Protestant vision for life with God and human flourishing.[1] Because of space limitations, however, I will set forth in broad strokes where such a vision overlaps with Catholicism, thereby highlighting the commonalities between Protestantism and Catholicism. Then I will offer an Evangelical Protestant assessment of Catholicism, showing particularly where the Catholic worldview differs from the worldview I affirm and defend. Finally, I will make a concluding appeal to readers not to forsake Evangelical Protestantism for Catholicism.

Where an Evangelical Protestant Vision Overlaps with Catholicism: Commonalities

An Evangelical Protestant vision affirms certain essential elements that, in one sense, render it quite unremarkable, in that this vision is firmly rooted in a responsible interpretation of Scripture, coheres well theologically, and draws robust support from church tradition. Indeed, in the following areas, this Evangelical Protestant vision is the same as, or very similar to, Catholic theology:

- The existence and knowability of God; his triune nature as Father, Son, and Holy Spirit; his eternal plan or purpose according to which God is working all things, including the creation of the universe *ex nihilo* and his providential care for all that he has created[2]
- Divine revelation expressed in two modes, general and special revelation
- The creation of human beings in the image of God; their fall into sin and the reality of original sin, including guilt before God and corruption of their nature[3]
- The person and work of Jesus Christ; his full deity and full humanity, the hypostatic union, his miraculous conception by the Virgin Mary in the incarnation, his sinlessness, mediatorial work, crucifixion, resurrection, ascension, and future return[4]
- The Word of God, or Scripture, which is fully inspired, wholly true (inerrant) in all that it affirms,[5] and effective (an Evangelical Protestant vision includes other attributes of Scripture — sufficiency, necessity, [supreme] authority, and clarity — not affirmed by Catholicism); and the New Testament canon as consisting of twenty-seven books (an Evangelical Protestant vision affirms thirty-nine books of the Old Testament and does not include the Apocrypha as recognized by the Catholic canon)
- The accomplishment of salvation by the atoning sacrifice of Jesus Christ on the cross, followed by his resurrection from the dead
- The actualization of salvation with priority given to the gracious action of God, by which fallen human beings who are incapable of saving themselves are redeemed
- The person and work of the Holy Spirit; his full deity, his works of creation and providence, his inspiration of Scripture, and his multifaceted ministry in Christians and the church
- In general, the same broad contours of the future mighty acts of God, including the return of Christ, the resurrection, the

last judgment, the eternal condemnation of the wicked, and the new heaven and new earth

These commonalities arise from the fact that Catholicism and Protestantism are branches growing from the same trunk of the early church and, to some degree, the medieval church (it is in this period that the branching begins). This rich legacy needs to be embraced and appreciated by both parties; there is much that unites us under the broad rubric of Christianity.

At the same time, startling differences separate Catholicism and Protestantism.

WHERE AN EVANGELICAL PROTESTANT VISION DIFFERS FROM CATHOLICISM: DIVERGENCES

The major differences between Protestantism and Catholicism are divine revelation, specifically the issues of Scripture and Tradition, the apocryphal writings in the Old Testament, and the interpretation of the Bible; salvation, particularly the doctrine of justification; Mary and her role; the church; and eschatology, or a view of the future.

(1) Divine revelation that consists of written Scripture, which is sufficient, necessary, and authoritative (Protestantism), or divine revelation that consists of both Scripture and church tradition (Catholicism). A major point of division between Catholicism and Protestantism focuses on the issue of ultimate authority for the church. Catholicism embraces a triadic structure of authority, with written Scripture, church tradition, and the magisterium (the teaching office of the Catholic Church) constituting a threefold authoritative collective. This structure is akin to a three-legged stool; as the three legs prop up the seat, so Scripture, Tradition, and the magisterium support the Church and its doctrine and practice. In this first section about the differences between Catholicism and Protestantism, I will focus on written Scripture and church tradition; in the third section, I will focus on the magisterium.

A foundational tenet — called the "formal principle" — of Protestantism is that the ultimate source of divine revelation, and hence the supreme authority for the church, is the written Word of God only *(sola scriptura)* and not Scripture plus church tradition. This latter position is embraced by Catholicism, which views Tradition as consisting of teachings that Christ passed down orally to the apostles, who in turn passed them down to their successors, the bishops. This Tradition is maintained in the Catholic Church and occasionally promulgated as official church doctrine, including such dogmas as the immaculate conception of Mary and her bodily assumption.

At the heart of Protestantism's rejection of Catholicism's theology of divine revelation are the following: the idea of Tradition as supplementing written Scripture rests on poor biblical support, especially the Catholic misinterpretation of John 16:12[6]; Tradition as conceived by Catholicism is a late—fourteenth-century—development[7]; the Catholic Church's claim to be the maintainer and promulgator of such divine revelation is essentially a claim to be infallibly led by the Holy Spirit—apart from Scripture; Tradition contradicts both the sufficiency[8] and necessity[9] of Scripture; and the Scripture-plus-Tradition formula is inherently unstable, with Tradition trumping Scripture in terms of ultimate authority when the two are in conflict.[10] For these reasons, Protestantism champions *sola scriptura*: Scripture, not Scripture plus Tradition, is the sole source of divine revelation and hence of supreme authority for the Church.

(2) An Old Testament that corresponds to the Hebrew Bible used by Jesus and the apostles (Protestantism), or an expanded Old Testament that includes the apocryphal writings (Catholicism). Another major difference between Protestantism and Catholicism is the canon of Scripture. The focus of this issue is not the New Testament—both agree on the same twenty-seven writings—but the Old Testament. Protestantism insists that the church's Old Testament should be based on the Hebrew Bible, resulting in thirty-nine writings. Catholicism asserts that its Old Testament should incorporate some of the additional books found in the Septuagint (the Greek translation of the Hebrew Bible), resulting in a longer version that includes the apocryphal writings. The Apocrypha contains additional books—Tobit, Judith, Ecclesiasticus, Wisdom of Solomon, Baruch, and 1 and 2 Maccabees—not found in the Protestant Bible, and additional sections in Esther and Daniel, which it shares in common with the Protestant Bible.

This difference exists because the sixteenth-century Reformers rejected the Catholic canon for the following reasons: the apocryphal writings were not part of the Hebrew Bible of Jesus and his disciples;

the apocryphal writings were explicitly deemed noncanonical (that is, nonauthoritative) by church leaders[11] leading up to the time (the fifth century) of Augustine, who was responsible for this startling shift to include those writings in the Church's Old Testament;[12] some of the apocryphal writings included incorrect historical or chronological information; while deeply appreciative of, and often dependent on, Augustine and his theology, the Reformers sided with Jerome's principle — the church can read the apocryphal writings for its growth, but it should not consult those extra writings in the establishment of its doctrine — over against Augustine's insistence that the Apocrypha is divinely inspired and thus canonical; the Council of Trent in the middle of the sixteenth century was the first general council[13] to proclaim the Old Testament including the Apocrypha as the official canon of the Catholic Church.[14] Thus, Protestantism does not include the Apocrypha in its canonical Old Testament.

(3) The interpretation of Scripture that focuses on the clarity of Scripture and encourages personal responsibility for its understanding (Protestantism), or an official, authoritative interpreter, the magisterium (Catholicism). Another matter separating Catholicism and Protestantism in this realm of Scripture concerns its proper interpretation, and this section picks up the third element in Catholicism's triadic structure of authority. Catholicism insists that the prerogative to determine the correct and authoritative interpretation of Scripture belongs solely to its magisterium, or teaching office (consisting of the pope and bishops). This was a decision made in response to the growing Protestant movement by the Council of Trent (1546) in its declaration "that no one relying on his own judgment shall, in matters of faith and morals pertaining to the edification of Christian doctrine, distorting the Holy Scriptures in accordance with his own conceptions, presume to interpret them contrary to that sense which holy mother Church, to whom it belongs to judge of their true sense and interpretation, has held and holds…."[15] Thus, the Catholic magisterium claims that it possesses the sole right to interpret Scripture. This mere claim, however, does not guarantee a correct interpretation, as the misinterpretation of some Scripture by the magisterium is well in evidence.[16]

Protestantism's rejection of the Catholic magisterium and insistence on personal Bible study stem from its conviction that Scripture is clear for all Christians, who are also responsible and competent for the task of interpreting it. The clarity of Scripture[17] means that it is written in such a way that ordinary human beings who possess the normal acquired ability to understand written and oral communication can read Scripture with understanding or, if they are unable to read, can hear Scripture read and comprehend it (Deut. 29:29). Specifically, it is intelligible to Christians who diligently read it guided by the Holy Spirit (1 Cor. 2:10–16) and following sound interpretive principles (for example, understanding the text in its context, being sensitive to the genre), with the aid of the divinely ordained elders (1 Tim. 3:2; 5:17; Titus 1:9)—the "pastors and teachers" (Eph. 4:11)—of their church. Commands to give attention to Scripture (1 Peter 2:1–3; 2 Peter 1:19–21), examples of common people evaluating the religious claims of others by the Word of God (Acts 17:10–12), assumptions that Christians will understand Scripture, even when it narrates events far removed from the context of those Christians (for example, 1 Cor. 10:1–11; Rom. 4:22–24; 15:4), and examples of Scripture being understood (Neh. 8) encourage—and give the responsibility to—all Christians to read and study the Bible, with the expectation that they will indeed understand and benefit from it.[18]

(4) Salvation by God's grace alone without human cooperation (Protestantism), or salvation by God's grace that enables the meriting of eternal life (Catholicism). One of the most pronounced and crucial differences between Catholicism and Protestantism is their understanding of salvation.[19] Catholicism joins together justification with other acts of God in salvation, specifically sanctification and regeneration: "Justification is not only the remission of sins, but also the sanctification and renewal of the inward man."[20] Specifically, justification is tied to baptism, through which grace for regeneration is infused; it can and must increase through participation in the other sacraments, through which more grace is infused, and engagement in good works, and it may be lost through committing mortal sin, rendering any assurance of salvation impossible.[21] Thus, justification is a cooperative effort between God's grace and human effort; at the initiative of grace, sinful people are enabled both to express faith in Christ's atoning death and, moved by love and the Holy Spirit, to merit eternal life through involvement in the Church and good deeds.

Protestantism dissents from this view. Justification is the mighty act of God by which he declares sinful human beings to be not guilty—to be forgiven of sins—but instead righteous, because the righteousness of Christ is accredited to them. In Scripture, justification is presented as a forensic (legal) declaration, the opposite of condemnation (for example, Deut. 25:1; Prov. 17:15; Rom. 5:16, 18); indeed, as those justified by divine grace, Christians are assured there is "no condemnation for those who are in Christ Jesus" (Rom. 8:1; cf. Rom. 5:1, 9). While intimately linked with regeneration and sanctification, justification is distinguishable from those other two mighty works; Scripture itself notes these as different divine acts (1 Cor. 6:11).[22] Catholicism conflates these three: it mixes together the declarative work of God (justification, the pronouncement that sinful people are not guilty but righteous instead) with his transformative works (regeneration and sanctification, by which sinful people are born again to become new creatures and progressively renewed into Christlikeness in character). Confounding these three mighty acts results in Catholicism's false notion of justification: it is the infusion of righteousness instead of its imputation; it may increase or decrease instead of being either declared to be the case or not declared; it is tied to baptism and the other Catholic sacraments instead of being God's mighty act alone; it incorporates human cooperation; and it can be lost instead of providing the assurance that the future verdict—"no condemnation" but perfect standing before God because of the perfect righteousness of Christ—has already been rendered for those who embrace Christ by faith alone.[23] Out of deep gratitude for their justification, Christians obey God, exercise faith that works through love (Gal. 5:6), and engage in good works, because they have been born again and have a new nature—regeneration—and because they and God cooperate together in the ongoing process of greater conformity to Christlikeness—sanctification—not to merit the eternal life that has been graciously given to them but because they are new creations.

(5) *Singular focus on Jesus Christ plus appreciation for the role of Mary (Protestantism), or an honoring of Mary in her cooperative role with Jesus Christ (Catholicism).* Protestantism has a singular focus on Jesus Christ, while Catholicism adds some attention to Mary, his mother. Specifically, Catholicism believes in (a) the immaculate conception

of Mary, that is, she was "preserved from all stain of original sin" from the moment of her conception,[24] (b) her sinlessness throughout her entire life, (c) her perpetual virginity,[25] (d) her role as *Theotokos* ("mother of God"), (e) her presence at the cross by which she joined her Son in cooperation with the divine plan of redemption through suffering, and (f) her bodily assumption (she "was taken up body and soul into heavenly glory"[26]) immediately after her death. Because of Mary's personal history and the inseparable union with her Son, "the Blessed Virgin is invoked in the Church under the titles of Advocate, Helper, Benefactress, and Mediatrix."[27] Catholicism honors the maternal mediation and spiritual motherhood of Mary, acknowledging that she cooperates "in the birth and development of divine life in the souls of the redeemed."[28] Additionally, "the Church's devotion to the Blessed Virgin is intrinsic to Christian worship,"[29] specifically, the seventeen annual festival days dedicated to her, and the fifty "Hail Mary" prayers in the rosary.

Protestantism acknowledges the unique role played by Mary, agreeing that she is *Theotokos* in the sense of being the "God-bearer"; that is to say, the one to whom she gave birth—Jesus Christ—is fully God. Furthermore, it admires her faith and obedience (Luke 1:26–38) and calls her blessed (Luke 1:48). At the same time, Protestantism repudiates most of what Catholicism believes about her. Specifically, Protestantism recognizes that like Jesus' other disciples, Mary struggled to understand the significance of her Son (Luke 2:25–35; 11:27–28; Mark 3:20–35; John 2:1–11; 19:25–27), and it maintains that many of the claims made about her by Catholicism either are the result of poor interpretation of Scripture or arise from unchastened church tradition.[30]

Accordingly, Protestantism appreciates the role of Mary without allowing this value to escalate into an unwarranted honoring of her as Advocate, Helper, Benefactress, and Mediatrix, cooperating with her Son in his work of salvation and assisting fallen human beings to embrace that salvation.

(6) A church that closely follows the contours of Scripture (Protestantism), or a church that focuses on the sacramental economy (Catholicism). One of the most pronounced differences between Catholicism and Protestantism is in their understanding of the doctrine and role of the Church. For Catholicism, the Church is the means of grace neces-

sary for salvation, as evidenced by its idea of the "sacramental economy".[31] As Redeemer, Jesus Christ accomplished salvation through his Paschal (Easter) mystery—his passion, death, and resurrection—that occurred in history and that gave birth to the sacrament of the Church. As High Priest, he continues to accomplish salvation through the Church, with particular reference to the apostles and their successors, the bishops, who teach, govern, and sanctify the Church through the gospel and the seven sacraments. Thus, it is through the Catholic Church alone that the fullness of salvation is extended to a sinful world.

At the heart of this doctrine of the Catholic Church and its sacramental economy are the seven sacraments, through which the Church dispenses the grace of God: baptism regenerates those who are baptized, who in most cases are infants; confirmation confers the empowerment of the Holy Spirit upon baptized people; the Eucharist re-presents the once-and-for-all sacrifice of Jesus on the cross, the saving event that becomes present in the Catholic Mass when the bread and the wine are transubstantiated into his body and blood; penance reconciles to God and to the Church all who have committed postbaptismal mortal sins; marriage; holy orders for men as they are ordained to the priesthood; and the anointing of the sick for those who are ill and potentially in danger of death, so they will be prepared for the life to come. Because these Catholic sacraments confer grace, they are necessary for salvation.

No Protestant denomination or church conceives of and lives out the doctrine of the Church in a way that even remotely resembles this Catholic notion. Though often charged as being Church-lite, Protestantism may articulate a robust doctrine of the Church, focusing on the Church as part of the eternal plan of God (Eph. 3:3–6), as the body of the Son of God, who is supreme head of all things (Eph. 1:19–23), and as ingredient to the Son's mission to rescue humanity from sin (Matt. 16:13–21). At the same time, such a Protestant affirmation advocates a necessity for the Church that is derivative and instrumental, not causative and foundational.

Moreover, Protestantism dissents from Catholicism's authority structure of apostolic succession. What Jesus passed down to his disciples was not a self-perpetuating hierarchy, nor even the blueprints for such a line of succession. Rather he commissioned his disciples with the same commission that he had received from the Father (John 20:21), what is often termed the "Great Commission" (Matt. 28:18–20). Certainly, the apostles appointed leaders in the churches they had established (for example, Acts 14:23), but such appointments did not confer on their recipients apostolic authority. And the development of the episcopalian hierarchical structure that eventually progressed to the idea of apostolic succession was a pragmatic move, originating for good purposes—to ward off heresy and to maintain the unity of the church[32]—but which contradicted the biblical pattern of leadership: eldership as one office (with different words—*elder, bishop, pastor*— used for those serving in it),[33] and the deaconate as a second office of ministry or service (for example, Phil. 1:1).

Furthermore, Protestantism separates from Catholicism over its notion of the sacraments being valid and effective *ex opere operato* and being seven in number. According to the Catholic perspective of *ex opere operato* (literally, "from the work worked"), the sacraments are valid by the simple fact that they are performed in the appropriate Christian manner (for example, baptism in the name of the triune God), and they are effective in that they confer grace, regardless of the spiritual state of those who administer them and of those who receive them (though more benefit results, in terms of personal transformation by grace, for those who are properly disposed toward the sacraments). Protestantism maintains that only two—baptism and the Lord's Supper—were ordained by Christ (Matt. 28:19; Matt. 26:26–29; 1 Cor. 11:17–34) and have accompanying tangible signs (water; bread and wine).

In its theology of these two sacraments, Protestantism differs greatly from the Catholic understanding. Whereas Catholicism believes that baptism regenerates *ex opere operato*, Protestantism (of all varieties) denies that the Church's administration of water is capable of saving anyone. Whether in the case of infant baptism or in the practice of believer's baptism, Protestantism emphasizes the necessity of the Word of God and faith.[34] And whereas Catholicism maintains that the Eucharist confers grace as the bread and wine are transubstantiated, or changed in nature into the body and blood of Christ, Protestantism denies that transubstantiation has biblical, theological, philosophical, and historical warrant[35] or confers grace that saves *ex opere operato*.

(7) A personal eschatology of two eternal destinies (Protestantism), or a personal eschatology of two eternal destinies plus a temporal destiny of purgatory (Catholicism). Protestantism believes that human beings face one of only two eternal destinies: eternal life for all whom God saves through his grace as they embrace the gospel by faith, or eternal condemnation for all who reject this salvation. Although Catholicism agrees with these two eternal destinies, it adds a temporal destiny for most people: temporal punishment in purgatory. "All who die in God's grace and friendship, but still imperfectly purified, are indeed assured of their eternal salvation; but after death they undergo purification, so as to achieve the holiness necessary to enter the joy of heaven."[36] This temporal punishment for final purification is called purgatory.

Protestantism rejects this doctrine for the following reasons: the idea of purgatory is based on an apocryphal writing (2 Macc. 12:46), and Protestantism denies that the Apocrypha is canonical Scripture—and hence authoritative; the doctrine is based on poorly interpreted biblical passages (for example, 1 Cor. 3:15 describes the testing of human works by the divine fire of judgment, not purgatory as a place of punishment for ultimate purification); and the doctrine is based on an incorrect idea of justification.

Purgatory makes sense in a view of justification that combines a declarative act of forgiveness with inward renovation; in a case where this latter renewal process is not sufficiently advanced, such a sinful person is in need of further purification in purgatory. However, if through justification that sinful person is declared to be not guilty—to be forgiven of sins—but instead completely righteous, there can be no temporal punishment (because of his being imperfectly purified) awaiting him in a final purification of purgatory. The Protestant doctrine of justification leaves no room, because it has no need, for a doctrine of purgatory.[37]

Thus, Protestantism rejects the notion of purgatory as a temporal destiny for most people and holds to only two eternal destinies.

※

In summary, Protestantism and Catholicism significantly disagree on and divide over seven major areas: divine revelation, specifically the issues of Scripture and Tradition; the Apocrypha; biblical interpretation; salvation, especially justification; Mary; the Church; and eschatology.

CONCLUDING APPEAL

Evangelical Protestants become interested in and move to the Catholic Church for several reasons:[38] they desire certainty of salvation and truth concerning God and his ways; they want to feel connected to the church of the past and be organically related to Christians from ancient times; they long for unity of all churches because they are scandalized by the historic and current divisions among Christians; and they yearn for authority and thus are attracted by the authority of the Catholic Church and its magisterium. Though I have not had space to develop it, a robust Evangelical Protestant vision of human flourishing and life with God can address these deep longings.

For those searching for certainty of salvation and truth concerning God and his ways, the Evangelical Protestant vision offers such assurance. In terms of its "big picture," it embraces creation, fall, redemption, consummation — the very storyline of Scripture. It rests foundationally on the triune God and his works of creation, providence, and salvation. It embraces the inspired Word of God that is wholly true in all that it affirms, completely sufficient for salvation and for living a life that pleases God fully, authoritative to command faith and obedience, intelligible to all who read it, necessary for knowing God and his will, and powerful to rescue fallen human beings and transform them into the image of Jesus Christ. This vision magnifies the complete sufficiency of the death and resurrection of Christ and makes no provision for a cooperative effort by which people depend on the grace of God while working to merit eternal life. It highlights the multifaceted mighty works of God to actualize such salvation in human lives, from election to regeneration, from justification to sanctification, from perseverance[39] to glorification. This vision manifests itself in a church that closely follows the contours of Scripture with an emphasis on robust worship of God, proclamation of his Word, celebration of the two ordinances given by Jesus Christ, extensive engagement of non-Christians with the gospel, and much more.

The Evangelical Protestant vision offers certainty of salvation and truth concerning God and his ways.

As for being connected to the church of the past, this Evangelical Protestant vision embraces the essential doctrines that Christians have always believed, defended, and lived—core truths like the Trinity and Christology hammered out in the earliest centuries of Christianity. But it does not embrace key elements held by Catholicism, because the Evangelical Protestant vision is forged in the context of a chastened tradition, accepting those doctrines and practices that enjoy scriptural support and rejecting other beliefs that lack such warrant or are based on a faulty interpretation of Scripture.[40] Just because the early church and medieval church believed and practiced something does not mean that the Church today must believe and practice that as well. What is called for is a chastened tradition that distinguishes between doctrines and practices that have biblical justification and those that do not. And this Evangelical Protestant vision clings to that which is rightly warranted. Furthermore, it inherits proven doctrines and practices from the Reformation that were essential for the Church both in terms of modifying already existing beliefs and in terms of discovering new ones that came to light in that desperate situation of a carnal and spiritually bankrupt Catholicism.

A robust Evangelical Protestant vision is properly connected to the church of the past.

An intense longing for the unity of all churches so as to overcome the historic and current divisions between them is not satisfied by leaving Protestantism and joining the Catholic Church, for the latter does not even consider Protestant "ecclesial communities" to be true churches, a fact that patently does not overcome the problem of disunity.[41] This Evangelical Protestant vision will certainly not overcome this problem either, but it does embrace a universal church of which all genuine Christians—both those in heaven with Christ and those currently alive—are members and that manifests itself in local churches that establish strong connections with like-minded churches for high-impact ministries in their region. Such churches work hard to overcome disunity even among their own members (Eph. 4:3–6). And they long for the actualization of the vision of perfect unity still to come, when those "from every tribe and language and people and nation" will worship the Lord together (Rev. 5:9–10).

A healthy Evangelical Protestant vision encourages and provides for a realistic unity of churches now and a hope for perfect unity in the future.

As for the yearning for authority that attracts people to the Catholic magisterium, it is one thing to long for an authority that is perfect and inerrant, and quite another thing to long for an authority that rests on a mere claim of infallibility while simultaneously demonstrating that it is susceptible to error. With respect to the former, such perfect and inerrant authority belongs not to any human institution — religious or otherwise — but to God and his Word alone. With respect to the latter, the Catholic magisterium may be established as the official interpreter of Scripture and Tradition and may claim infallibility for (some of) its pronouncements, but because of its errors in interpretation and theological formulation, it must be regarded as other human authorities. It is certainly not a panacea that in reality satisfies the yearning for perfect authority. This Evangelical Protestant vision places such authority in its proper place — in God and his authoritative written Word. Certainly, Scripture must be interpreted, then believed and obeyed. And Scripture has been written clearly for Christians to understand, and they have the responsibility to read and embrace it. Furthermore, God has ordained and gifted local church pastors and elders to preach and teach his Word to help their members understand it rightly and live it obediently and faithfully. Such clarity of understanding lived out in faith and obedience is adequate for our journey of faith in this earthly life.

A healthy Evangelical Protestant vision places authority in its proper place.

Accordingly, to readers contemplating a move from Evangelical Protestantism to Catholicism, let me emphasize that you are moving not from lesser faithfulness to greater faithfulness but from greater faithfulness to lesser faithfulness, and let me urge you to reconsider and abandon such a move.

Stay the course on the journey of faith of Evangelical Protestantism.

✣

CHAPTER 6

CATHOLICISM REJOINDER

Francis J. Beckwith

Iwould like to thank Professor Gregg Allison for his clear and direct essay. In an age in which theological beliefs are often treated as devoid of cognitive content, it is refreshing to read an author who takes theology seriously and is unapologetic in offering an account of why he believes that his tradition, Evangelical Protestantism, is the most authentic form of Christianity.

In the few pages allotted to me for this response, I raise a few conceptual questions that came to mind when reading Allison's chapter.

I. BRANCHES FROM THE SAME TREE

Allison writes that those beliefs that Evangelicals and Catholics hold in common "arise from the fact that Catholicism and Protestantism are branches growing from the same trunk of the early church and, to some degree, the medieval church (it is in this period that the branching begins)." Although I certainly applaud his ecumenism, the actual history of doctrinal development is not congenial to Allison's account. The beliefs we hold in common—for example, Trinity, deity of Christ, two natures of Christ—were in fact disputed in the early church and were resolved only after the pronouncement of ecumenical councils, while the sorts of beliefs and practices that virtually all Evangelicals find objectionable about Catholicism—for example, infused grace, apostolic succession, baptismal regeneration, eucharistic realism— were so uncontroversial from the time of the early church until the time of the Reformation that both Eastern Orthodoxy and Eastern Rite Catholicism embraced them as well and still embrace them today.

Thus, it seems to me impossible to sustain, as Allison believes, that these Catholic beliefs and practices are a medieval invention of Latin Christianity.

II. JUSTIFICATION

Allison is correct that the primary difference between the Catholic and Evangelical views on justification is over the nature of grace, whether it is infused or imputed. It is not over the necessity of works, as Allison implicitly concedes by eloquently describing the Evangelical belief that good works follow from justification.

Thus, both Catholics and Evangelicals see the works that follow from conversion as consequences of that initial grace. Among Evangelicals, this gets cashed out in interesting ways. For example, for the Evangelical, the person who answers the altar call at a Billy Graham Crusade and says the sinner's prayer but shows no evidence of regeneration, that is, no good works, may not in fact be saved. For this reason, he may be asked by his pastor to walk the aisle yet again, to rededicate his life to the Lord. On the other hand, for the Catholic, as I noted in my chapter, a believer's works are the result of cooperating grace and thus are properly ascribed to God. Consequently, the believer's works no more detract from *sola gratia* than the human authorship of the Bible detracts from Scripture's status as entirely the Word of God. In both traditions, there is a place for works, yet each eschews works as a means by which to earn God's grace. Thus, it seems that the real divide is over whether justification — the righteousness of God — is a divine quality that changes nature or merely a divine declaration that changes status.

In note 22, Allison maintains that my scriptural case for the Catholic view does not attend to several distinctions central to Evangelical soteriology. But these distinctions, it seems to me, do not arise naturally from Scripture. They are, to be sure, theological categories that provide insight to the Evangelical reader who stands in a nearly five-century tradition of Reformed hermeneutics. And as I note in my chapter, I believe that the Reformed view is biblically defensible, but it is not the only legitimate reading of Scripture on the matter of justification. In fact, it seems less plausible than the Catholic view when one carefully attends to the history of theology and biblical hermeneutics in the first fifteen hundred years of Christian history. For this reason, the Catholic view has a distinct advantage: it is in continuity with the views of those Christians whose Church, Allison concedes, was all trunk and no branches. This is why in my chapter I circumspectly connect the soteriology of Saint Augustine (AD 354–430) and the Second Council of Orange (AD 529) with the views of Saint Thomas Aquinas (AD 1225–74), the Council of Trent (AD 1545–63), and the *Catechism of the Catholic Church* (1994).

III. JUSTIFICATION AND PERSPICUITY OF SCRIPTURE

The doctrine of justification in the first fifteen hundred years of Christian history poses a peculiar problem for the Protestant view that "Scripture is clear for all Christians, who are also responsible and competent for the task of interpreting it." "The clarity of Scripture," according to Allison, "means that it is written in such a way that ordinary human beings who possess the normal acquired ability to understand written and oral communication can read Scripture with understanding or, if they are unable to read, can hear Scripture read and comprehend it...."

Given this belief—sometimes called the "perspicuity of Scripture"—it seems difficult for Allison to account for why the Protestant view of justification is not front and center in the Church's first fifteen hundred years. For if that view were the obvious and clear reading of Scripture, one that literate Christians of ordinary wit should find in the Bible with ease, then its absence from deliberations of every church council as well as the Church's sacramental life and the writings of its leading theologians means that either the Protestant view of justification is right and Scripture's perspicuity wrong or Scripture's perspicuity is right and the Protestant view of justification wrong. Thus, it seems to me that the Reformation's legitimacy depends on two apparently contrary beliefs both being true at the same time.

IV. SCRIPTURE AND TRADITION

Although Allison eschews the normative role that Tradition plays in the development of Christian doctrine, he seems to rely on it on several key points. For example, on the content of the biblical canon—whether the Old Testament includes the deuterocanonical books (what he calls "the Apocrypha")—Allison appeals to the writings of several church fathers as well as the Old Testament that Jesus and his disciples allegedly embraced. Setting aside the question of whether Allison is right about what the early church as well as Jesus and his disciples believed about the scope of the Old Testament canon,[1] his argument is certainly a legitimate one to make. It is, however, an extrabiblical argument, one that appeals to an authoritative leadership that has the power to recognize and certify books as canonical that were subsequently recognized as such by certain Fathers embedded in a tradition that Allison considers more authoritative than the tradition that certified a different canon.[2] But if Jesus and his disciples are the appropriate authority for Old Testament canonicity, and if there is an authoritative tradition that properly passed on this correct canon, then what of New Testament canonicity, which was determined long after Christ and his first followers had departed this mortal realm? So, ironically, if we accept Allison's ecclesiology, then the sort of authority and tradition that apparently provides Allison warrant to exclude the deuterocanonical books from Scripture—binding magisterial authority with historical continuity—is missing from the Church during the development of New Testament canonicity.

The Catholic Church, on the other hand, maintains that this magisterial authority was in fact present in the early church and thus gave its leadership the power to recognize and fix the New Testament canon. So, ironically, Allison's case for the Protestant Old Testament canon depends on Catholic intuitions about a tradition of magisterial authority.

V. *SOLA SCRIPTURA*, THE PRIORITY OF THE CHURCH, AND THE SCOPE OF THE CANON

This leads to two other tensions in Allison's chapter. First, in defense of the Protestant Old Testament canon, Allison argues that although some of the Church's leading theologians and several regional councils accepted what is known today as the Catholic canon, others disagreed and embraced what is known today as the Protestant canon. It is not clear how this helps the Protestant case, since by employing this argumentative strategy, Allison concedes the central point of Catholicism: the Church is logically prior to the Scriptures.

That is, if the Church, until the Council of Trent's definitive declaration, can live with a certain degree of ambiguity about the content of the Old Testament canon, that means that *sola scriptura* was never a fundamental principle of authentic Christianity. After all, if Scripture alone applies to the Bible as a whole, then we cannot know to which particular collection of books this principle applies until the Bible's content is settled. Thus, to concede an unsettled canon for Christianity's first fifteen centuries, as Allison does, seems to make the Catholic argument that *sola scriptura* was a sixteenth-century invention and thus not an essential Christian doctrine.

Second, because the list of canonical books is itself not found in Scripture—as one can find the Ten Commandments or the names of Christ's apostles—any such list, whether Protestant or Catholic, would be an item of extrabiblical theological knowledge. Take, for example, a portion of the revised and expanded Evangelical Theological Society statement of faith suggested by two ETS members following my return to the Catholic Church.[3] (The proposed change failed to garner enough votes for passage, losing by a two-to-one margin.[4]) It states that "this written word of God consists of the sixty-six books of the Old and New Testaments and is the supreme authority in all matters of belief and behavior." But the belief that the Bible consists only of sixty-six books is not a claim of Scripture—since one cannot find the list in it—but a claim about Scripture as a whole. That is, the whole has a property—"consisting of sixty-six books"—that is not found in any of the parts. In other words, if the sixty-six books are the supreme authority on matters of belief, and the number of books is a belief, and one cannot find that belief in any of the books, then the belief that Scripture consists of sixty-six particular books is an extrabiblical belief, an item of theological knowledge that is *prima facie* nonbiblical.

For the Catholic, this is not a problem, since the Bible is the book of the Church, and thus there is an organic unity between the fixing of the canon and the development of doctrine and Christian practice. Thus, while the Church's theology and liturgy developed, the books that eventually became the New Testament canon were promulgated and gradually recognized as Scripture.[5] In fact, many of these books, including some that did not make the final New Testament canon

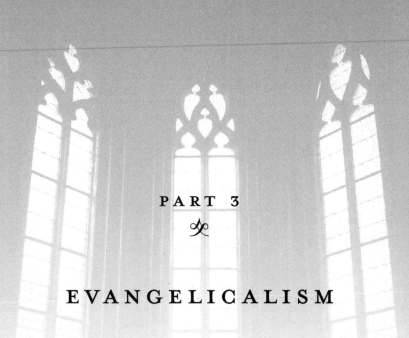

PART 3

EVANGELICALISM

CHAPTER 7

⚭

A JOURNEY TO EVANGELICALISM

Chris Castaldo

I loved Catholicism, and in some ways I still do.

I love the grandeur of the sanctuary with its carved wood, arched windows, and stained glass. I love the deep, resonate amalgam of voices confessing the Nicene Creed, and the honesty and humility expressed in the *Kyrie*: "Lord, have mercy; Christ, have mercy; Lord, have mercy." I love memories of simple things, like braiding cruciform palm leaves for Easter.

With fondness I remember my first Holy Communion, when we received strict instructions: "When your name is called, walk to the front, head bowed slightly, hands praying fingertip to fingertip, reverently stick out your tongue and (after saying amen) pause, sign the cross, and return to your seat." For days I awoke frightened by the thought that I would somehow mess it up. Then came the big day: Girls appeared like tiny brides clutching shiny new rosaries and purses, while we boys, holding pocket-sized prayer books, strutted along in stylish white suits like John Travolta. Moms and dads looked on, beaming with pride, as we followed in the footsteps of those who went before us.

Oh, what I wouldn't give for one more Knights of Columbus dinner, with trays of pasta fra diavolo, risotto parmigiano, and pignoli nut cookies prepared by my uncles. These were the occasions in which boys became men, learning how to eat for God's glory.

I vividly recall our confirmation retreat at the nearby cenacle. In the tranquil surrounding of a Marian grotto, we learned stories of heroic saints like Perpetua and Felicity, martyrs who stared down lions in the name of Christ. Dominick, my best friend, suggested that I choose Saint Jude as my personal saint, since Jude was the saint of lost causes. Despite our juvenile banter, we were challenged to be courageous for God.

As I grew older, I did what every Italian Catholic in New York does—visit Little Italy for the Feast of San Gennaro to watch the statue processed around Mulberry, Hester, Mott, and Grand Streets. With festive banners overhead displaying the green, white, and red of Italy's flag, and food vendors selling the most scrumptious sausages, meatballs, and cannoli, the lines of religion and culture intermingled seamlessly.

Most of all, I loved our priest, Father Tom, who occasionally visited our home. His black clerical shirt with unfastened collarino (collar in which the white plastic insert fits) expressed the nature of his relationship to us. It said, "I am here not only as your priest but also as your friend," like Bing Crosby's character, Father O'Malley, in whose presence one gets the feeling that "God is in his heaven; all is right with the world."

I enjoyed watching television reruns of Archbishop Fulton Sheen with his long, flowing cape and clever quips, marveled during Lent at the seemingly endless number of recipes we had for preparing tuna fish, and took great pleasure in walking to the altar with my family during Mass to present the gifts of wine and bread. This was my identity—a member of the Catholic Church—and I loved it.

But I had to leave.

SEARCHING FOR HOPE

Everyone is searching for hope, even when we don't realize it. From early years, we give expression to this desire by asking questions, often with a single word: "Why?" If you have talked with a child between the ages of two and five, you know precisely what it's like. Their adorable and sometimes irritating refrain of interrogatives bears witness to the natural curiosity that is common to humanity. Deep down we all wonder—and a primary reason for our wondering is our inexorable need for hope. We want to understand why the world operates as it does, and ultimately we want to know the one who created it. As Ecclesiastes 3:11 states, God has set eternity in our hearts.

While my experience of growing up in the Catholic Church was positive, I never found the hope for which I was searching, at least the kind that endures. I enjoyed life in our parish; I was happy to have completed religious training and the sacrament of confirmation, but the idea of redemptive grace escaped me. At the end of the day, I found Catholic faith to be frustrating because it never provided confidence that I was fully and finally accepted by God. Even when I successfully observed the Church's precepts — regulations such as attending Mass weekly, observing holy days of obligation, or abstaining from eating meat on Lenten Fridays — I knew it was only a matter of time before I violated another religious stipulation and thus removed myself from God's favor. Therefore, at age nineteen, I embarked upon a quest to find hope in other religious traditions.

I started my search by pursuing transcendental meditation with the Maharishi Mahesh Yogi. After a few months of uttering strange noises in a lotus position, I understood why the Beatles became disenchanted with Mr. Yogi's method. From there I went on to attend seminars through the Learning Annex, studying under world-class gurus like M. Scott Peck and Deepak Chopra.

While working with New York Telephone in Manhattan's Greenwich Village, I was surrounded by a broad range of religions and philosophies. The Village became my classroom. For instance, when I wanted to learn from someone in the nearby Buddhist Center, I arranged for a personal meeting. My method for doing this was dubious, even though at the time it made sense. After locating the center's phone terminal, I disconnected their cross-connection wires, reported the trouble, took the repair, and rang the Center's doorbell, to be received by a grateful host. Once inside, I found the person to interview, sat beside a wall jack in her office, pretended I was on hold with the central switchboard, and asked questions. As I recall, I think the Buddhist lady even made me a cup of coffee.

The apex of my spiritual journey was a "fire walk." It was at New York's Jacob Javits Center, where over a thousand people waited to hear motivational speaker Tony Robbins. After three hours of his encouraging affirmations, neurolinguistic programming, and some New Age meditation, our massive herd shuffled outside into the parking lot, where we were greeted by long stretches of burning coals and embers. According to Robbins, the experience was designed to be a metaphor for overcoming our fears and improving life. Never before had a metaphor looked so hot and potentially harmful!

When the lady ahead of me proceeded to walk across the twelve-foot path of fire, I inhaled deeply. Tony Robbins's wife (who happened to be facilitating my line) put her hand on my shoulder and said, "You can do this!" I noticed that she was wearing shoes and was at least twenty inches from the nearest coal; nevertheless, I stepped forward and walked as quickly as my trembling legs could carry me.

I don't know how it worked; all I can say is that I walked on the fire without getting burned. After I stepped from the coals, someone immediately hosed down my feet with cold water to extinguish any embers that may have been stuck between my toes. There was a celebration afterward, and in good New York fashion, we exchanged stories over schmeared bagels. It was a thrill, yet the bareness of my heart persisted, and my journey on the wide road continued.

THE TURNING POINT

As a Catholic, I was unfamiliar with Protestantism. The only Evangelical people I encountered were of the fanatical "born-again" variety. These folks resembled the character Euliss "Sonny" Dewey played by Robert Duvall in *The Apostle*. You may recall the scene in which Sonny overcomes his psychosomatic demons by standing waist-deep in water and baptizing himself as "the Apostle." Somehow these wide-eyed country souls found their way to East Coast civilization, even to New York.

I remember talking to an Evangelical Christian shortly after Jeffrey Dahmer, the infamous serial murderer, was killed and it became known that Dahmer had converted to Christianity before his death. The Evangelical spoke confidently about Dahmer's conversion and asserted that if it was genuine, he would be completely forgiven simply because he had "trusted in Jesus." After hearing about "unfathomable grace" numerous times and the phrase "personal relationship with Jesus," I responded with an impassioned tirade. It went something like this:

"You know what annoys me most about Jeffrey Dahmer? It wasn't his cannibalism, though it was disgusting. Seventeen murders, eleven corpses in his apartment, dismembered bodies. Then there was his trial, his seemingly remorseless, motionless, regretless face; I wanted to jump through the television screen and slap him around. If evil has a face, this was it. But that is not what irritates me the most. You know the most outrageous part? His conversion! How is it that a monster like Dahmer can perpetrate such atrocities and then be totally forgiven?"

After venting my religious spleen, I completed my remarks with a statement I shall never forget. With more than a little hubris, I announced, "This religion of complete grace is an irresponsible cop-out, and it is why I will never become a born-again Christian."

My movement toward Evangelicalism began just after my commute to work one morning. After I reached my Manhattan office, my grandfather phoned. In a serious tone, he spoke a brief message: "It's your dad; come home." Somehow I knew not to ask questions. It turned out to be a severe heart attack. The waterline of fear and anxiety quickly rose above our heads.

After days of sitting beside Dad's hospital bed, I left my job at New York Telephone to manage the family business. It was a midsize printing company with a dozen employees. With a deepening level of stress, Mom's emotions crashed, and I started having panic attacks. Into this dark valley appeared a new employee named Jan. I soon learned that she was a born-again Christian.

One day, while hanging up the phone with the cardiologist, I noticed a handwritten index card on my desk, displaying a paraphrase of Psalm 1:2–3: "The one who delights in the Law of the Lord is like a tree planted by streams of water that yields its fruit in its season, and its leaf does not wither. In all that he does, he prospers."

It was from Jan. Each day, she selected a Bible verse for me. I normally would have dismissed her notes as religious propaganda from a flaky employee, but now, after weeks of despair, I was attentive and collected them in my desk. Eventually the day came when Jan invited me to her church. Free to choose, and naturally disposed to decline, I listened to the words proceed from my mouth in response to her invitation. I, more than anyone, was surprised by what I heard. "Yes."

I knew nothing about Protestantism and, quite frankly, I didn't care to. Protestantism, in my view, was an imitation of the one true Church. As I had told Jan when she first mentioned the idea of my visiting her midweek service, "If you own a set of Big Bertha golf clubs, why be concerned with imitation knockoffs?" But now, on account of my dad's heart attack and the myriad challenges that it provoked, my stress had grown to unmanageable proportions.

The parking lot of Faith Evangelical Church was packed. In amazement I looked around, thinking, "It's a Wednesday night; these people must get a life!" With a mixture of humiliation and curiosity, I entered the building and sat in the rear pew of their "worship center." Devoid of any wood carvings, arched windows, or stained glass, it was simply a large room with a stage. Worse than austere, it was ugly.

Occasionally I looked through my peripheral vision at Jan. Her eyes remained closed as she sang. Oh, and did we sing! After forty minutes of choruses that seemed familiar to everyone but me, the senior pastor finally entered the pulpit. With a style combining Al Pacino and a young Billy Graham, he quoted John 15:5–6: "I am the vine; you are the branches. If you remain in me and I in you, you will bear much fruit; apart from me you can do nothing. If you do not remain in me, you are like a branch that is thrown away and withers; such branches are picked up, thrown into the fire and burned."

The preacher continued:

> Humanity attempts to produce its own fruit. We run around exploring this and that religion, this and that philosophy, and by the end of the day, when we lay our heads down upon our pillows, our souls are still empty.
>
> The Bible says in Psalm 121, "I lift up my eyes to the hills. From where does my help come? My help comes from the Lord, who made heaven and earth." And what do we find when we look up to the Lord? The Lord Jesus says, "Come to me, all who labor and are heavy laden, and I will give you rest."
>
> In what are you resting? In what does your life find meaning and purpose? What will be there for you the second after you take your last breath and depart in death? Consider the good news! Jesus the Messiah died for our sins, rose from the dead, reigns in eternal glory, and at this moment is calling you to repent and embrace him.
>
> Everyone on earth faces the same fundamental choice. Will we

continue to live independent of Christ, in restlessness of soul, eventually to be gathered like a useless branch into a pile to be burned? Or will we submit to his authority and abide in his peace? The former person dies in a never-ending state of alienation; the latter enjoys God's acceptance now and for eternity. What will it be?

I don't know how to properly describe what came next. Anticipation surged through my veins, and my mind swirled with questions. Then suddenly the eyes of my soul opened. They immediately blinked, blinked again, and again, as though they'd been awoken from sleep by a flash of light. The object of my vision appeared so new and bright that my initial response was to retreat.

As my inner eyes tried to adjust, I sensed an imposing presence. I didn't see the angelic host or hear them singing. Instead I felt divine mercy and grace closing in on me. After a moment, it reached out to grasp my guilt and shame—previously reasons for hopelessness—and it brought to mind three simple words: "It is finished."

In that moment, I finally understood the meaning of Jesus' cross and resurrection. My search for hope had ended. The Lamb of God had died in my place, not simply as an offering for "sin" in a general sense but for me personally. Not Christ accruing superabundant merits to be stored in a heavenly treasury and dispensed to me as I participated in religious rites but the complete satisfaction of God's wrath and forgiveness of my sins.

The joy of redemption became a reality. At once I identified with the penitent thief on the cross who encountered the Lord's promise, "Today you will be with me in paradise" (Luke 23:43), the adopted orphan-turned-son (John 1:12–13), and the rescued rebel delivered from the domain of darkness (Col. 1:13). Why such a dramatic change? In Jesus' words: "Very truly I tell you, whoever hears my word and believes him who sent me has eternal life and will not be judged but has crossed over from death to life" (John 5:24).

Like converts such as Augustine, Pascal, Luther, Newton, and a host of others throughout history, I encountered God in such a profound way that my life was permanently changed. To this day, I don't have a better way to describe it than with the words of Charles Wesley in his famous hymn "And Can It Be That I Should Gain":

Long my imprisoned spirit lay, fast bound in sin and nature's night;
Thine eye diffused a quickening ray, I woke, the dungeon flamed
    with light;
My chains fell off, my heart was free;
I rose, went forth and followed Thee.

In retrospect, I believe this was the day when I ceased to be a Roman Catholic.

FORMER CATHOLICS TESTIFY

Catholic journeys of faith come in all shapes and sizes. After two years of interviewing former Catholics for my book *Holy Ground: Walking with Jesus as a Former Catholic* (Zondervan), this fact became clear. Some Catholics walked with Jesus before moving in an Evangelical direction, while others were converted to Christ as they made the move. In either case, the fundamental reason for leaving one's Catholic background was the same: a different understanding of the ultimate source of authority for Christian faith. No longer did we look to the institution of the one, holy, catholic, apostolic church as the final arbiter of orthodox belief and practice. Instead we started looking to the Bible.[1]

Over time, I discovered five major reasons why I and hundreds of former Catholics whom I interviewed left the Catholic Church of our childhood for Evangelical pastures. In virtually every case, it came down to a disagreement over how the Catholic Church lays claim to authority. Here are the top five concerns. Of them, the final one, "religious guilt," repeatedly surfaced as the most significant:

1. Clericalism, the notion that clergy operates on a higher spiritual plane
2. Rules-keeping to the extent that it eclipses one's personal relationship with Jesus
3. Priestly or sacramental mediation as a normative means of accessing sanctifying grace
4. Objects of devotion (such as Mary and the saints) that inadvertently compete with Jesus
5. An injurious form of religious guilt that hinders one from trusting God

It should be acknowledged that these problems also apply to Evangelical churches; in fact, I recently visited such a congregation. The church "bylaws" were a collection of rules and regulations, some of which existed in written form, while others were conveyed through oral tradition. The degree of emphasis placed upon these stipulations created an ethos that affected the entire ministry. I could go on with such observations, but suffice it to say that for every critical finger that we Evangelicals point at Catholics, there is one or more pointing back at us.

If I were to boil down the concerns of former Catholics into a single reason for leaving, it would be weariness with the vast array of religious rules, regulations, and traditions which seemed to have little or nothing to do with the gospel. Here, for instance, is the way it was communicated in *America*, a national Catholic weekly magazine published by the Jesuits. In January 1991 it ran an article titled, "Coming to Grip with Losses: The Migration of Catholics into Conservative Protestantism" by Mark Christensen. In the following excerpt, the author explains how the gospel remained obscure to him despite his years of participation in the Catholic Church: "The effect of the obscurity for me was that, while I certainly grew up knowing about Jesus, I never realized who He is or why He came to earth in the first place. I knew Catholicism ... I have been shaped by Catholicism as a religious system and culture — but, I never heard the Gospel."[2]

I can just see Catholic religious leaders pulling their hair out at that statement: "What do you mean, you never heard the gospel! What do you think we've been proclaiming the last two thousand years in the Eucharist?" Yes, I realize the preeminent place Christ holds in the Mass. I know that Scriptures are read every Sunday. I know the magnificence and purity of the Nicene Creed. I've no interest in slandering an institution for which I hold tremendous respect. I have to report, though, what I hear coming from the mouths of ex-Catholics as they describe their number one reason for leaving Catholicism: "How could it be that I spent twenty-two years in the Catholic Church," one friend said angrily, "and never heard the gospel?"

WHAT ARE THE REAL ISSUES HERE?

At first I wondered if we defectors were just buying into a new terminology rather than a new spirituality when we left Catholicism.

Maybe Evangelicals just had a prettier package on the same truths. But I tell you that I have asked dozens of Catholics in the last eight years if they know who Christ is or why he came to earth. Overwhelmingly, they just don't know. I'm not talking about fundamentalist lingo here. I'm talking about the great apostolic message, uncluttered by jargon and qualification: Christ came to free us from the encumbrance of sin, providing us with what we could not provide for ourselves — restoration with God for eternity.[3]

In March of that same year, *America* published a follow-up to Christensen's article because, in the editor's words, it "elicited many heated responses, both pro and con." Go figure! The raw emotion of these rejoinders further illustrates the controversial nature of the salvation discussion between Catholics and Evangelicals.

If Christensen's thesis sounds outrageous, consider Catholic Peter Kreeft's words in this vein: "There are still many who do not know the data, the gospel. Most of my Catholic students at Boston College have never heard it. They do not even know how to get to heaven. When I ask them what they would say to God if they died tonight and God asked them why he should take them into heaven, nine out of ten do not even mention Jesus Christ. Most of them say they have been good or kind or sincere or did their best. So I seriously doubt God will undo the Reformation until he sees to it that Luther's reminder of Paul's gospel has been heard throughout the church."[4]

The Journey Continues

The year was 1994, and it had been just a few months since my conversion at Jan's Evangelical church. I took a position with the Martin J. Moran Company, a professional fundraising firm that worked almost entirely in Catholic dioceses across the country.

The position was ideal. Almost every day I conversed with priests. Many of these men were Jesuits who had forgotten more than I had ever learned about theology, but that didn't stop me from engaging them in dialogue. Over dinner and walking the fairway of the Okeeheelee Golf Course, they often urged me to "stop this talk about Protestantism and enter the Catholic priesthood."

It was the learning experience of a lifetime, and to this day, advice from some of these priests rings in my ears. Most of all, I cherish the mentoring I received from Monsignor Irvine Nugent of St. Helen's Church in Vero Beach, Florida. A little leprechaun of a man, he was full of humor and wit. For as long as I live, I'll always remember his advice to me when I announced that I was preparing for ministry in the Evangelical tradition. With a twinkle in his eye and a cheerful Irish brogue, he replied, "Chris, remember, don't take yourself too seriously; save that for God."

Perhaps the most instructive lesson during my time with the Moran Company came during a black-tie affair held at the Breakers Resort on Palm Beach Island. In a large dinner room, there sat a packed audience of wealthy potential donors. Before the bishop opened in prayer, our team reviewed the agenda one last time. It was then we discovered the blunder. All the campaign elements were in place — volunteers, video, brochures; the problem was the food. On the menu was an entrée of filet mignon, twice-baked potato, and vegetable. At any other time of the year, steak would have been fine; unfortunately, this particular Friday was during Lent, a special religious season when Catholics must abstain from eating meat. To knowingly and willfully consume meat on a Friday during Lent constitutes a mortal sin.[5] If one should die after doing so, it would put that person into the flames of eternal damnation. This was a serious problem!

In actuality, many Catholics eat meat on Friday during Lent, but they don't do it when dining with the bishop and clergy. And it's unthinkable that the Church would host such a meal. The salad and a dinner roll would buy us about twenty minutes. The Lord's multiplying of fish came to mind.

While our team of fundraisers nervously stared at one another in silent bewilderment, the bishop spoke. He reiterated what we already knew about Lenten food laws and the implications of our predicament. He continued, "As the bishop, I have the authority to declare a special dispensation which will allow us to eat meat during Lent. If there is ever a time for such a provision, it is now." I then watched the bishop pray, announce the menu, and before guests connected the doctrinal dots, he pronounced a special blessing to sanction the meal. My eyes turned toward old Joe Sedlak, who sat beside me thinking that if he had choked on his steak and died apart from the bishop's blessing, he would have been roasted. But now, after the bishop's prayer, he could feast in peace.

That evening, I left the Breakers finally understanding that the issue of Church authority is the fulcrum which separates Catholics from Evangelicals. Do you recognize authority in the bishops by means of apostolic succession? If you say yes, you are a Catholic. If instead you see ultimate authority in Scripture alone, you are essentially an Evangelical.

THE CATHOLIC VIEW OF AUTHORITY

Like a line of falling dominos that diverges into two lines, the Catholic and Evangelical approaches to theology emerge from a common Bible[6] and creedal confessions (for example, the Apostles' and Nicene creeds) but thereafter begin to separate. This divergence is based upon a different understanding of how the infallible revelation and authority of Jesus applies to his Church, and by extension to the world. In other words, when Catholics identify the tangible presence of Christ in the world, they normally point to the institution of the one, holy, catholic, and apostolic church. Evangelicals, on the other hand, while acknowledging a union between the risen Christ and his Church, are nonetheless more inclined to see the infallible manifestation of Christ's revelation and authority in the text of Scripture. This is the basic point where our theological dominos separate.

Let's begin by considering more closely the Catholic position. The *Catechism of the Catholic Church* gets us started with the following summary:

> The Church is both visible and spiritual, a hierarchical society and the Mystical Body of Christ. She is one, yet formed of two components, human and divine. That is her mystery, which only faith can accept.[7]

> The Church in this world is the sacrament of salvation, the sign and the instrument of the communion of God and men.[8]

The reason why the Catholic Church considers herself to be a sacrament with a divine character may be summarized in one word — *incarnation*.[9] Most Christians have probably heard the term during Advent and Christmas. It describes the redemptive historical event in which the second person of the triune God became flesh. On this much, Catholics and Evangelicals agree — born of a virgin, Jesus of

Nazareth is fully God and fully man. In Catholic thought, however, the term *incarnation* has a broader meaning. Consider, for instance, the following statements, the first of which is from Pope Benedict XVI.

> The notion of the body of Christ was developed in the Catholic Church to the effect that the Church designated as "Christ living on earth" came to mean that the Church was described as the Incarnation of the Son continuing until the end of time.[10]

Another way to describe the ecclesial incarnation of Christ is in terms of "prolongation," as Hans Urs von Balthasar writes:

> The Church is the prolongation of Christ's mediatorial nature and work and possesses a knowledge that comes by faith; she lives objectively (in her institution and her sacraments) and subjectively (in her saints and, fundamentally, in all her members) in the interchange between heaven and earth. Her life comes from heaven and extends to earth, and extends from earth to heaven.[11]

Finally, there is this statement from Father Yves Congar:

> Since the medieval era ... we have witnessed a particular fondness for St. Augustine's formula, "the whole Christ," or for the formula of St. Joan of Arc, "I think that between our Lord and the Church — it is all one," ... or for the theme of "continuing incarnation."[12]

I emphasize the above point because this concept — the continuous incarnation of Christ in his Church — is enormously helpful for understanding so many things that happen in Catholic theology, especially the function of revelation and authority.

The critical difference between Catholics and Evangelicals on this point concerns the relationship of Jesus' incarnation to his Church. According to Rome, the incarnated presence of Jesus (the "head") is manifested in his Church (the "members") to make up the body of Christ.[13] As the *Catechism* puts it, Christ and his Church thus together make up the "whole Christ" *(Christus totus)*.[14] In this way, incarnation is not simply a historical event from two millennia ago; it is *also* an ongoing process that applies to his body today.[15]

The Catholic position says, in effect, that if you want to see the presence of Jesus in the world, look to the institution of the Roman

Catholic Church, because it is the embodiment of Jesus on earth.[16] What Jesus Christ entrusted to his apostles, they in turn passed on in their preaching and writing, under the Holy Spirit's inspiration.[17] This revelation consists of Scripture *and* Sacred Tradition, which together "make up a single sacred deposit of the Word of God."[18] While distinct, these modes are bound closely together, flowing out of the "same divine wellspring," in the words of Vatican II. This Word of God—Scripture and Sacred Tradition together—is authentically interpreted by the Church (alone) in her teaching office, which is called the magisterium, that is, the bishops in communion with the successor of Peter, the bishop of Rome.[19] In keeping with the principle of continuous incarnation, there is an organic connection between divine revelation and the magisterial authority that interprets it. Thus, Scripture, Sacred Tradition, and magisterium are commonly identified as the three basic elements of Catholic revelation and authority.

It's probably a minority of Catholics who can explicate the relationship of Scripture, Tradition, and magisterium. Perhaps more familiar to most is the presence of Jesus in the sacraments, particularly the Eucharist, which is the centerpiece of Catholic worship, or, in the words of Vatican II, the "source and summit of the Christian life."[20] The Eucharist is "[t]he ritual, sacramental action of thanksgiving to God which constitutes the principle Christian celebration of and communion in the paschal mystery of Christ."[21] It is the reason why Catholics cross themselves when driving by a parish; it is the reason why they genuflect before the tabernacle before entering the pew; and it is the most commonly cited reason for going to church on Sunday morning.[22] In other words, as one of my Catholic students in last week's class mentioned when I asked him to identify the place where Catholics encounter Jesus Christ, "We receive Jesus in the Eucharist."

THE EVANGELICAL VIEW OF AUTHORITY

While Evangelicals may not use the word *sacrament* to describe the body of Christ, we wholeheartedly affirm the existence of a mystical union between Christ and his Church, a union that manifests the transforming grace of God to the world.[23] Evangelicals stand with Catholics in affirming that Jesus Christ is our head (Eph. 4:15), the firstborn (Rom. 8:29), the one onto whom we are grafted (Rom.

11:17) and with whom we are clothed (Gal. 3:27). We agree that, as God's Word, Jesus speaks to and from his Church, the result of which impacts the world in tangible ways. In this regard, we use the term *incarnation* quite regularly to describe our desired approach to gospel outreach. In fact, I daresay that you would be hard-pressed to find an Evangelical conference these days that doesn't have at least one speaker whose title or talk concerns "incarnational ministry." So where do we differ from Catholics?

From an Evangelical point of view, the Catholic position of incarnation ecclesiology—the notion that Christ's infallible revelation and authority subsists in the one, holy, catholic, apostolic church—is unsustainable from Scripture. It's not an infallible Church that God gives us; it's the infallible Word, the Bible.[24] This conviction, that Scripture is the supreme source of divine revelation and therefore our ultimate authority, is what Evangelicals mean by the Latin phrase *sola scriptura*.[25]

A helpful way to think about the concept of Scripture alone is in terms of the correlation between Jesus the *living* Word and Jesus' authoritative *written* Word (the Bible).[26] The inspired text is the way in which Jesus' revelation and authority extend to the Church and by extension to the world.[27] In the words of Alister McGrath, "When the first generation of Protestants spoke of the 'authority of the Bible,' this was to be understood as 'the authority of the risen Christ, mediated and expressed through the Bible....'" Precisely because Jesus Christ stands at the heart of the Christian faith, Protestants argue, so must the Bible. There is the most intimate interconnection between the Bible and Christ in the Protestant tradition. The Bible is the means by which Christ is displayed, proclaimed, and manifested."[28]

A clear distillation of what Evangelicals mean by "Scripture alone" is found in the Chicago Statement on Biblical Inerrancy, crafted by more than two hundred Evangelical leaders in October 1978. It begins with the following words: "The authority of Scripture is a key issue for the Christian church in this and every age. Those who profess faith in Jesus Christ as Lord and Savior are called to show the reality of their discipleship by humbly and faithfully obeying God's written Word. To stray from Scripture in faith or conduct is disloyalty to our Master. Recognition of the total truth and trustworthiness of Holy Scripture is essential to a full grasp and adequate confession of its authority."[29]

While all nineteen articles of the Chicago Statement relate to "Scripture alone" in some way, number 2 strikes at its heart with the following words:

> **We affirm** that the Scriptures are the supreme written norm by which God binds the conscience, and that the authority of the church is subordinate to that of Scripture.
>
> **We deny** that church creeds, councils, or declarations have authority greater than or equal to the authority of the Bible.[30]

If, as Catholics believe, the bishops are "endowed with the authority of Christ" and share in Christ's infallibility,[31] then Christian authority is rooted in the institution of the Church. If, however, the inspired revelation of Jesus is the written Word alone, then Scripture is the supreme authority. On this point, the Chicago Statement offers another helpful summary:

> By authenticating each other's authority, Christ and Scripture coalesce into a single fount of authority. The biblically-interpreted Christ and the Christ-centered, Christ-proclaiming Bible are from this standpoint one. As from the face of inspiration we infer that what Scripture says, God says, so from the revealed relation between Jesus Christ and Scripture we may equally declare that what Scripture says, Christ says.[32]

When we discuss the doctrine of "Scripture alone," a qualification is in order. Our view of biblical authority should not undermine one's appreciation of biblically rooted traditions. Certain standards, routines, and customs may not be explicitly stated in a chapter and verse but nonetheless provide tangible forms in which to encounter and express authentic faith. These conventions will naturally look different depending upon one's context. So long as they are consistent with Scripture, however, such traditions should be employed for the glory of God.

I often think that the language of "Scripture alone" is a bit unfortunate, because at face value it sounds as if Protestants are espousing a misnomer commonly referred to as "*nuda scriptura*,"[33] a practice which removes tradition from the ongoing life of the church, insisting that the Bible functions as the *only* source of authority for Christian faith and practice. While this definition may sound like what the Protestant Reformers meant by "Scripture alone," it is actually quite different.

In actuality, the language of "Scripture alone" is trying to express what was essentially the concern of Jesus in Matthew 15:9 (cf. Isa. 19:13), where the Lord warns against presenting the "commandments of men" as God's word, since such development of dogma may obscure or in some instances even contradict the teaching of Scripture. From an Evangelical point of view, this is how aspects of Catholic teaching like purgatory, indulgences, and Mary's comediation function. Instead of serving divine revelation, these traditions threaten to undermine it. Professor Tony Lane captures the heart of the concern when he writes, "*Sola Scriptura* is the statement that the church can err."[34]

I like how the late Harold O. J. Brown described the problem of *nuda scriptura* when he said, "If we consider faith as a climber trying to scale a snowy mountain peak, the one group [Catholics] will have him so packed in flowing garments that he can hardly move, while the other [Evangelicals] might have him naked and barefoot—or to be more decent, in shorts and sneakers—and in imminent danger of hypothermia."[35]

Unfortunately, when Catholic apologists critique *sola scriptura*, it is often the flawed view—what we're calling *nuda scriptura*—that is the object of their critique.[36] Although perhaps more troubling from my perspective is when the same mistake is made by Evangelicals (since it's our doctrine, we should at least understand it). When it's all said and done, I agree with the conclusion of Brown, who says, "We need to accept tradition in principle, and at the same time we need to be critical of traditions, both our own and those of others, lest they become the 'commandments of men' about which Jesus warns us."[37]

A BRIEF DEFENSE OF *SOLA SCRIPTURA*

If you ever happen to write a book on Catholicism while also maintaining a blog, I can assure you of one thing: you will receive a lot of feedback from Catholics. I'm sure my friend Frank Beckwith, who contributes the Catholic journey of faith in this volume, would testify to the same experience from the other direction. After a year of reading and responding to comments from these Catholic friends (and

I'm grateful that many have in fact become friends), I have identified four common protests which they tend to express toward the Evangelical teaching of "Scripture alone." Unfortunately, space won't permit more than a passing comment on each.

(1) "Unless there is an official teaching office to interpret and guard the faith, we will be left with the cacophony of views, which is Protestantism." Speaking as someone who lived and worked in the Catholic Church for years, I'm not convinced that Catholic unity actually rises to the level that some claim. But, of course, I'm now a (biased) Evangelical Protestant pastor, so don't take my word for it. Here is how journalist Peter Feuerherd, a thoughtful and committed Catholic, describes it: "In reality, Catholicism includes those with disparate authority and opinions about almost everything under the sun. There are liberal bishops and conservative bishops. The pope sometimes differs with his own Curia. American Catholic voters are regularly viewed by experts as a crucial swing group in every national election, too diffuse to truly categorize. In fact, some scholars of religion refer to Catholicism as the Hinduism of Christianity, because it is infused with so many different schools of prayer, ritual and perspective, much like the native and diverse religions of India now referred to under the single rubric of Hinduism."[38]

Feuerherd's point is helpful to keep in mind. It's easy to see the common clerical attire of priests, the standard liturgical order of the Mass, and the hierarchical structure that unifies parishes and conclude that there is general unity in the Catholic Church. In actuality, Catholic tradition comprises a wide variety of ideologies and practices—from progressives to conservatives, charismatics to stoics, feminists to male elitists, postmodern relativists, liberation theologians, traditionalists, mystics, and virtually everything in between.[39]

Another reason for such diversity among Catholics is the Protestant-like turn which Catholic hermeneutics takes before the process of interpretation is completed. Here is how the late Avery Cardinal Dulles explained it: "The meaning of magisterial decisions, in turn, has to be studied with reference to the way they are understood and interpreted by pastors, theologians, and the faithful. The study of the Magisterium, therefore, *would be incomplete* without some attention to the process of reception."[40] In other words, when it's all said and done, the Catholic approach to interpreting truth—relying on the insights of "pastors, theologians, and the faithful"—is strikingly similar to that of Protestants.

(2) "The Evangelical appeal to Scripture as the final authority fails to recognize that it was the Church which canonized these documents. In fact, the appeal to canon shows the necessity of a unified, central ecclesiastical authority. To suggest otherwise violates the law of causality—the principle of logic that requires a cause (the Church) to possess greater authority than its effect (the biblical canon)." This might be a valid argument if not for the reality of God's activity operating through men and women. Let me explain how this works by giving a few examples from Scripture.

Paul says in 1 Corinthians 15:10, "I worked harder than all of [the other apostles]—yet not I, but the grace of God that was with me." Who did the work? Paul. Who is the ultimate cause, the one responsible for it? God.

Later in his ministry, Paul said these words: "Work out your own salvation with fear and trembling, for it is God who works in you, both to will and to work for his good pleasure (Phil. 2:12–13 ESV). As the Church, we do something, "work out [our] salvation." But who is the ground or cause of this work? God.

One last example is Paul's statement in Romans 15:18, "I will not venture to speak of anything except what Christ has accomplished through me to bring the Gentiles to obedience—by word and deed" (ESV). Who did the accomplishing? Ultimately, it was God.

The technical term for what we're describing is *monergism*. The word simply describes an accomplishment that is attributed to *one* source. In Christian theology, it is used of God's sovereign work through men and women, a notion that is quite common in Catholic thought, thanks to Augustine. My friend Frank Beckwith makes this point when he explains why he believes that Catholicism is a religion of grace and not of meritorious works (because, in Augustine's words, "When God crowns our merits he crowns his own gifts").[41] I simply want to apply this principle to the development of the canon and suggest that it is perfectly tenable to understand that God guided his Church in the process of recognizing his inspired Word, without having to posit the institution as a self-existent authoritative cause.

To summarize, the early church recognized the inherent authority of certain documents (the Old Testament and the New Testament) as uniquely inspired by God. In so recognizing this inherent authority, the early church did not make such documents contingent on or subservient to the recognizing party. In fact, it was God who both uniquely inspired the documents and enabled the early church to perceive rightly the authority of such works.

(3) "Sola scriptura *separates faith from reason."* In this context, the word *reason* refers to the positive contributions of philosophy which have enabled thinking people to better understand God and creation.[42] Catholic thought regards faith and reason to be complementary and inseparable. To remove reason from faith leaves one with superstition, and to take faith from reason leads one to relativism.

Sometimes Catholics employ the phrase "dehellenization of Christianity" to describe the Protestant tendency of emphasizing Scripture at the expense of philosophy. A description of this perspective is presented by Scott Hahn, for example, who quotes Pope Benedict XVI on this point: "The premise [of dehellenization] is false because, as Benedict argues, 'the encounter between the biblical message and Greek thought did not happen by chance.' He cites St. Paul's vision of a Greek man calling Paul to 'come over to Macedonia and help us' (Acts 16:6–10). Benedict interprets the vision as indicating 'the intrinsic necessity of a rapprochement between Biblical faith and Greek inquiry.'"[43]

In addition to articulating the Catholic concern, the above quote also demonstrates why Evangelicals are cautious in employing categories of Greek philosophy. It is because Hellenistic questions, ideals, and assumptions are often forced into the driver's seat, leaving Scripture to sit quietly in the back. Such is the unintended effect of Pope Benedict's interpretation of Paul's Macedonian vision, I'm afraid. The pontiff's exegesis leads readers to scratch their heads in bewilderment in search of a contextual warrant for his conclusion. Without a methodological interest in applying Hellenistic thought, such a reading appears to emerge *ex nihilo*.[44] In the final analysis, there is no reason why *sola scriptura* must marginalize philosophical reflection. There is sufficient room in the passenger seat for philosophy.[45]

(4) *"The doctrine of* sola scriptura *fails to appreciate contributions from the history of Christian thought, particularly from the church*

fathers." This is a fair critique. As described earlier in the caution against *nuda scriptura*, it is common for Evangelicals to exchange the richness of Christian history for the subjectivity of private opinion, all in the name of "Scripture alone." Many of us don't realize that this move is a departure from what Protestants originally meant by the concept. As James Payton Jr. points out, we fail to realize that "for the Reformers, *sola scriptura* found its boundaries in the faithful teaching of the church fathers, the ancient creeds and the doctrinal decrees of the ecumenical councils."[46] In other words, responsible interpretation requires more than me, my Bible, and my religious imagination. God has provided us with the community of faith in which to work out the meaning of Scripture. This community is local, and, in another sense, it is the body of men and women in every age who have faithfully given themselves to following Christ.

At present, there appears to be a resurgence of interest among Evangelicals in studying the history of Christian thought. You see evidence of it, for example, in your local bookstore, where you'll find numerous titles featuring key terms like "patristic," "Fathers," "Tradition," or "rule of faith." This proliferation is now in the mainstream, and it is bigger than ever. There is, however, an important caveat.

In the language of James Payton Jr., quoted above, the boundaries of *sola scriptura* were found in "the *faithful* teaching of the church fathers" (emphasis added). Payton elaborates this point: "The Protestant Reformers would not allow that any of these ancient worthies could initiate truth on their own: that was the prerogative of Scripture alone, which was the touchstone of all Christian teaching. If any church father defaulted in humility before a faithful exposition of Scriptural truth, that writing or father could be dismissed from consideration."[47]

We must quickly point out that the Catholic Church affirms the need for church fathers to be submitted to Scripture and that she seeks to limit her Sacred Tradition to faithful teaching. It would be incorrect and uncharitable to suggest otherwise. However, from an Evangelical point of view, when bishops of the Church function as infallible interpreters of the Christian tradition, regardless of how ancient or brilliant these individuals might be, the result, however unintentional, is to deprive the Bible of its authority. In other words, once the Church pronounces on a subject, the Bible is no longer allowed to contradict magisterial conclusions, thus muting Scripture's voice and marginalizing its message.[48] When this happens, contributions from the history of Christian thought no longer serve Scripture; they begin to subvert it.

THE HOPE OF SALVATION

Having explored some basic differences between Catholics and Evangelicals with regard to Christian authority, we now consider the implications of these positions on our doctrines of salvation. In terms of the diverging dominos metaphor from earlier pages, it is here, in our understanding of the gospel message, that Catholics and Evangelicals can be farthest apart. So, for instance, in the case of Catholics, the impartation of divine grace through the sacraments, particularly the Mass, is an extension of Christ's ecclesial incarnation in the Church. Similarly, the Evangelical's Word-centered focus grows from our doctrine of *sola scriptura*. One way to appreciate the nature and extent of our divergence is to ask the question, What must I do to be saved? To this question we now turn; however, before doing so, we should remember an important reality.

During seminary, I took a class at Harvard Divinity School with visiting professor N. T. Wright. In addition to attending Wright's lectures, students met in hour-long breakout sessions following each class. If I were to describe the ethos of these meetings in one word, it would be *eclectic*. It was partially a function of Harvard; the other reason was the popularity of Professor Wright. In either case, students came from a wide range of religious backgrounds.

In one session, our student leader started with a fascinating statement. She said, "All religions of the world seek to answer the question, How can I be saved? We may define 'saved' differently; nonetheless, we all share a desire to be delivered from one state of affairs unto a greater level of existence." She then pointed to various students around the table and asked them to provide an answer to her question from the vantage point of their religious tradition. What came next I shall never forget.

"Enkyo, how would you answer the question?"

Enkyo explained, "Buddhism says that we suffer because our base desires crave that which is temporary. The solution to this is to cease all desire in order to realize the nonexistence of the self, otherwise known as nirvana."

"Gloria, how would you answer?"

Gloria was a young woman who was less than fond of the male gender. She thought for a moment and responded, "God, the divine Mother, nourishes her creation with the milk of her cosmic spirit. We will observe salvation when humanity stops discriminating on the basis of biologically determined qualities like sex."

"Vishnu, how would you answer the question?"

Vishnu was evidently preparing his answer while the others spoke, because he quickly retorted, "As Hindus, we believe that, by nature, man is good and made of the same essence of the divine. Man's problem is that he is ignorant of his divine nature. We must realize our divinity and must then strive to detach ourselves from selfish desires in order to attain enlightenment."

"Peter, how would you answer the question?"

Peter, a Catholic student, thought for a moment, then simply recited the Apostles' Creed: "I believe in God, the Father Almighty, the Creator of heaven and earth, and in Jesus Christ, his only Son, our Lord: who was conceived of the Holy Spirit, born of the Virgin Mary, suffered under Pontius Pilate, was crucified, died, and was buried. He descended into hell. The third day he arose again from the dead. He ascended into heaven and sits at the right hand of God the Father Almighty, whence he shall come to judge the living and the dead. I believe in the Holy Spirit, the holy catholic Church, the communion of saints, the forgiveness of sins, the resurrection of the body, and life everlasting. Amen."

His answer was striking, for it was the one that I might have given.

From Peter's answer, I learned a profound lesson. While there are many important doctrines that divide Catholics and Evangelicals, there is also much on which we agree. The incident helped me see our similarities in ways I hadn't previously. This same insight would surface again before the end of the semester as Peter and other Catholics from Boston College offered crushing arguments against our liberal Protestant classmates. Not only did they provide compelling refutations to those who denied the empty tomb; they also explained the resurrection in ways that stirred the soul. Despite significant doctrinal differences, these Catholic students were our allies in theological debates.

I share the above story because it's easy for Catholics and Evangelicals to so concentrate on our differences that we lose sight of common ground. In the course of contending for the faith, we unwittingly become theological pit bulls—gnashing teeth, foaming at the mouth, attacking the poor soul who has the audacity to defy us. Meanwhile, a watching world looks on in astonishment at how graceless we who preach grace can be. In the words of the apostle Paul, *me genoito* (may it never be)!

Of course, we also see the other extreme, when we are so open-minded that our brains fall out of our heads. This theologically compromised, lowest-common-denominator approach fails to take God and his revelation seriously. Reasons for this are legion, including laziness, selfishness, or sheer indifference toward the authority of God's Word. This too must be disregarded. If God is God, and if his revelation is true, then theological reflection deserves our best time and attention. With that little qualification, we'll now attempt to answer our question.

On one level, the question, What must I do to be saved? is simple; at the same time it's quite complex. There are several issues that contribute to this. On the Catholic side, these include the perpetual sacrifice of the Mass, works of supererogation, purgatory, the treasury of merit, transubstantiation, the Canons of the Council of Trent, the mediating role of Mary, penance, and others. For Evangelicals, there are questions pertaining to the extent of depravity, the ground of election, the scope of the atonement, the nature of faith, and the role of obedience. A proper treatment of the question, What must I do to be saved? should address each of these subjects. However, with limited space remaining, I will focus on the question that factored most heavily in my journey of faith and in the journeys of those whom I interviewed: how to deal with the problem of guilt.

After two years of conducting focus groups among former Catholics throughout the nation, I learned that the biggest dilemma with the Catholic doctrine of salvation is the oppressive imposition of unhealthy religious guilt. It is a nagging fear that preoccupies the soul, a root of doubt that questions whether one is truly forgiven in

Christ. In my case, I would often go to bed and wonder, "Has my behavior been good enough to merit divine approval?" Like Martin Luther, who attempted to find a gracious God, I never knew whether I was fully accepted.

Historian Martin Marty describes the religious journey of Martin Luther by saying, "He makes most sense as a wrestler with God, indeed, as a God-obsessed seeker of certainty and assurance in a time of social trauma and of personal anxiety, beginning with his own."[49] By observing a range of austere religious works, Luther sought to grow in holiness and thereby find himself pleasing to the Divine Judge. In his own words,

> I greatly longed to understand Paul's Epistle to the Romans and nothing stood in the way but that one expression, "the justice whereby God is just and deals justly in punishing the unjust." My situation was that, although an impeccable monk, I stood before God as a sinner troubled in conscience, and I had no confidence that my merit would assuage him.
>
> Night and day I pondered until I saw the connection between the justice of God and the statement that "the just shall live by his faith." Then I grasped that the justice of God is that righteousness by which through grace and sheer mercy God justifies us through faith. Thereupon I felt myself to be reborn and to have gone through open doors into paradise. The whole of Scripture took on a new meaning, and whereas before the "justice of God" had filled me with hate, now it became to me inexpressibly sweet in greater love. This passage of Paul became to me a gate to heaven....[50]

It should be noted that post-Vatican II Catholicism is far less legalistic and guilt-oriented than it was previously. Statements such as the Joint Declaration on the Doctrine of Justification and books like Pope Benedict XVI's *Saint Paul*, for example, bear eloquent testimony to this fact.[51] Yet, at the same time, it's fair to say that certain theological paradigms and formulations are so deeply established in Catholic thought that their influence continues.

As it relates to the doctrine of salvation, one such formulation is the eucharistic sacrifice of Christ — the Church's participation in Christ's continuous self-offering, as the Lord offers himself at the heavenly altar. Accordingly, the sacrifice of Jesus is thought to be pro-longed (or in the language of Vatican II, "perpetuated") so that Christ is regarded as continually offering himself to the Father.[52] If you have been reading this essay from the start, then it's possible that the words *continual*, *prolonged*, and *perpetual* are ringing some bells for you. If so, your intuition is correct: the doctrine of continuous incarnation exerts influence here, with regard to the doctrine of salvation, as it does in regard to authority and revelation. And, as in the case of authority, our divergence on salvation marks a key point at which Catholics and Evangelicals sing from a different sheet of music.

The Catholic Church teaches that in the offering of the Mass, the Lord Jesus Christ is presented as a victim under the appearance of bread and wine.[53] As Christ offered himself directly to the Father from the cross, he is thought to also do so in the Mass through the hands of the priest, such that "[t]he sacrifice of Christ and the sacrifice of the Eucharist are *one single sacrifice*."[54]

It's important for Evangelicals to understand what Catholicism is *not* teaching here. Contrary to popular opinion, the Catholic Church doesn't believe that Christ is *re-sacrificed* in the Mass. The Eucharist is not a repetition of the cross; rather it is a re-presentation of it.[55] Simi-larly, the Church doesn't say that Christ *dies* at the Mass; rather he is "immolated," which means that he is presented in a state of victimhood.

The continuous nature of Catholic salvation, of which the doctrine of immolation is part, directly relates to the question, What must I do to be saved? and also to the challenge of dealing with injurious religious guilt. Because the death of Christ is ongoing, there is never a sense that justification (being made right with God) has been fin-ished in this life. It continues into the future as a process and finally depends upon one's ability to successfully cooperate with Catholic teaching. The result is what some have called "salvation on probation," the feeling that a person is secure in his or her relationship with God so long as one is good in the eyes of the Church. In this system, the idea of being secure as a son or daughter of God is missing.

I once taught a lesson at College Church in which I addressed this problem of salvation on probation. It was titled "Why I Believe in Pur-gatory." If you ever want to draw large numbers of people to hear you speak, and don't mind a lot of emails in your inbox beforehand, you should consider using this title. The facial expressions of those sitting in the class before I started to speak were priceless. It was like the boy who looked up at Joe Jackson, after the famous White Sox player was found guilty of fixing the 1919 World Series, and exclaimed, "Say it ain't so, Joe." Many evidently thought that it would be my theological coming-out party—true confessions of a closet Catholic. It probably didn't help that I started the lesson stating, "I believe in purgatory."[56]

At one point my wife glared at me as if to say, "Please, stop keeping these people in suspense." I realized that it was time to explain. My comments went something like the following:

> Some of you are wondering how it is I can believe in purgatory. Let me tell you. The word *purgatory* describes purification or purging from sin. In the Catholic tradition, this is believed to happen after people die, in order for them to enter heaven spotless and pure. I also believe in purgatory; however, I believe that it happened once and for all on the cross of Jesus Christ. When the Lord hung between heaven and earth and shed his blood, he did so as a substitute for humanity. He paid the penalty for our guilt once and for all, even as it says in 1 Peter 3:18: "For Christ also suffered once for sins, the righteous for the unrighteous, to bring you to God. He was put to death in the body but made alive in the Spirit."
>
> Having died and risen from the grave, Jesus is no longer a victim of death, as Paul declares in Romans 6:9: "We know that Christ, being raised from the dead, will never die again; *death no longer has dominion over him*" [ESV, emphasis added].
>
> In his death, Jesus perfectly satisfied the righteous requirement of God's law, which is why the Bible says in John 19:30, "When he had received the drink, Jesus said, 'It is finished.' With that, he bowed his head and gave up his spirit."
>
> In Christ, the work of purging is finished. We are fully accepted by God on account of what Jesus has done for us. This is the gift that keeps on giving; it's not guilt, it is grace.

CONCLUSION

So harkening back to my opening statement, in what sense do I still love Catholicism? Most people who come from a Catholic background will probably identify with my sentiment, while those who weren't raised Catholic probably won't. It's the kind of affection you have for that eccentric cousin whom you see once a year at Christmas. Despite your common upbringing, the two of you are now entirely different. He is a Marxist, vegan atheist whose views are diametrically opposed to yours on absolutely everything. He runs marathons, TiVo's professional wrestling, enjoys dancing the polka, and somehow always manages to perform his Bob Dylan impersonation when the family is assembled.[57] However, as first cousins, you have a deep, abiding affection for one another. Despite your differences, you share a common history that reaches back to your earliest memories, on the basis of which you possess a relationship that is deeper and richer than words can express. So it is for many of us who were raised Catholic. We disagree with certain aspects of Catholic faith, but these differences can't erase the positive, Christ-honoring memories which we continue to cherish.

This is where my journey of faith has led. I identify with the Evangelical tradition because I believe that its approach to biblical authority and the gospel best reflects the will of God as revealed in Scripture. Insofar as the term *Evangelical* describes such a person, despite its flaws and negative connotations, I hope to be this kind of man, comporting myself and relating to others—including my Catholic family and friends—with the character of Christ. I hope that these pages have served you in this respect: to prompt you to more intentionally embody the grace and truth of Jesus Christ, our reigning King, to whom be honor and eternal dominion. Amen.

CHAPTER 8

A Response to Evangelicalism

Brad S. Gregory

As a historian who has been reading Reformation-era doctrinal controversy between Catholics and Protestants in multiple languages for more than twenty years, I have no illusions about what a short (or even long) essay in critique of contemporary Evangelical Protestantism is likely to accomplish. The principal arguments and tit-for-tat biblical prooftexts were all well-known centuries ago and remain well-known now; there seems little point in rehashing them again. In themselves, they are unlikely to unseat faith commitments interwoven with the personal relationships and significant individual experiences that characterize virtually all serious religious believers, Christian or non-Christian, simply insofar as believers experience their lives meaningfully as members of their respective communities of faith. For this reason, my critique will not depend on anything substantively faith-based, even though I am a committed Catholic and regard Catholicism as the fullest expression of Christian truth. (Thus I consider lives lived in radical holiness in accord with Catholic teachings as the most authentically evangelical human lives.) Nor will my critique concern itself with the obvious sociological facts that so many Catholics are ill-informed about their own Church's teachings and reject in various ways the authority of its magisterium, failing to see how obedience to it as the arbiter of orthodoxy is only a starting point, not the fulfillment, of what it means to be a Christian. These are both genuine problems for the Catholic Church but irrelevant to the issues in dispute between Catholicism and contemporary Evangelical Protestantism.

The ecumenical efforts of the past half century, in part by emphasizing the many beliefs that (at least some) Evangelical Protestants share with what the Catholic magisterium teaches, have undeniably improved relationships between Catholics and some Protestants.[1] Reformation-era controversialists, by contrast, almost always concentrated on their points of disagreement and were often bitterly hostile toward each other. The recent change is surely a good thing; to be not only civil but also friendly, and indeed to love one another as brothers and sisters in Christ despite ecclesial divisions, is certainly preferable to the animosity that was so often evident for centuries after the Reformation. Furthermore, it seems to me that any Christian who cares about Jesus' prayer for his disciples, "that they may all be one" (John 17:21 NRSV), in addition to dedicating herself to proactive evangelization can and should continue to work for the eventual reconciliation of all divided Christians to the end that our descendants might endeavor to live the shared life in Christ willed by him, so that, as Paul puts it, "together you may with one voice glorify the God and Father of our Lord Jesus Christ" (Rom. 15:6 NRSV), insofar as there is "one Lord, one faith, one baptism, one God and Father of all, who is above all and through all and in all" (Eph. 4:5–6 NRSV).

Still, much as we might wish for a more usable and less painful past, the religious disagreements of the Reformation era were not a mere matter of unfortunate misunderstandings, disputatious personalities, or incendiary rhetoric. They were theologically substantive, concretely divisive, and enormously consequential. Now transformed, they persist as marginalized realities within a secularized Western world whose governing institutions and dominant ideologies were unintentionally precipitated by Christians' rancorous and unresolved doctrinal disputes.[2] As a matter of logic, it is of course impossible that all of the respective competing views might actually be what they claim to be, namely true, on the points at which they contradict one another. Reformation-era controversialists understood this better than do many present-day Christians, some of whom seem to think that in the special case of religious truth claims, the principle of noncontradiction is magically suspended in order to accord with politically protected civil rights to individual religious freedom. In my view, the principal virtue of this volume of essays is its implicit acknowledgment that not all Christian (or other) truth claims can be what they purport to be. Such a view respects reason, logic, and truth.

I am grateful for Chris Castaldo's frank explanation of his spiritual journey, but with limited space, my critique of Evangelical Protestantism will concentrate on what seems to me to be its weakest point.

Like Catholics who know their faith and understand their Church's tradition, committed Evangelical Protestants love Scripture and understand its central importance in Christian life. As far as devotion to God's Word per se is concerned, this is a very good thing. On the other hand, Catholics who do *not* know their faith and their Church's tradition well — who pay too little attention to the extent to which the liturgy is essentially a biblical prayer,[3] for example, with the Liturgy of the Word including readings from Scripture, and the homily devoted to their explication — could benefit from observing the dedication with which many Evangelical Protestants read the Bible. It might motivate some lackadaisical Catholics to do likewise, and inspire uninformed ones to learn more about the centrality of Scripture in the history of their own Church, from the letters and gospel narratives that began circulating in manuscript copies as "living texts," along with many other Christian writings from the second half of the first century, to the mostly stable canon of twenty-seven books recognized as the New Testament by church leaders at the Council of Hippo and the Third Council of Carthage at the end of the fourth century. They might learn also about the deep and rich tradition of patristic, monastic, scholastic, humanist, and post-Tridentine scriptural commentary and preaching in the Latin West and familiarize themselves with the biblical mastery exhibited by contemporary Catholic scholars such as Raymond Brown and John Meier as well as church leaders such as Pope Benedict XVI.[4]

The ability of some Evangelical Protestants to quote biblical verses from memory or to refer to specific scriptural passages to illustrate their beliefs, ideas, and feelings, while often impressive, is less obviously of benefit to Catholics. Its value presupposes that those quoting or referring to the passages not only have memorized or cited the ones most crucial for Christian faith and life but also have properly understood them. But which passages are most important and how they are to be rightly understood and applied, and indeed what Christian faith and life *mean*, are precisely the issues in question—not only in disagreements between contemporary Evangelical Protestants and Catholics but also more significantly for analytical purposes, as we shall see, in the disagreements that have characterized non-Catholic Western Christians from the outset of the Reformation to the present. If Catholicism is true, then it is certainly better to be a well-formed Catholic who pursues holiness in accord with the Church's teachings but never reads Scripture individually than to be an Evangelical Protestant who has memorized hundreds of biblical verses but understands them within an errant theology and without either the grace conferred by the sacraments or the fullness of ecclesial life in the body of Christ. Here I agree with Saint Augustine, who despite being steeped in Scripture wrote in *De doctrina Christiana* that "a person strengthened by faith, hope, and love, and who steadfastly *[inconcusse]* holds on to them, has no need of the Scriptures except to instruct others."[5]

Evangelical Protestantism's central problem has nothing to do with whether large numbers of people in their respective churches and parachurch communities of faith find particular interpretations of biblical passages convincing, meaningful, and foundational for their lives. Obviously, they do—why else would they memorize and seek to live by them? The same applies to devout Muslims who commit Koranic verses to memory. Nor does it have anything to do with whether Evangelical Protestants, such as Chris Castaldo, have had personally powerful, subjective experiences that have changed their lives. Obviously, they have, analogous to the experiences of countless men and women from many different religious traditions. The central problem consists rather in the very notion that the Bible *can* function in the way that Evangelical and many other Protestants historically have claimed that it functions, namely as a perspicuous, self-sufficient authority that needs no interpreter—or is "self-interpreting"—because its meaning is clear on all fundamental matters of religious importance.[6] Empirically, the entire history of Protestantism not only offers no evidence for this claim but also provides abundant evidence against it. And this is so whether or not Catholicism is true, indeed even if it is complete nonsense.

By the Leipzig Disputation in July 1519, Martin Luther articulated what turned out to be the foundational principle for what would become the Reformation: that Scripture alone is the sole legitimate basis for Christian faith and life, independent in principle of papal, conciliar, patristic, canon-legal, and any other alleged ecclesiastical authorities and traditions. As the saving Word of God, the Bible was its own authority and it needed no interpreter, but only a humble openness to its manifest meaning and liberating message of grace gratuitously given, guaranteed in the receptive heart of the sincere Christian by the self-authenticating testimony of the Holy Spirit within what Luther would call the "priesthood of all believers." "No faithful Christian can be forced beyond the sacred Scripture," Luther said at Leipzig, "which is nothing less than divine law, unless new and approved revelation is added. On the contrary, on the basis of divine law we are prohibited to believe, unless it is approved by divine Scripture or palpably obvious *[manifestam]* revelation."[7] Hence only those decisions of church councils and opinions of church fathers consistent with Scripture were acceptable; the others were objectionable additions and distortions. The long-sought reforms of medieval Christendom depended on a return to God's saving Word in the Bible, uncorrupted by the mere "traditions of men" and undistorted by pagan philosophies. As Luther recognized, this raised some important issues. "Yet you might ask," he wrote in 1520 in his *Freedom of a Christian*, " 'What then is this Word, or in what manner is it to be used, since there are so many words of God?' "[8] These were excellent questions. Indeed, given that the content of true Christian faith and life was now to be based on Scripture alone *over against* the Church's tradition wherever the latter had (supposedly) departed from true Christian doctrine, these were the most important questions of the Reformation. How were they answered by those who came to reject the authority of the Catholic Church?

The answer is: in an open-ended range of exegetically discrepant and therefore doctrinally divergent and therefore ecclesially and socially divisive ways that began in the early 1520s and has never gone away. This is the indisputable empirical and historical answer—as distinct from the very many incompatible confessional and theological answers that have been and continue to be given by Evangelicals and other sorts of Protestants, from Unitarians to Pentecostals. Anyone with a textbook knowledge of the Reformation (and who does not confuse its history with Luther's or Calvin's biography or theology) knows that despite *agreeing* about the foundational importance of Scripture as the sole legitimate authority for Christian faith and life, anti-Roman reformers *disagreed* vehemently among themselves in multiple ways about what the Bible said, and thus about what Christians were to believe and do. By March 1522, for example, Luther's senior colleague in Wittenberg, Andreas Bodenstein von Karlstadt, disputed Luther's marginalization of the book of James, plus his views on the character of the Old Testament, eucharistic practice, the oral confession of sins, and the allowability of religious images.[9] As a result and with reciprocal animosity, they went their separate ways. Which of the two interpreted Scripture correctly? Luther and Philip Melanchthon disagreed with Huldrych Zwingli and the latter's reforming colleagues about the nature of Christ's presence in the Lord's Supper, which precipitated a vitriolic pamphlet war and the nonresolution of the Marburg Colloquy in October 1529.[10] This proved to be the beginning of the doctrinal — and thus also the ecclesial and social — division between Reformed Protestants and Lutherans, one that in crucial ways has persisted throughout the intervening centuries to the present. Which of the two traditions was (and is) biblically faithful concerning the Eucharist? Zwingli also disagreed with his former colleagues Balthasar Hubmaier and Conrad Grebel about the biblical basis for infant baptism, with its profound implications for the very nature of the Christian community that resulted in the emergence of Anabaptism beginning in 1525.[11] Hubmaier, Grebel, and other Anabaptists rejected Zwingli's newly established Church in Zurich just as the latter had rejected the established Roman Church, and for the same reason: because they were convinced that it taught unbiblical lies in place of biblical truth. Who was faithful to Scripture? Many biblically based expressions of Christian fraternity in the most widespread, socially adamant expression of the early German Reformation, the so-called Peasants' War of 1524 – 26, utterly rejected Luther's opinion that the gospel as such had nothing to do with the remaking of the hierarchical political structures or the altering of the inequitable socioeconomic relationships characteristic of sixteenth-century Europe.[12] Were they mistaken? These few examples from central Europe in the 1520s could be multiplied at great length.

The unwanted disagreements that resulted from the shared anti-Roman commitment to Scripture were not restricted to the tempestuous years of the early German Reformation. It might be thought that initial contestation was only to be expected before things "settled down," before agreements started to coalesce concerning the difference between "central Reformation principles" and "secondary issues" or even *adiaphora*, indifferent matters.[13] But there was no such coalescence. As we shall see, the Reformation "settled down" not because anti-Roman Christians moved toward agreement about "central Reformation principles" but because political power was exercised and effectively suppressed most of their rival claims about God's truth. Not only did the divisive disagreements persist, but also the distinction itself simply begged the question about what was central and what was secondary, providing something else about which anti-Roman controversialists could and did disagree, notwithstanding whatever rapprochements occurred among various groups from time to time. Was baptism a secondary issue of sacramental theology? Not according to all of the diverse Anabaptist groups, for whom it went to the essence of being a Christian, and whose members were judicially executed by Lutheran and Zwinglian as well as Catholic authorities for their biblical rejection of infant baptism.[14] Was the Eucharist a secondary issue? Not according to either the Lutherans or Reformed Protestants, whom it divided notwithstanding everything else they shared in common, with theologians on each side defending their respective views based on learned exegesis. In 1522, Zwingli assured readers that "I know for certain that God teaches me, because I have experienced it."[15] By contrast, Luther during the initial eucharistic controversy warned readers to "beware of Zwingli and avoid his books as the hellish poison of Satan, for the man is completely perverted *[gantz verkeret]* and has completely lost Christ."[16] It sounds as though the issue were central to Luther — as it was also to Zwingli, or else he presumably would have acquiesced at Marburg in 1529 for the sake of Christian concord. That many Evangelical Protestants *today* might rate the sacraments as less important than did sixteenth-century reformers demonstrates only that they interpret the Bible differently and understand discrepantly its relationship to Christian faith and life. But whence all the disagreements and divergent priorities, among the sixteenth-century reformers, between them and present-day Evangelicals, and among present-day Evangelicals, if the Bible's meaning is clear and Scripture is its own authority?

In terms of the proliferation of rival views about what Scripture meant, things never settled down. Just like Luther, John Calvin, for example, was involved in doctrinal controversies with other Protestants throughout his reforming career, between the first publication of his *Institutes* in 1536 until his death in 1564.[17] Within their respective traditions, Gnesio-Lutherans and Philippist Lutherans opposed each other bitterly and worshiped separately in the decades after Luther's death in 1546, as did Arminians and Calvinists in the Dutch Republic and England in the early seventeenth century.[18] To assume that at least "the essentials" were shared presupposes mistakenly what was in fact contested. What *were* "the essentials"? What *are* they? And what happens to shared life in Christ when Christians disagree about what is essential to the faith and act on their disagreements in concrete ways? Damage, diminution, dilution, dissipation, destruction, disappearance.

"The Bible, I say, the Bible only, is the religion of Protestants!" William Chillingworth famously declared in 1638. This simply restated with an exclamation point the root of the problem, as would be dramatically demonstrated in England during the next two decades in an efflorescence of rival Protestant claims and groups unseen since the early German Reformation.[19] Those who follow in Chillingworth's footsteps fail to see that a commitment to "the Bible only" does not and — based on the historical evidence of nearly five hundred years — *cannot* establish a foundation for shared Christian truth. Rather *it is itself the cause* of an apparently insuperable exegetical, doctrinal, ecclesial, and social fissiparity. From the very start, Protestant Christianity foundered on its own foundation — even though there is no reason to doubt that today Pentecostals, liberal Methodists, Old Order Amish, nonfundamentalist Evangelicals, young-earth-creationist Evangelicals, and all other sorts of Protestants find meaningful and consider true their respective, contrary views about what the Bible says. Otherwise each of them would presumably believe something else. No one's sincerity or heartfelt experience or personally meaningful journey of faith is in question. The point is simply that it is logically impossible for them all to be correct about their respective truth claims on the matters about which they disagree. Just as in the 1520s, as their antagonistic, anti-Roman predecessors well understood.

It is sometimes claimed that the advocates of *sola scriptura* differ from hermeneutical individualists who in effect champion *nuda scriptura* apart from any ecclesiastical tradition and do indeed foment an objectionable exegetical anarchy. Some Evangelicals seem to think that *sola scriptura*, whether among sixteenth-century Protestant reformers or today, yields or can yield a coherent affirmation of legitimate conciliar decrees and faithful opinions of the church fathers that link contemporary Evangelicals substantively and historically to the tradition of the early church. (For example, see Chris Castaldo's essay in this volume.) Unfortunately, such arguments are perfectly circular, relying as they must on one *contested* interpretation of the Bible among others for their evaluative criteria of legitimacy and fidelity. Reference to the biblically "faithful teaching" *within* the Church's tradition both begs the question about the correct interpretation of the Bible and implicitly undermines the notion that Tradition *has* any independent authority apart from Scripture, thereby rendering *sola scriptura* and *nuda scriptura* indistinguishable. A particular biblical reading among many rivals has *already* been deemed the criterion according to which conciliar decrees, patristic statements, and any other sort of Christian expression will be judged. Choose a rival reading, and different decrees and statements become correlatively legitimate and faithful. (Just try it.) Truth be told, Tradition has *no* independent authority for Evangelicals apart from the particular interpretation of Scripture that a given reader happens to favor, and so is nothing but a corollary of that individual preference. Thus, however it is supplementarily clothed with creedal statements, conciliar decrees, patristic ideas, doctrinal formulations, confessions of faith, and theologians' opinions, *sola scriptura* always veils a preferential reading of *nuda scriptura*. In the end, they cannot be distinguished. Else what is the point of insisting on the Bible as its own self-interpreting authority in the first place?

In early modern Europe, Scripture as interpreted by hermeneutic authorities and backed by political authorities led to confessional Protestant states, territories, and cities, whether Lutheran or Reformed Protestant (including the post-Henrician but non-Marian Church of

England, which is only anachronistically called "Anglican" before the Restoration of 1660). These Protestant regimes stipulated and policed their respective versions of biblical truth in a manner analogous to Catholic political regimes. Scripture "alone," on the other hand, *without* an alliance between anti-Roman reformers and political authorities, resulted empirically in a vast range of irreconcilable truth claims about the meaning and implications of God's Word. The latter phenomenon is most obvious in the early German Reformation during the 1520s and in England during the 1640s and 50s, less dramatically in the Golden-Age Dutch Republic (whose ruling urban regents made Reformed Protestantism the "public church" without mandating it as the state religion, and thus oversaw an expansive Protestant pluralism in the seventeenth century).[20] We see the same concrete result of Scripture "alone" in the history of the United States, which, because it has never had an established Church, has always manifested the open-ended arbitrariness of the Reformation unfettered, whether in the colonial period, in the vast proliferation of Protestant claims and correlative groups in the first third of the nineteenth century, or today, as is implicit in the entries under "churches" in the yellow pages of American telephone books.[21]

In attempting to understand the Reformation, most scholars and nonscholars have interpreted the largely effective *political* control of most anti-Roman interpretations of Scripture between the Anabaptist Kingdom of Münster in 1534–35 and England in the 1640s as evidence for a "settling down" of exegetical disputes or a movement toward agreement about "central Reformation principles." This is a mistake. It conflates the longstanding and widespread demographic influence of Lutheranism and Reformed Protestantism (including the Church of England) with doctrinally normative Christianity (bracketing for the moment the divisive differences between and within these traditions). But there is no necessary connection between these two things, and to conflate them simply begs yet again the Reformation's core question about the meaning of Scripture. Lutheranism and Reformed Protestantism were not the Reformation's norm but rather its *great exceptions*—because among the many anti-Roman competitors about the meaning of God's Word, only they secured lasting political support. Hence only they, like post-Tridentine Catholicism, had an impact on the lives of millions of early modern Europeans in multiple countries. Persecuted and proscribed "radical Protestants," by contrast, shaped far fewer human lives, even though they offered many *more* interpretations of what God's Word meant. Because of an analytical failure to distinguish the interpretation of the Bible from the exercise of political power, Lutheranism and Reformed Protestantism have been and still tend to be regarded in the opposite way — not as the Reformation's politically privileged exceptions but as somehow its *doctrinal* norm, as "mainstream." No Anabaptist agreed in the sixteenth century that Lutherans or Reformed Protestants understood the Bible correctly, just as no Mennonite agrees today. Commitment to the authority of Scripture alone as the basis for Christian faith and life led neither obviously nor necessarily to justification by faith alone or to salvation through grace alone, for example, as the cornerstone doctrines of Christianity. There is no intrinsic relationship between *sola scriptura* on the one hand and *sola fide* or *sola gratia* on the other, as the biblical interpretations of many other anti-Roman Christians made abundantly clear. So it was in the sixteenth century, and so it is today. Rival appeals to the Holy Spirit's authenticating testimony, too, settle as much now as they did then — that is, nothing at all. "What am I to do," Erasmus asked in 1524, "when many persons allege different interpretations, each one of whom swears to have the Spirit?"[22] Precisely.

Like every other text — or in this case, like every collection of texts written, redacted, selected, and compiled through extraordinarily complex historical strands of oral and written transmission and translation in multiple languages across a far-flung geographical region over more than a millennium — the Bible does not interpret itself. Or at least there is no evidence that it ever has, and there is no reason to think it ever will. Scripture alone sits on shelves between the covers of Bibles and now reposes in digital databases. *Human beings* interpret the Bible, just as they interpret other texts, and their interpretations do not concur. So it is impossible that they are all correct. The unavoidable question is thus *whose* interpretations one accepts, and on what basis — particularly if one cares about shared life in Christ, the possibility of its sustenance and vigor over time, and about genuine prospects for resolving disputes that inevitably arise and threaten with socially divisive schism the shared life willed by Christ. Of course, this presupposes that one believes that Christ wills that his followers "may all be one" (John 17:21) and live together in what Saint Paul calls "the fruit of the Spirit," namely "love, joy, peace, patience, kindness, generosity, faithfulness, gentleness, and self-control" (Gal. 5:22–23), rather than believing that Christ wills that individuals should live in indefinitely many socially divided communities of faith depending on how they contrarily interpret the Bible and experience their personal journeys of faith.

If those sixteenth-century reformers or subsequent anti-Roman Christians who insisted on *sola scriptura* and abominated interpretative individualism had agreed among themselves about what the Bible taught and so about what Christians were to believe and do, there would be historical evidence for the claim that Scripture is its own authority and interprets itself. Had this happened, it would have been impressive. It would have constituted a formidable fact with which to counter Catholic claims about the Church's magisterium as the authoritative interpreter of Scripture. Presumably, then there would also be some evidence that the comparing of biblical passages with each other tends to produce agreement among hermeneutical antagonists, rather than the perpetuation of interminable exegetical controversy. Then, too, "Protestantism" might meaningfully be compared with "Catholicism" in substantive ways as something with discernibly coherent doctrines, worship, institutions, and devotions, instead of being simply an umbrella designation of groups, churches, movements, and individuals whose only common feature is a rejection of the authority of the Catholic Church. But from the beginning of the Reformation to the present, those who *agreed* that the Bible was the Christian faith's self-sufficient authority disagreed about what it said. Thus they functionally constituted *themselves*—against their intentions but as the result of their actions—as their own rival authorities. Rejecting the Catholic Church's tradition as the mere "tradition of men," mere men started many competing traditions of their own. And so can anyone else who establishes himself as its allegedly authoritative interpreter precisely in being bewitched by the chimera that the Bible is a self-interpreting authority.

Among the ironic, long-term consequences of the Reformation era's doctrinal disagreements has been the marked modern trend toward the wholesale subjectivization of belief and relativization of truth, both of which have powerfully contributed to Western secularization. Indeed, the open-ended doctrinal pluralism of Protestantism can suggest to the analytically unwary that *all* religion is nothing but a matter of individual, subjective, and irrational personal preference, a theater of Feuerbachian and Freudian projection. Certainly, many contemporary secularists seem to see things this way. Moreover, because of early modern Europe's concretely disruptive and destructive religious disagreements, modern political institutions were created that protect exactly the interpretative arbitrariness condemned by sixteenth-century Protestant reformers. In sharp contrast to the Catholic magisterium, there are no shared criteria, authorities, institutions, or mechanisms that *can* resolve Protestant exegetical, doctrinal, or moral disagreements. Nor are there realistic prospects for devising any, because efforts to settle such questions can unfold only based on competing criteria that are themselves in dispute, and all proposals of new criteria only compound the problem. Or so it has been for nearly five centuries. Perhaps the future will be completely different.

Those who dispute this conclusion should study the history of anti-Roman Western Christianity since 1500 *comparatively across its full breadth* and consider the *full extent* of its present-day doctrinal pluralism and social realities. One cannot see the problem if one preferentially decides in advance what *Evangelical* means and then notes with satisfaction how much one shares with others who also happen to accept one's definition—as if this constituted, after all, evidence about Scripture as a self-sufficient authority. Heartfelt apologetics and advocacy is not analysis, nor can it see the problem. Today, in the absence of anything resembling consensus or convergence among those who reject Catholicism, the decision to be an Evangelical in contrast to some other sort of Protestant—and indeed, more fundamentally, the move even to define *Evangelical* in the first place—is quite literally arbitrary in the etymological sense: it is a function of the *arbitrium*, the individual human will. What one decides is a matter of self-determined personal preference; one is one's own authority. In what must be one of the greater ironies in the history of Christianity, Luther himself understood this: "Whoever has gone astray in the faith may thereafter believe whatever he wants to, everything is equally valid."[23] A prophet indeed. In the midseventeenth century, that learned exegete and passionate Protestant keen to reform the Reformation, John Milton, saw what had been implicit in it from the beginning, adumbrating despite himself the preferential arbitrariness that modern institutions would eventually protect: "[T]he Scripture only can be the final judge or rule in matters of religion," he wrote, "and that only in the conscience of every Christian to himself," for "every true Christian, able to give a reason of his faith, hath the word of God before him, the promis[e]d Holy Spirit, and the mind of Christ within him."[24] But among those who allege the self-sufficient perspicuity of Scripture, there is no more agreement about the Word of God, the promised Holy Spirit, or the mind of Christ now than there was then, or has been at any time in between.

❧

CHAPTER 9

EVANGELICALISM REJOINDER

Chris Castaldo

Thanks to Brad Gregory for his thoughtful response. This interchange would be far more enjoyable over espresso somewhere on Notre Dame's campus. Perhaps that day will come, but in the meantime here is my humble rejoinder. I begin with a few observations about the enterprise of interpretation.

Gestalt psychologists are known to point out that perception is profoundly influenced by expectation. Two people looking at the same picture will often perceive different patterns, depending upon their particular presumptions. A motif may be hidden to the person whose eye has not been trained to find it. At the same time, a design can be imagined into existence by one who believes that it should be there.

In much the same way, we observe theological patterns which are intrinsic to the Bible. The Church is called to sit in humble submission to the content of God's Word, and, in the context of a believing community, to allow doctrinal formulations to arise from that content. Because Evangelicals understand God's Word to consist of the inspired text of Scripture, and not the patterns of Tradition that have emerged over the course of church history, we are committed to a serious study of the Bible, a study guided and governed by the larger canonical context. When Christian theology loses sight of the centrality of the biblical text, it becomes vulnerable to losing its bearings.

There are some common ways that we lose our textual bearings. First, we miss the bits that comprise the whole, the trees from the forest, the exegetical parts that hang together to constitute the overarching narrative of redemption. On the other hand, we may get bogged down in the atomistic minutiae such that we fail to see the larger structure in which those smaller parts fit. In this instance, the interpreter's nose remains so closely pressed against the page that it is well-nigh impossible to see the big picture. We Evangelicals struggle in both of these respects.

There is also a third problem. Continuing the art interpretation metaphor, it is the members of the curator guild who insist on providing the only valid interpretation of the picture, the artistic experts who speak with infallibility and thus reign supreme in matters of interpretation. This group posits itself as the authority that adjudicates the importance of particular patterns, how they are to be rightly understood and applied, and indeed what they *mean*. In my opinion, this is where Catholicism struggles.

Undoubtedly, the Lord gives his Church certain individuals who are more gifted in matters of grammatical, historical, and literary analysis and more capable of bringing leadership to the interpretive enterprise. However, we must be careful that such people are not isolated as religious elites who operate on an exclusive plane above and beyond the rest. The proper domain of theological interpretation and arrangement is the whole Church. The task of biblical interpretation and application ought to reflect the organic functioning of the community, with each part complementing and sharpening the other. The foot cannot say, "Because I am not a hand, I do not belong to the body" (1 Cor. 12:15).

The imbedding of theology in Scripture does not guarantee that the Church will always agree, as Brad Gregory points out, but it is nonetheless the proper context for maintaining fidelity to the structure and substance of Christian theology—to the material norm of divine revelation—namely, Scripture itself. Sacred Tradition and statements of magisterial consensus may help to clarify the meaning of Scripture, or they may just cloud and confuse it. Such is the way that many Evangelicals view aspects of Catholic teaching: doctrines such as transubstantiation, papal infallibility, Mary's immaculate conception, the assumption, and purgatory, for example.

Personally, I remain unconvinced of the so-called unity of Catholic dogma, for at least two reasons: First, if you probe below the surface, you discover that such agreement often doesn't go beyond a common liturgy and clerical attire. As I mentioned earlier, quoting Catholic journalist Peter Feuerherd, significant disagreement and fragmentation is found even at the highest levels of Catholic authority. Second, infallible statements of interpretation fail to solve the problem at the end of the day, precisely because they beg the question of who gets to interpret the interpretation, as the statement by Avery Cardinal Dulles pointed out. Perhaps more problematic is the conscious step away from divine revelation that Sacred Tradition and magisterium represent, since these sources, understood by Catholics to possess the quality of infallibility, inevitably function as the "commandments of men" about which Jesus warns us.

Nevertheless, Evangelical readers would make a grave mistake if we didn't hear Gregory's point concerning our problem of hyperindividualism. Not only does this tendency wreak havoc on biblical interpretation; it also encourages a shallow, self-centered consumerism that constructs faith with the material of spiritual platitudes to the exclusion of theological substance. Very often this is what disgusts Catholics, and it should repulse us too. It's not fair for Catholics to caricature all of Evangelicalism as an open-ended range of exegetically discrepant and therefore doctrinally divergent and socially divisive communities, nor is it right for Evangelicals to pretend that the problem of individualism doesn't exist.

So what of the Evangelical notion of perspicuity — that the Bible is sufficiently unambiguous on the whole for well-intentioned persons with Christian faith to understand with relative adequacy? Recognizing that none of us, even the most hermeneutically savvy, is immune to the cataract of confusion that inhibits a perfect reading of the text, is the doctrine of Scripture's clarity rationally and empirically defendable? In the balance of this rejoinder, I would like to respectfully disagree with Gregory's argument by suggesting that the doctrine of perspicuity is indeed supported by reason and by history.

The first hurdle that perspicuity must clear is the accusation that it, along with *sola scriptura* in general, is "perfectly circular." Logically speaking, an explanation of one's ultimate beliefs always involves a degree of circularity. The Protestant relies on Scripture to define his belief in Scripture as the supreme source of authority; the Catholic relies upon the institution of the Church to define authority by that institution; the Muslim relies on the Koran for his Koranic religion; and the secular humanist clings to his own reason. This is not to espouse fideism — that faith is independent of reason. The foundation of our beliefs should be regularly scrutinized. Intellectual honesty requires it, as does the deepening of our faith. Nevertheless, the circular pattern of ultimate truth claims is an unavoidable function of the fact that every view stands upon some sort of epistemic ground. In other words, there is no such thing as a view from nowhere. However, our commitment to this ground shouldn't inhibit further investigation. As imperfect interpreters, we must carefully assess and measure evidence to determine which rendering of the data is most tenable. Short of core tenets of faith, such as what we have in the Apostles' and Nicene creeds — primary doctrines which God's people have agreed upon from time immemorial — honesty and humility requires that we remain open to doctrinal reform.

Evidence for perspicuity is based on the premise that God has spoken in order to be understood. Accordingly, the Hebrew prophets addressed themselves to regular people, not only to religious leaders (Deut. 6:6–7; Ps. 119:105). Scripture is said to be clear enough for the "simple" to understand and benefit from its message. "The statutes of the LORD are trustworthy, making wise the simple" (Ps. 19:7). Again, we read, "The unfolding of your words gives light; it gives understanding to the simple" (Ps. 119:130).

The New Testament attests to the same emphasis by Jesus and the apostles. When Jesus encountered individuals who misunderstood doctrine, their confusion was never blamed on the imperspicuous nature of Scripture; instead our Lord responded with statements such as "Have you not read ..." (Matt. 12:3, 5; 21:42; 22:31, ESV), "You are wrong because you know neither the Scriptures nor the power of God" (Matt 22:29 ESV; cf. 9:13; 12:7; 15:3; 21:13; John 3:10; et al.), or even "How foolish you are, and how slow to believe all that the prophets have spoken!" (Luke 24:25). In each of these instances, Jesus expected his interlocutors to have understood the proper meaning of Scripture.

The epistles of the New Testament are further proof of the Bible's clarity. Paul's letters were written not to church leaders but to entire congregations, for example, "to all the saints in Christ Jesus who are at Philippi" (Phil. 1:1 ESV; cf. 1 Cor. 1:2; Gal. 1:2). Peter addressed believers scattered throughout Asia Minor (1 Peter 1:1). Although Peter acknowledged that Paul's letters contain some things that are hard to understand, he nowhere lets readers off the interpretive hook, but instead places the blame on the "ignorant and unstable people" who distort these passages "as they do the other Scriptures, to their own destruction" (2 Peter 3:16).

In his book *On Christian Doctrine*, Augustine deals with the issue of interpreting obscure passages, describing how they reveal our sin-darkened intelligence. What's interesting is that Augustine says nothing of a Church magisterium as the solution to these conundrums; rather he portrays hard sayings as purposefully arranged by God to subdue our pride and feed charity.[1] Augustine's view on this point is also the biblical portrait. Scripture has no example of an infallible teaching office, nor does it have a revealed interest in one. Instead it portrays an eschatological reality in which we now see but a poor reflection as in a mirror, awaiting the day when we will see truth face-to-face (1 Cor. 13:12). This reality should infuse the activity of biblical interpretation with a conscious balance of grace and truth, or, in Richard Baxter's words, "unity in necessary things; liberty in doubtful things; and charity in all things." We contend for the faith (Jude 1:3) while simultaneously preserving the unity of the Spirit in the bond of peace (Eph. 4:3).

What about Professor Gregory's challenge to Evangelicals to furnish evidence of perspicuity in history? Here is one example: the Third Lausanne Congress on World Evangelization, held October 17–25, 2010, in Cape Town, South Africa. Out of four thousand delegates, 197 nations were represented. A spectrum of churches and ethnicities were included, speaking eight official languages: Arabic, Chinese, English, French, German, Portuguese, Russian, and Spanish. Centered upon a common commitment to the gospel, this global church council (including cardinals of the Catholic Church representing the Vatican) gathered as brothers and sisters in Christ to prayerfully seek the Lord's wisdom to address the challenges and opportunities for the spread of the gospel in today's world. Christian humility born of the recognition of our sin-stained hearts and minds prevented any one Church from claiming dominance over the other; nevertheless, participants engaged in discussion with an absolute regard for truth.

PART 4

ANGLICANISM

✻

CHAPTER 10

A JOURNEY TO ANGLICANISM

Lyle W. Dorsett

In the 1980s my wife and I had the privilege of spending part of several summers in England with world-renowned journalist Malcolm Muggeridge and his wife, Kitty. As we got to know their family better, we learned that they had a son who belonged to a conservative Brethren congregation, a daughter in the Dutch Reformed Church, and a son who worshiped in the Catholic Church. The Muggeridges counted Father Alec Vidler, an Anglican priest, as one of their closest friends and spiritual advisors, yet they left the Anglican tradition and converted to Catholicism. The mantel of their fireplace displayed a photograph of Mother Teresa, as well as a picture of one of the Booth women who served as a general officer in the Salvation Army.

One evening I asked Mr. Muggeridge what he made of all these friends and relatives worshiping and serving the Lord in such diverse traditions. The octogenarian instantly replied, "They serve in different regiments of the same army, my man." I liked that response, and it has worn well with me over the years. Indeed, I quote Mr. Muggeridge often. I like the charity manifested in his answer. Likewise, the metaphor holds up to the tests of Scripture, church history, and my own experience.

A spiritual war has been raging ever since Jesus Christ proclaimed he would build his Church and "the gates of hell shall not prevail against it" (Matt. 16:18 ESV). Saint John the Evangelist echoed our Lord when he wrote that "the reason the Son of God appeared was to destroy the works of the devil" (1 John 3:8 ESV).

From the time that Herod set out to destroy the baby Jesus, the Evil One has unleashed his demons and inspired his human servants to destroy the bride of Christ. Because our adversary is real, Saint Peter has warned us that he is "like a roaring lion, seeking someone to devour" (1 Peter 5:8 ESV), and Saint Paul exhorts us Christians to behave like good soldiers and take up our "sword" of the Spirit and wear "the whole armor" provided by God (Eph. 6:10–20 ESV). C. S. Lewis put it well when he wrote, "Enemy occupied territory—that is what this world is. Christianity is the story of how the rightful King has landed, you might say landed in disguise, and is calling us to all take part in a great campaign of sabotage."[1]

Unfortunately, different regiments in the Lord's army have frequently fought one another, failing to see that our enemy is much greater than our differences. It is in a spirit of camaraderie with brothers and sisters of all traditions of God's army who want to fight the good fight and finish the race that I explain and celebrate my own choice of a regiment. The international Anglican communion, in the Episcopal Province of Rwanda, is where I have felt led to serve. Or to put it another way, my wife, Mary, and I are in the "room" of the Anglican Mission in the Americas, a chamber off the great hall of the universal church, to use C. S. Lewis's illustration in *Mere Christianity*. Like the late professor and celebrated author, we neither think we are in the only true room nor think we are necessarily in the best one. Instead we are in the room where we find fellowship that best suits us.[2] If other folks choose to join us, we welcome them.

To the point, my purpose in writing this overview of my religious journey is not to recruit men and women from other regiments of God's army to become Anglicans. Our North American ranks are growing, to be sure, but not because recruiters are raiding other camps. Instead it is because increasing numbers of folks like me are longing for *something more* and are finding it in the Anglican tradition that has enriched my walk with the Lord and given me more appreciation of the importance of the Church.

✂

The story of my Christian pilgrimage cannot be complete without my mentioning the bestowal of God's grace before I knew anything about him. Several weeks after my birth, my parents had me baptized in a Lutheran church in Kansas City, Missouri. When I was twelve or thirteen, the pastor of First Lutheran Church in Birmingham, Alabama, confirmed me. I do not remember his name, but I do recall his warm care for me, as well as the engaging way he taught the Ten Commandments. There must have been careful instruction on God's grace, but I do not remember it. We confirmands did memorize the Apostles' Creed, but neither the importance of that creed in understanding God's grace nor the place of the sacraments as means of grace lingered with me.

As far as I could tell, the Lutheran Church played only marginal importance in the life of our family. And for me it seemed totally dispensable. In retrospect, I am certain that my parents' indifference to church attendance — even on Sundays — helped convince me that church ranked near the bottom of our list of priorities.

Years later, when I was in my forties, the Holy Spirit began to show me that in those two Lutheran churches, I received blessings too subtle for my youthful mind to discern. In moments of quiet reflection, I could close my eyes and see the Kansas City pastor in his elevated pulpit and hear him saying these words from Habakkuk 2:20: "The LORD is in his holy temple; let all the earth keep silence before him" (ESV). One evening I called my father and asked if this long-buried memory could be true. He assured me that the pastor always opened worship services with those words of the prophet. On another occasion, again during a quiet time, I saw Miss Johnson in a white robe leading the choir down the church's center aisle. They were singing, "Holy, Holy, Holy." Again I called my father. "Did they do that every Sunday too?" I inquired. He said they processed in every Sunday singing a hymn of praise to God. But he was certain it was not always "Holy, Holy, Holy."

Obviously, the Lutheran Church served as a channel of God's grace beyond my awareness and despite our family's casual attitude toward worship and church attendance during my early years in Kansas City and adolescence in Birmingham. The holiness, majesty, and awesomeness of God had been implanted in my young, impressionable soul.

❧

Much less subtly and indeed quite surprisingly, the Holy Spirit spoke to me during the summer of my fifteenth year. We Dorsetts were still living in Birmingham and only occasionally going to church. One evening during the summer, I walked toward my home after performing a weekly task of changing the marquee at a local movie theater. Taking a shortcut across the Howard College campus, I came upon a big tent on the football field and observed a crowd seated in front of a nattily dressed young man pacing back and forth across an elevated platform. I stood outside the tent, listened while the dynamic preacher talked about the parable of the prodigal son, and then experienced a deep resonance in my soul when this evangelist named Eddie Martin called prodigals in the congregation to "come home to Jesus."

I did not go forward at the preacher's invitation. I feared it would be inappropriate inasmuch as I was not part of the congregation seated inside. But after the invitational music ended, Eddie Martin said he knew there were more prodigals who needed to come home from the far country, and if God would give him one more night to live, he would be back the next evening to reiterate the call so that more sinners could be led into the presence of God.

This old-fashioned big-tent revival meeting stood in stark contrast to everything I had witnessed in two different stained-glass-adorned Lutheran churches. Nevertheless, I returned to the tent the next night, waited through the sermon, and eagerly anticipated the invitation the preacher had promised twenty-four hours earlier. When that call came, up to the front I sprinted. Within a few minutes Eddie Martin came off the platform, pulled me down on my knees next to him, wrapped an arm around my shoulders, and led me in a "sinner's prayer." While he prayed a phrase and asked me to repeat it, I acknowledged my sinfulness, asked the Lord Jesus to forgive me, and promised to go to church regularly and obey the Lord all the days of my life.

Just twenty-four hours earlier, I had walked home from work oblivious to spiritual reality and unburdened by a sense of sin. But before this second evening at the big-tent preaching event, I knew beyond a doubt that I had rebelled against God, that I lived in the far country and needed to get home to my heavenly Father before it was too late. On this second evening, I became powerfully aware of spiritual reality. I prayed like I had never prayed, and my young soul danced for joy with a keen sense of God's loving presence and forgiveness. But even more astonishing, while the evangelist prayed with me,

I also heard the Lord Jesus tell me that I must preach the good news about him just as Reverend Martin had been doing.

Immediately after this prayer and a simultaneous call from God to preach, the evangelist inquired if my family and I belonged to a church. "Yes, of course," I replied, and I explained that we were members at First Lutheran Church. But I left off the part about our quite intermittent attendance. It made no difference to Eddie Martin. He explained that my family and I all needed to be in a good Baptist church and be baptized by immersion. He made it seem as urgent as getting out of the far country.

Within a day or two, Ruhama Baptist Church near Howard College contacted me and my parents. The following Sunday, we all showed up there. Within a few weeks, my mother, father, and I were all baptized by immersion in a deep tank behind the choir benches.

In the wake of what Eddie Martin explained was my "new birth" experience, my parents seemed to have "born again" experiences themselves. Whether we were already members of Christ's kingdom because of our previous baptisms and confirmations, none of us had any theological categories to make that claim. But one thing became clear. What happened to our family proved to be profound. My mother and father began attending church regularly, and they faithfully tithed. My father became so committed to Jesus Christ that the pastor asked him to become a deacon. But dad refused. He said he enjoyed the odd beer and his New Year's Eve cocktail. He argued that Jesus approved of drinking because he turned water into wine. And what was good enough for Jesus certainly settled it for my father. The preacher did not argue. He made dad a member of his "informal cabinet." He also visited us twice and stayed in our home after we moved back to Kansas City for reasons related to my father's career.

⚭

Although my parents put their hands to the plow and never looked back, I eventually became a true prodigal. My trip to the far country did not come with a one-time decision. I simply drifted. The gradual move away from the Christian faith began with wanting friends more than I wanted intimacy with Christ. And despite my early pronouncements of being called to ministry, by my senior year in high school

I laid that calling aside like an outgrown coat that gradually ceased to fit. Then during four years of university, my still malleable mind was reshaped by professors who delighted in telling gullible undergraduates that intelligent and reflective people did not believe in God, because no evidence existed for such supernatural nonsense. Furthermore, one psychology professor explained that most people who claimed to have had supernatural religious experiences, and especially "encounters" with God, had probably been emotionally stirred up by preachers who knew how to manipulate people.

Gradually my mind and interests turned from Christ to history. Teaching American history at the university level became my new calling. Never one to do things halfheartedly, I immersed myself in this purpose and spent the next few years in graduate school earning master of arts and PhD degrees in history. Eventually I embarked upon a career as a university history professor.

After teaching stints at the University of Southern California and the University of Missouri, St. Louis, I married and soon accepted an offer to teach American History at the University of Colorado. After we were married, my wife, Mary, expressed a desire to attend church. When we first met, I learned that Mary had been raised a Catholic, had attended Catholic elementary and high schools, and had done undergraduate work at St. Louis University. But Mary had grown disillusioned with Catholicism, and her difficulties with that tradition squared quite well with Martin Luther's. Consequently, we attended a Missouri Synod Lutheran church near our St. Louis home, and when we moved to Boulder, Colorado, we naturally began attending a Lutheran church. A few months after regularly attending the church, Mary truly "heard" the gospel. Although I willingly accompanied her and our growing family to church, I felt spiritually comatose and could never quite get beyond the agnosticism I had acquired during my years as a university student.

During the next four and a half years, I watched Mary grow in grace, devour Scripture, and gain confidence in her freedom in Christ. During this time, I accepted an offer at the University of Denver, but we continued to live in Boulder. Several factors conspired to soften my heart toward the gospel. First, just watching Mary change caused me to pause, being reminded of my parents' palpable transformation once they fell under the pastoral care of the Birmingham Baptist minister. Second, one of my students at the University of Denver, Lauren Pfister, gathered enough courage to question my materialist worldview, and he challenged me to read G. K. Chesterton's *Orthodoxy* and C. S. Lewis's *Surprised by Joy* and *Mere Christianity*. He also irenically confronted my occasional veiled suggestions in class that intelligent and thoughtful people are not Christians. Because I admired this brilliant, charitable, and charismatic young man, we had frequent conversations over lunch and during outings to bookstores off campus. Besides the prayers and witness of Mary and this purposive student, the radio in my car became stuck on KPOF, a metro Denver radio station that offered hourly news and a few hours of classical music. During the other twenty or twenty-one hours, KPOF broadcast a variety of Bible teachers and preachers, as well as stories of great Christians. Because the radio remained stubbornly riveted on KPOF, I listened to Evangelical teaching and preaching during my daily round-trip commute of nearly sixty miles. Especially penetrating were sermons, commentary, and references to Christian history by the Reverend Dr. Robert Dallenbach, director of the station. An unusually intelligent, articulate, and persuasive Christian, this man with an M.A. from New York's Columbia University and a PhD from the University of Colorado spoke to my mind and heart. Indeed, one night I felt constrained to drive to the radio station in hopes of meeting him. Although the station door was locked, he let me in, listened to my questions, and prayed for me. He finally sent me away with some soul-piercing literature. Over the years, Dr. Dallenbach and his wife, Pauline, have continued to deeply bless and encourage me.

My wife's witness and prayers, the gentle evangelistic efforts of my student, and the radio ministry all combined to bring me to a point of crisis. In the wake of a demanding academic leave to write a history of Denver, Colorado, and during a season of life when I drank alcoholically, I cried out while awakening from a drinking binge, "God, if you are there, will you help me?" A presence came to me. It was the one who had spoken to me in the big tent a quarter century earlier in Birmingham. Astonished again, I knew that the Lord Jesus was with me and that he loved me. In brief, to use the words of the English poet Francis Thompson, "the Hound of Heaven" who had been pursuing me via family, radio, a student, and books, appeared when I cried for mercy. The prodigal had come home, and he found a welcoming Father.

⚭

The Lord delivered me from the bondage of alcohol, and he gradually restored my battered soul. Within two or three years after this mystical experience, the words of the prophet Joel became quite personal. As I awkwardly and imperfectly began to "rend my heart and not my garments" (see Joel 2:13), the Lord Jesus Christ became increasingly real and intimate. I longed to know him better and began to imbibe ever-larger helpings of Scripture and books by C. S. Lewis and G. K. Chesterton, as well as biographies and autobiographies of men such as Peter Marshall, George Mueller, Sir Wilfred Grenfell, William P. Jacobs, Saint Francis of Assisi, Dr. George Washington Carver, and Oswald Chambers.

⚭

Gradually, in the aftermath of this conversion experience or explosive understanding of what God had done for me through infant baptism, confirmation, and the mystical experience under the Baptist big-tent revival meeting, the Lord gracefully restored the call to preach. But walking out the call and finding a regiment in which to serve did not happen quickly.

When I described my mystical experience to the servant-hearted Lutheran pastor whose preaching had led Mary into the knowledge that salvation comes by grace through faith in the Lord Jesus Christ, especially when I told him that I had been "born again" as the Lord answered my cry, he said, "Lyle, you now *understand* what God gave you in your baptism and confirmation." Looking back over the years, and seeing a continuous pattern of God's graciousness toward me, I acknowledge there is much to what he said. Nevertheless, I had no ears to hear it. Instead I did not like his response. When I argued that what happened to me was qualitatively so far greater than my baptism and confirmation experiences and that he did not know what he was saying, he urged me to read some theology because my ignorance and emotions clouded my understanding of those earlier experiences.

Although I did begin to read theology—studying a bit of Luther and talking to the pastor about various means of grace—I selfishly felt hurt and grew convinced I had been put down and misunderstood.

Craving fellowship with men who could resonate with my comprehension of a "new birth" experience, I found some like-minded friends in an Alcoholics Anonymous group. We had much fellowship, told AA visitors about the saving work of the Lord, and encouraged one another to remain sober and close to Jesus Christ.

Several of us "new birth" AA men found our way to a program called Bible Study Fellowship, founded several years earlier by A. Wetherell Johnson. I remained involved in BSF for three years, growing in knowledge of Scripture and getting an eye-opening education about the differences among regiments in God's army. Most of the BSF leaders I grew to know and love described themselves as Evangelicals. This was all new to me. Indeed, they made it clear that they were not Lutheran. Furthermore, they counseled against my forays into Lutheran theology. Instead they pointed me to John Calvin, and even beyond the Geneva reformer to dispensationalism of the Lewis Sperry Chafer and Dallas Theological Seminary premillennial variety.

Even though these labels and theological persuasions were new to me, they became a blessing because all these new terms and regimental identities demanded still more reading. During conversations with my Lutheran pastor, I inquired if he considered himself Calvinist or dispensationalist. After all, most of these new friends were "Reformed" in theology. Because Lutherans were certainly children of the Reformation, I assumed we were at least "Reformed." But I learned from the pastor that we were neither Reformed nor dispensationalist. We were Lutherans.

The more I talked to the Lutheran pastor and engaged in fascinating conversations with BSF leaders—some of whom were Presbyterians but most of whom were in Baptist or "Bible" churches—the more I realized that these regiments were each rather different. At minimum, their rhetoric concerning the atonement, means of grace, and last things were less than similar. My end of innocence about Christian traditions became at once disillusioning and educational. I was driven to Christian bookstores and the library at the University of Denver. And to my delight, I discovered the library at the Iliff School of Theology, the United Methodist Seminary that was located next to the University of Denver, which, at that time, maintained ties to the United Methodist Church. The Iliff library was open to me as a faculty member at the university. I frankly liked the idea that Iliff was Methodist, because my secular education in history had introduced me to John Wesley, and I greatly admired his concern for the poor and his strong antislavery stand.

In the meantime, I had begun to visit seminaries of different traditions to find a place to study and pursue ordination. But alas, I did not seem to fit anywhere. Many of the Lutherans saw the BSF folks and Evangelicals as "fundies"—their derisive label for fundamentalists. The Evangelicals, for their part, labeled the Lutherans and other sacramentalists as "liberals," and this meant they were nearly as bad as pagans. A tendency toward separation and exclusivity seemed strong in both camps, and particularly at one Presbyterian seminary I visited.

During the spring of 1980 two events conspired to bring clarity to my confusion. First, Mary insisted that inasmuch as I felt called to do the work of an evangelist, I should contact the Billy Graham Evangelistic Association for advice on how to get started. Doubtful that anyone in that large organization would answer my letter addressed "To Whom It May Concern," I explained my "conversion," my sense of calling to preach the gospel, as well as my ignorance of how to begin. To my utter surprise, a few days later Mr. John Dillon, the director of the Billy Graham Schools of Evangelism, called me. He urged Mary and me to attend Billy Graham's Crusade at Indianapolis in early May. He promised to give us a small stipend for travel, as well as free lodging during five days of meetings. Mr. Dillon said that Dr. Graham would be preaching each night, and during the day a School of Evangelism for pastors would be offered. And while neither Mary nor I were pastors, we would be welcome to attend. Additionally, Mr. Dillon pointed out that during the daytime sessions Billy Graham, Leighton Ford, and several evangelists would offer plenary sessions, and several seminary professors of evangelism would speak as well. Mr. Dillon was confident that we would find direction in Indianapolis.

The Billy Graham School of Evangelism proved to be every bit as helpful as Mr. Dillon predicted. Besides learning much from many speakers, we met Dr. Robert E. Coleman, author of dozens of important books, among them the widely read classic *The Master Plan of Evangelism*. Dr. Coleman's plenary message illumined my mind and warmed my heart, strongly confirming a call to preach. Also, his breakout session on the master plan of evangelism made clear the importance of making disciples—disciples who will reproduce their kind—rather than mere converts.

Having the opportunity to meet Dr. Coleman affected the direction of my calling and ministry from 1980 to the present. He became my mentor. His books and our one-to-one meetings over the years helped focus me on Jesus Christ and the methods he practiced. The Master's Plan of evangelism, discipleship, education, spiritual warfare, and prayer—just to mention a few—gradually became the core of my methods as a pastor, preacher, and teacher.

Dr. Coleman also helped me grapple with the theological confusion I experienced listening to the voices of Calvinists, Lutherans, dispensationalists, Pentecostals, Evangelicals (both charismatic and cessationist), as well as the Methodists I knew at the Iliff School of Theology. Coleman, I discovered, served as the McCreless Professor of Evangelism at Asbury Theological Seminary, an independent institution of Wesleyan-Arminian persuasion. Educated in a secular state university in Texas, he went on to earn master's degrees at both Princeton Theological Seminary and Asbury, and then a PhD in religion at the University of Iowa. When I asked him how well his Reformed (Princeton) and Wesleyan (Asbury) educations meshed, he said they complemented one another. He also stressed how important it is for an evangelist to avoid preaching a systematic theology. Instead the evangelist must lift up Christ and eschew entering into divisive theological debates. To be sure, a preacher must pick his regiment (Coleman did not use that term), because he needs to be ordained and for a host of other important reasons.

After several one-to-one sessions with Dr. Coleman, and in the wake of two opportunities to hear him give lectures, I decided to pursue ordination in the United Methodist Church. Coleman cautioned me to be very prayerful about this choice because not all Methodist bishops and pastors assume the inerrancy and inspiration of the Bible. This surprised me because my reading on Wesley suggested that the eighteenth-century evangelist boasted he was "a man of one book but a student of many."

To make a convoluted and long story brief, Mary and I joined a Methodist church in Boulder. The pastor took me under his wing and became my advocate as I pursued ordination. I went from sitting in on classes at Iliff to taking them for credit. And my ordination process in the Rocky Mountain Conference of the United Methodist Church began to move forward with deliberate speed.

Alas, the process came to a halt in 1983. One of my ordination committee members took me aside and said I needed to stop quoting Robert E. Coleman because neither he nor his seminary were well regarded in the Rocky Mountain Conference of the Methodist Church. Coleman, he argued, preaches and teaches doctrines of judgment and eternal damnation. Around the same time, my district superintendent, at the order of the bishop, insisted that all pastors instruct their churches that gay and lesbian lifestyles are not sinful and in fact are quite redemptive for many people. Then the seminary prohibited all use of what was described as "gender exclusive God-language." God could be not referred to as "he." Even Jesus Christ, who could be called "he" if referring to the historical Jesus, could not be labeled "he" if the writer or speaker was referring to the Messiah. At the seminary, I protested that it is heresy to lift up Jesus as anything less than fully God and man. I was informed that "some Christians" believe that, but those committed to love and unity do not.

Once again I came face-to-face with regimental warfare. There were, after all, unsaved people who needed to hear about Jesus Christ. To stay and argue with my fellow Methodists seemed unwise.

Mary and I decided that we were tired of Christian civil wars. Therefore we concluded we would plant our feet in the soil of "nondenominationalism."

⚹

In the spring of 1983, I was ordained by the elders of an independent, nondenominational church in Decano, Colorado. Then I was offered a position at Wheaton College in Illinois as professor of history and the curator of the Marion E. Wade Center, where the world's largest collection of C. S. Lewis materials is housed.

Soon after arriving in Wheaton, the Dorsett family joined College Church in Wheaton — one of the most prestigious and vibrant nondenominational churches in America. The senior pastor, Dr. Kent Hughes, became a dear friend. His preaching and friendship became second only to that of Dr. Coleman, who by this time had become director of the School of World Missions and Evangelism at Trinity Evangelical Divinity School in Deerfield, Illinois.

Fellowship with Dr. Hughes, unquestionably one of the most outstanding preachers in America, enriched our hearts and minds. Although I frequently filled pulpits on Sundays in a variety of churches in metro Chicago, I loved and served College Church as an adult Sunday school teacher. Occasionally Dr. Hughes invited me to preach, and I served a three-year term on the board of elders.

For twelve years Mary and I worshiped God at College Church in Wheaton. We prospered in that rich environment where the Bible was confidently taught as the inspired and inerrant Word of God. Refreshingly, the regimental battles were not fought there. Of course, College Church, like Wheaton College, stood in marked contradistinction to the growing liberal strain of Christianity in which the Bible was viewed as only one way to learn about God and what he requires of us. And to be sure, at College Church there were people with differing points of view. Many had Calvinist leanings, some claimed to be Wesleyan or Arminian, and there were people with varying millennial views. In the same vein, not everyone agreed on how the gifts of the Holy Spirit as set forth in 1 Corinthians and Romans were manifested today, if at all. It was encouraging, however, that people did not argue or divide over these issues.

For the most part, both College Church and Wheaton College brought glory to God by allowing some freedom within the perimeters of historic Evangelical orthodoxy. At College Church, infants were baptized or dedicated, depending upon the desire of parents. One pastor had a sacramental view of Holy Communion and always referred to it as a sacrament, whereas some other pastors on staff saw communion as a memorial service and referred to it as an ordinance. Hymns by Frederick Faber, Martin Luther, Edward Perronet, Charles Wesley, and Isaac Watts, as well as songs by Fanny Crosby, P. P. Bliss, Charlotte Elliott, and H. G. Spafford, were sung with gusto, and only occasionally did anyone complain about doctrinal emphases in the music. Generally speaking, these charitable nondenominationalists embraced these nonnegotiables:

1. The Bible is inspired and inerrant.
2. People are saved by grace through faith in the Lord Jesus Christ.
3. Salvation—whatever the length of the gestation period—is manifested by a new birth that will be evident in a life of piety and obedience to God.
4. Evangelistic and missionary zeal.
5. Demonstrating love for God by loving neighbors.

These essentials became the rallying point of unity; nonessentials such as the mode and age of baptism, and definitions about communion, called for liberty; and all things required charity. At least, this is the way I saw College Church and much of the nondenominational environment. The church also trained interns to become pastors and missionaries. And nearly fifty cents of every dollar went to home and foreign missions.

For twelve years I enjoyed this environment. This regiment of God's army became a place for growth and healing in contradistinction to the fratricidal battles Mary and I experienced in Colorado. Certainly, the nondenominational churches took a militant stand against creeping secularism and an increasingly militant and unbiblical drift in the old-line denominations, but Calvinists and Wesleyans, amillennialists, and pre- or postmillennialists were simply too busy doing evangelism and supporting missions to fight one another.

❧

In the mid-1990s, Mary and I together agreed that although we were being fed, befriended, and encouraged in our regiment, deep inside our souls we longed for "something more." It is not that we craved something new or novel. On the contrary, we gradually recognized that our longing was for something very old.

Throughout the period from 1983 to the early 1990s, we had made numerous trips to Great Britain and several journeys to continental Europe. Again, it was neither one thing nor a moment of crisis that changed us. Rather it was an accumulation of nudgings and illuminations that left us increasingly aware that despite the richness of our nondenominational experience, we craved more of what we frequently experienced while abroad. For instance, in either the Czech Republic or Slovakia, I can't remember which, there was a Protestant church with a relief sculpture that stood out in its simplicity. At the place where two arches converged, there was a sculpture of an open Bible upright behind a chalice. The thought "Word and Sacrament" immediately came to mind. It occurred to me that the early evangelists and missionaries, part of that ever-spreading flame that burned across the world, took Word *and* Sacrament to the uttermost parts of the earth.

The centrality of Holy Communion in the early centuries of the Church is unmistakable, from its institution by Jesus in Matthew 26:26–29 to the words of Saint Luke: "They continued steadfastly in the apostles' doctrine and fellowship, in the breaking of bread, and in prayers" (Acts 2:42 NKJV).[3] That something beyond a fellowship meal is taking place here gains credibility when keeping in mind that Saint Luke, in his gospel, points out that the Lord revealed himself in the breaking of bread (Luke 24:30–31) on the third evening after his crucifixion.[4]

This centrality of the Eucharist in worship becomes clear in the liturgies and practices of traditions maintaining that they are apostolic in origin. During our eight summers in Britain, we worshiped God each Sunday in a variety of regiments, including churches of England and Scotland, Baptist, Brethren, and the Salvation Army. It was in the Church of England where we began to experience more of what we were longing for. In the Anglican Church, the Nicene Creed was normally recited each Sunday. The phrase "one, holy, catholic, and apostolic church" took on significance as we said it each week. The Anglicans—at least the conservative ones like those found at St. Aldate's (Oxford), where Michael Green served as rector during much of our sojourn—saw themselves in apostolic succession and as part of *one*, holy, catholic, or universal, church. This apostolic and catholic fabric was manifested in the Scripture read and proclaimed, the creed recited, a time for confession of sin and absolution, and then the highest point of the worship service—the celebration of Holy Communion.

For us, St. Aldate's Anglican Church, across the road from Oxford University's Christ Church, the college attended by both John and Charles Wesley, became an oasis in the spiritual desert we found in so much of England. The "something more" we longed for became increasingly clear during each summer visit there. The Word was preached with fervor, as it was in College Church. But at St. Aldate's, we had Holy Communion every week, celebrated with the assurance that this sacrament was a means of grace, not simply an occasional act of obedience to an ordinance. Rather than just a memorial service—although it was that—it was much more. "Christ has died, Christ is risen, Christ will come again" became the proclamation of our past, present, and future unity with the Lord Jesus Christ.

In St. Aldate's Anglican Church, where Dr. J. I. Packer experienced his personal conversion on Sunday, October 22, 1944,[5] we began to "taste and see that the LORD is good" (Ps. 34:8 ESV). We also liked the fact that this Anglican regiment eschewed chronological snobbery and unashamedly carried on the apostolic tradition, including the teaching of the apostles, and a laying on of hands for ordination that could be traced back to the apostles.

We felt connection to Christ and the historic church, and we enjoyed being part of the universal church of international scope. Anglicans have local churches in thirty-eight provinces throughout the world.

⁂

Even when we were back in America, I sensed a pull to the ancient, catholic, and apostolic church's Anglican regiment. I became seriously interested in John Wesley because he still towers as one of the greatest evangelists and disciple makers of all time. The Wesley brothers were ordained in the Anglican Church and remained communicating members until their deaths. My study of John Wesley's journals, as well as his sermons, letters, and papers on a variety of subjects, convinced me that the Anglican tradition has deep roots in the ancient church. Reading Wesley introduced me to the ante-Nicene church fathers, making it clear that the Wesleyan wing of Anglicanism had been nurtured by the likes of Polycarp, Irenaus, and Ignatius of Antioch, as well as Augustine and the sixteenth-century continental reformers. This side of Anglicanism also drew upon the eighteenth-century German Pietists, providing a balancing complement to Anglicans like George Whitefield, who imbibed deeply from the fountains of John Knox, John Calvin, and the Puritans.

If my growing interest in Anglicanism came from visits to Oxford and increasingly careful study of the Wesley brothers and Whitefield, it was markedly influenced by the life and writing of C. S. Lewis.

As mentioned earlier, Lewis's apologetic works were signposts on my journey back to Christ while a young professor at the University of Denver. But this proved to be a mere prelude to his influence on my spiritual formation and ultimate selection of the Anglican regiment in which to live and serve.

In 1983 I published a biography of C. S. Lewis's wife, Helen Joy Davidman.[6] Research for this book took me to England, Scotland, Wales, and Northern Ireland to conduct oral history interviews. Eventually I interviewed approximately four dozen people who knew Lewis well. Among these folks were Lewis's relatives, including his stepson, Douglas Gresham, and many of Lewis's friends, former students, and people associated with him in diverse capacities.

Besides interviewing over forty people and corresponding with many others, I also had the privilege of reading somewhere between two thousand and three thousand letters that Lewis wrote to friends, fans of his books, and spiritually hungry people who sought his counsel. As a consequence of researching the story of Joy Davidman, I necessarily studied the life of the famous writer. All this research led me to write a book on Lewis himself. Essentially, it is a spiritual biography titled *Seeking the Secret Place: The Spiritual Formation of C. S. Lewis.*[7]

Research for this book spanned at least a decade. As a result, I became a serious student of Lewis's writing and spiritual formation. Lewis himself once said that people should be careful what they read. In the same vein that Professor Lewis read deeply in sixteenth-century English literature as an agnostic, only to discover that most all of his favorite authors were Christians, so I began to see that many of my favorite theologians and Christian leaders of past centuries were Anglicans.[8] Among these are C. S. Lewis, Dorothy L. Sayers, J. I. Packer, John Stott, Charles Simeon, and G. K. Chesterton (until the last decade of his life).

Several friends who encouraged my pilgrimage to know Christ better and love him more also pointed to the richness of the historic Anglican tradition by simply talking about their own journeys. Dr. Thomas Howard, one of the most insightful students of the writings of Lewis, shared ideas on several occasions. And during a conference where both of us were reading papers on the celebrated English author, Howard conveyed his personal delight in how the liturgy and the colors, signs, symbols, and vestments employed by the Anglican Church led him to Anglicanism from the Brethren tradition.

The late Robert Webber, a colleague at Wheaton College and the author of numerous books on the history and practice of Christian worship, agreed to have lunch and talk about evangelism. He believed that all churches should be evangelistic—even on Sunday morning. What Webber said that set my thoughts in a new direction was this: "The most seeker-friendly thing a pastor can do on Sunday morning is celebrate Holy Communion by using the Anglican liturgy." This statement astounded me, and at first blush I disagreed. But the irenic Webber said that if a preacher merely offers an invitation to come to Christ at the end of every sermon, and especially if he has twisted his explication of the text to make it evangelistic, he might actually put off listeners. On the other hand, when he celebrates Holy Communion, the gospel is clearly presented.

In the wake of that conversation, I necessarily admitted that mere human efforts to win souls to Christ were unbiblical. Many of my own efforts during evangelistic meetings and one-to-one witnessing encounters were replete with my own passion and arguments. Over the years, I saw the fruitlessness of such tactics, after observing folk fall away when someone more persuasive than I argued them to a different place. Webber caused me to acknowledge the significance of Christ's own words: "I, if I am lifted up from the earth, will draw all *peoples* to myself" (John 12:32 NKJV). Of course, Jesus is pointing here to his crucifixion, but it is also true that when Jesus and what he has done for us are lifted up in the eucharistic liturgy, he draws sinners to himself. "Other sheep I have which are not of this fold; them also I must bring, and they will hear My voice" (John 10:16 NKJV). "When He [the Holy Spirit] has come, He will convict the world of sin, and of righteousness, and of judgment" (John 16:8 NKJV).

The efficacy of trusting Jesus and the work of the Holy Spirit to prepare hearts to hear the gospel, and my growing confidence in pointing to Christ through the natural flow of the communion liturgy, as well as in biblical, Christ-honoring sermons, caused me to develop a close relationship with another man. As the curator of the Marion E. Wade Center, I inherited an advisory board. Father William Beasley, rector of the Episcopal Church of the Resurrection in

West Chicago, served on the board. We became good friends, and occasionally I accepted his invitations to preach on Sunday or speak at one of his church's midweek services.

Eventually, Father William asked me to consider joining him as an unpaid assistant to help with the college students who increasingly crowded his small church building. I acknowledged the attractiveness of his offer but firmly refused. I told William that I had pursued ordination in one denomination that had changed John Wesley's quadrilateral of Scripture, reason, experience, and Tradition—with the Bible as the base—and turned it into an equilateral where experience, reason, and Tradition could trump the Bible whenever challenges arose in regard to what God requires of us. Therefore I would never again formally join a denomination where I had to debate what ought to be assumed.

Some months later Father William Beasley left the Episcopal Church USA. He handed the keys to the parsonage and sanctuary to his bishop who refused to make Scripture the basis for faith and conduct. Soon after this courageous act emboldened other clergy in the upper Midwest and other parts of the nation to stop serving under apostate bishops, William came and asked Mary and me if we would consider helping him minister in his rented worship facility where hundreds of people—including many college students—were flocking for Word and Sacrament, as well as healing prayer. He only half-jokingly said, "Lyle, you know John Wesley would love our church. We stand on the foundation of Scripture but apply reason, Tradition, and experience. And like Wesley, we are purposively evangelistic with a heart for the wounded and poor."

I liked that touch, and furthermore, Mary had been visiting Beasley's "renegade" Episcopal church when she could be free to do so. Mary received deep blessing from the liturgy, the weekly celebration of Holy Communion, and a strong sense of Christ's real presence. She was being fed, as C. S. Lewis put it when describing communion, because "a hand from the hidden country touches not only my soul but my body ... [T]he veil between the worlds ... is nowhere else so thin and permeable to divine operation."[9] Beyond the sacrament, the pastor and the congregation manifested faith in the real presence of the transcendent God among his people.[10]

Because Mary found "something more" at Father Beasley's new Church of the Resurrection, I too visited from time to time. On one

Sunday when Mary was out of town, I quietly slipped into the back of the congregation to worship. After going forward for Holy Communion, I sought out a prayer minister and asked for anointing with oil and prayer for a gimpy knee I had injured years before but had rather severely reinjured the day before. Although no instantaneous change came to my knee, my soul was strangely warmed by a keen sense of God's presence in the prayer of a saintly woman for my healing. At home several hours later, a sensation like electrical charges began to course through the lame knee. Suddenly the tingle in the knee became warm. I cautiously stood up, moved my leg, and enjoyed total healing. To this day, the knee that had been intermittently painful for decades in the wake of a football injury has felt like new.

⚒

Mary and I continued to seek God's guidance, and soon after the healing, we realized that both of us were closer to the "something more" we had been craving for years. Much of our longing found fulfillment in the "real presence" of Holy Communion as taught and celebrated by Anglicans. This is not transubstantiation as claimed by the Catholic Church. In fact, leaders of the Anglican Reformation, in the Articles of Religion, specifically refute this doctrine of transubstantiation. Instead most Anglicans are taught that Holy Communion celebrates Christ's Spirit as "really present" in ordinary bread and wine as explained by Richard Hooker in the late 1500s. His view has been embraced by most Anglicans, including C. S. Lewis, down through the centuries.[11]

The Blessed Sacrament, plus the visual richness accompanying worship with an historic liturgy composed of Scripture and prayer, more fully tied us to the ancient creedal tradition for which we longed. Certainly, involvement with several other clergy and laypeople seeking fellowship in similar Anglican-style churches also brought much joy. But neither of us became fully satisfied until we found Episcopal oversight from conservative, Bible-based Anglican bishops in Rwanda and Singapore.[12] What we had lacked was a truly Anglican connection to the global communion among the thirty-eight provinces across the world. Until that point, as long as we were without that Episcopal connection, we remained nondenominational churches, albeit markedly closer to historic Anglicanism. This problem of connection and episcopacy was eventually solved when oversight for our congregation was provided by the Anglican Province of Rwanda.

This Episcopal oversight from the Global South finally brought us home. Now we were fully tethered globally and historically to the great creedal tradition with its deep roots in an ancient church and tradition that included the Protestant Reformation, to be sure, but also the ante-Nicene church.

⁂

Looking back over the grace upon grace bestowed upon Mary and me from the days of our marriage and through each of our calls "to surrender to Christ as Lord and Savior," it is no coincidence that we began to yearn for "something more" at about the same time. In the same vein, it is significant that we both found completion in the Anglican Mission in the Americas (AMiA).

In summary, we found that the best regiment for us, where we can abide, serve, and find fellowship, is in the AMiA. The historic Anglican tradition not only anchors us to the ancient Great Tradition; it gives us a place where we can worship God in three streams: Spirit, Word, and Sacrament. In the stream of the Holy Spirit, we have the freedom to be unapologetically charismatic, where all of the gifts set forth in 1 Corinthians 12–14 and Romans 12 complement one another to build up a strong body of people who grow in Christ within a worshipful environment where we expect to meet our transcendent God. For us, the Word stream means that we are a Bible-based community. The daily office in our prayer book invites the Church to read from the Bible daily. Here the Scripture is read and speaks for itself inasmuch as no sermon or homily is required. Beyond the daily office, our Book of Common Prayer contains a lectionary. And from this our churches gather each Sunday and hear four readings from Scripture, including texts from the Old Testament, Psalter, Epistles, and Gospels. The Word, of course, is not only read; it is proclaimed. The third stream is Sacrament. This stream ensures that we meet Christ not only in the gifts of the people and in Scripture read and preached but also in the blessed sacrament of communion.

Like the nondenominational regiment where we were so wonderfully blessed, we Anglican Mission people are decidedly Evangelical and therefore strongly committed to evangelism and missions. Indeed, the AMiA is an African mission to reach the unchurched people of North America, and we North Americans are privileged to be part of it. And beyond these blessings, we are part of an extended family of Anglicans in almost every country around the globe. In fact, as J. I. Packer has often explained, we Anglicans are at once local, national, and worldwide. Likewise, we Anglicans are episcopal. The Bible in no way requires episcopal polity for churches, but it clearly presents this as an effective way to keep church order and protect people from heresy and disorder. For my part, as an ordained Anglican priest, I welcome the oversight of a godly bishop. As a child of America's individualistic culture, for too long I eschewed boundaries. I needed to submit to Bible-based authority, and I thank God for my bishop, who is a pastor to us otherwise pastorless shepherds who need nurture and accountability.

Finally, I feel at home in the Anglican tradition because historically it has been the *via media* that emerged from the English Reformation. It is a middle way between the austerity of some radical Puritans who determined to cleanse the Church from all "vestiges of popery," going so far as to call for the abolition of everything not expressly required in the Bible, and the Catholics on the other hand who placed Tradition and the Church above Scripture to an extreme where they promulgated some doctrines that stand in contradistinction to Holy Writ. It was Richard Hooker who most thoughtfully expressed the need for a via media. He synthesized the best of the past with the clarifying insights of the English Reformation in his important book *The Laws of Ecclesiastical Polity*, published in England during the late 1500s.

Anglicanism is often criticized for not having a systematic theology like the Presbyterians with John Calvin's *Institutes* and the Westminster Confession. We do, however, have the Articles of Religion that provide perimeters for our faith. To be sure, they do not provide a systematic theology, but they do specify the via media where we stand between radical Puritanism and Roman Catholicism. Peter C. Moore put it well in *A Church to Believe In*: "The essential contribution of the Anglican way is found in its distinction between things essential and things indifferent. The Anglican watchwords are unity, diversity, and charity: 'unity in essentials, diversity in nonessentials, and charity in all things.'" Moore goes on to say that "[t]he Anglican Church sees itself as a church that majors in the majors, and minors in the minors."[13]

Bishop John Jewell (1522–71) served as Richard Hooker's mentor. He argued that the Anglican Reformation called for a return to the standards of Christ Jesus, the apostles, and early fathers—the "faith once believed" that had been distorted by the medieval church. And as Moore wrote, "By the same token, Anglicanism's historic critique of many of the post-Reformation churches is that they neglect the core of the Apostolic tradition by stressing their own particular emphases."[14]

Anglicanism embraces diversity within the boundaries of historic Evangelical orthodoxy. And this is at once its strength and its weakness. This regiment where Mary and I worship is far from flawless. Like all other regiments, it has factions that are prone to wander from the great tradition, "the faith that was once for all delivered to the saints" (Jude 3 ESV). Nevertheless, this is where I will abide and serve until our Lord returns and unites his bride that too often, alas, fails to bring him glory.

CHAPTER 11

✄

A RESPONSE TO ANGLICANISM

Robert A. Peterson

My assignment differs from that of other respondents in this volume. It is my task to respond not to Eastern Orthodoxy or Roman Catholicism but to a fellow Protestant tradition—Anglicanism.[1] Readers have a right to ask about my vantage point and attitude toward Christian traditions other than my own, so here is a previously published description of my religious identity: "Some questions have more than one correct answer. If I were asked to describe my religious identity, I could give four correct answers: 'I am a Christian, a Protestant, an Evangelical, and a Presbyterian.' All four are true. I am a Christian, not a Hindu, a Buddhist, or a Muslim. I am a Protestant Christian, not a Roman Catholic or Orthodox Christian. I am an Evangelical Christian, not a liberal one. I am a Presbyterian, not an Episcopalian, a Lutheran, or a Baptist. Furthermore, not all of these designations are equally important to me. Being a Christian is more important to me than being a Protestant, which is more important than being an Evangelical, which is more important than being a Presbyterian."[2]

Given that description, readers will not be surprised to learn that I have more to appreciate in the Anglican tradition than I have to critique. So first I will appreciate and then, in light of the appreciation, I will respectfully critique.

THINGS I APPRECIATE ABOUT ANGLICANISM
It Respects the Church Fathers

Though some Christians today are rediscovering the church fathers, too many lack a sense of history, especially when it comes to the early church. Anglicanism has a deep sense of history because of, among other things, its adherence to the two most ancient Christian creeds and its scholarship on the church fathers. C. F. Allison, writing on Anglican communion in the *Evangelical Dictionary of Theology*, explains, "The Nicene and Apostles' creeds are accepted as confessing the faith of Scripture and classical Christianity."[3] This is so much the case that when Anglican bishops met in Chicago in 1886, seeking to list fundamental points which all non-Catholic Christians in America could accept, their first two points were: "(a) The Holy Scriptures of the Old and New Testament, as 'containing all things necessary to salvation,' and as being the rule and ultimate standard of faith; (b) The Apostles' Creed, as the Baptismal Symbol; and the Nicene Creed, as the sufficient statement of the Christian faith."[4]

In addition, Anglicans have excelled in the study of the church fathers. According to *The Oxford Dictionary of the Christian Church*, "Anglican scholars have been in the forefront of historical and patristic studies."[5] A standard Roman Catholic theological encyclopedia agrees: "There has always been among Anglicans a sense of the continuity of the Church, and a considerable devotion to patristic studies."[6] Representative noteworthy Anglican scholars, past and present, with significant publications in the field of patristics include J. B. Lightfoot, James Bethune-Baker, Frank L. Cross, J. N. D. Kelly, and G. R. Evans.

Its Roots Are Reformational

Gerald Bray, in a candid essay titled "Why I Am an Anglican," admits the difficulty of defining his own Anglican communion, which includes persons characterized as high church (descendents of Anglo-Catholics), low church (Evangelicals), and broad church (those in between). He does, however, point to some distinguishing features. Anglicanism has a hierarchy of bishops, as do Catholic and Eastern Orthodox churches, but unlike them, it is not defined by that hierarchy. The archbishop of Canterbury is viewed by many as a key figure, but he is not even the head of his own Church of England; that role falls to the monarch. Bray continues, "Most Anglican churches subscribe to the Thirty-nine Articles of Religion, which were passed by the Church of England in 1563, but not all of them do and there are many

Anglicans for whom the Articles are a dead letter."[7] He also points to the 1662 Book of Common Prayer, to which we will return later.

The Thirty-nine Articles, produced by Thomas Cranmer and a few associates and revised early in Elizabeth I's reign (1558–1603), are, in Bray's words, "a remarkably concise expression of Anglican doctrine. They are particularly impressive when we remember that at that time, they were the most systematic attempt to express Protestant teaching then available. They were never intended to be a comprehensive exposition of theology, but they point the way to the sources of Christian teaching in a clear and effective manner. For example, they list the canonical books of Scripture in a way that had not been done before, despite the Protestant insistence on *sola scriptura*, and they lay down the important Anglican principle that whatever cannot be proved from the Bible must not be imposed on the church as its doctrine."[8]

There is much here to commend, and all churches would do well to establish themselves upon sound theological principles ensconced in doctrinal statements. But, as I will show in the critique section, this doctrinal base has not kept some Anglicans from drifting from biblical faith and ethics.

It Is Worldwide

"At the beginning of the twenty-first century, Anglicans numbered approximately 73 million and were found in 167 countries as members of 38 national or regional churches. Numerically speaking, the largest of the churches in Anglicanism remains the Church of England, with over 20 million members."[9] This number, though technically correct, is misleading, because the active membership of the Church of England is around 1 million. By contrast, the active members of the Anglican Church of Nigeria number anywhere from 11 million to 17 million. Indeed, the center of the Anglican Church has shifted dramatically, so that "today more Anglicans (approximately 37 million or close to 50 percent of the global Anglican community) live in Africa south of the Sahara than in any other part of the world."[10]

Its Worship Is Beautiful

While admittedly worship is heading in various directions today, many Evangelicals desire more liturgy and beauty in worship services.

And for some of them, this means a turn to Rome or one of the Orthodox churches. From its inception, Anglicanism has fostered beautiful worship through its Book of Common Prayer. Tom Phillips, the man who led me to Christ over forty years ago, was a Baptist attending what was then called Reformed Episcopal Seminary in Philadelphia, a school with a high view of Scripture and an emphasis on Reformed theology. Tom, like most of the students, did not belong to the Reformed Episcopal Church, but, again like most, developed an appreciation for the Scripture-saturated devotion of the Book of Common Prayer.

With roots in the work of Cranmer and associates, the Book of Common Prayer may be the single most identifiable symbol of Anglicanism. Gerald Bray's high regard for it comes through in these words:

> The pattern of worship provided by the Book of Common Prayer is a model of balance in a field fraught with the dangers of succumbing to the excesses of personal taste. The BCP provides daily services for morning and evening prayer, as well as a rite of Holy Communion explicitly designed to teach the doctrine of salvation by grace through faith alone. It is reverent without being superstitious and comprehensive without being exhaustive (or exhausting). Those who have had to sit through the seemingly endless prayers of pastors who say whatever comes into their head and who end up repeating themselves over and over again have every reason to be grateful for Thomas Cranmer's remarkable economy of words and mastery of English style. There is nothing to compare to the elegant simplicity of classical Anglican worship. Furthermore, virtually every word in the Prayer Book comes from the Bible; in a very real sense, it is the Scriptures turned into devotion.[11]

Its Evangelical Scholars Have Taught Me Much

My first encounter with the Anglican communion was with James Pain, my doctoral mentor. Dr. Pain was a gentleman, deeply versed in Scripture, a solid Evangelical with an encyclopedic knowledge of historical theology, and a shepherd and trusted friend to students of all theological orientations. I am thankful to Jim for his role in shaping me as a historical and systematic theologian.

I have many Anglican scholars to thank, more than I have space to list. J. I. Packer helped me early on in my Christian development, with his *Fundamentalism and the Word of God* and *Knowing God*. He has continued to help me personally by kindly writing forewords, recommendations, and chapters for books I have written or edited. John Stott's writings strengthened my faith, and I continue to use *The Cross of Christ* as required reading in my systematics course, Christ and Salvation. My longest research interest has been on the atonement, and no one taught me more than Leon Morris, who wrote at least four books on the subject.

Philip Hughes's commentaries on 2 Corinthians and Hebrews benefitted me, and *The True Image: The Origin and Destiny of Man in Christ* was featured in my latest writing project, a book on the work of Christ. I am indebted to Gerald Bray for the outstanding theology series that he edits, IVP's Contours of Christian Theology, and especially for his contribution to the series, *The Doctrine of God*. I value Peter T. O'Brien's commentaries on Colossians, Philippians, and Hebrews. Many Evangelicals, including me, have learned from N. T. Wright and Christopher Wright. I could list many more but will stop, for I have made my point—Anglican Evangelicals have made significant contributions to scholarship and have taught me much.

A CRITIQUE OF ANGLICANISM

Writing part 1 of this essay was more enjoyable than writing part 2. But to complete my assignment, I must critique Anglicanism. There is much for an Evangelical Presbyterian to appreciate in the Anglican communion, but there are also things with which I disagree, sometimes seriously.

Its Doctrinal Latitude

It is true that the Thirty-nine Articles of Religion and the Book of Common Prayer are foundational to Anglicanism and that they still exert positive influence wherever they are used. The problem is that in many places they are not used. Combine that neglect with the Anglican commitment to openness, and big theological and ethical problems can arise. Do not misunderstand me; that openness is both a strength and a weakness. It is a strength in that it counters a doctrinaire spirit which snipes at others for the slightest departure from a particular theology. Indeed, part of me resonates with the Anglican "flavor," expressed well by Bray: "Concentrating on the essentials, affirming what needs to be affirmed, denying what needs to be denied and leaving the rest open to individual conviction has always been the hallmark of true Anglicanism, and when these principles have been observed, they have helped Anglicans maintain the preaching and teaching ministry that Christ gave his disciples."[12]

However, the weakness of this stance is that it sometimes has led to openness to false teaching on major matters. Plainly, some of the Church's leaders and scholars have denied Christian essentials, with disastrous results. Once more, Bray is candid: "It is also sadly true that the Anglican communion harbors openly heretical elements that are difficult to expunge, precisely because of this extraordinary tolerance. But people like David Jenkins (the former bishop of Durham who denied the bodily resurrection of Christ) and John Shelby Spong (the retired bishop of Newark, New Jersey, who has denied almost everything) come and go, rattling a few cages during their brief time in the spotlight and then disappearing into eternal darkness. The church will survive them as it has survived countless others in the past who have done similar things."[13]

Every Church has problems, and mine — the Presbyterian Church in America — is no exception. But some problems are more serious than others, and some strike at the vitals of the Christian religion. My own communion, and many other conservative denominations, would not tolerate Jenkins or Spong; they would be censured and, if not repentant of their heresies, excommunicated. And this is as it should be, for Scripture warns the Church not to abide heresies and their proponents (Gal. 1:6–9; Titus 3:10–11; 2 Peter 2:1–3; 1 John 4:1–6; 2 John 10). A spirit of Christian love and openness is one thing; allowing heretics to remain as teachers in the Church is another.

In 1999, *The Encyclopedia of Christianity* listed the main theological problems of the Anglican Church as "the ordination of women (only in November 1992 did the Church of England decide to ordain women), the practice of baptism, confirmation and admission to the Eucharist, divorce and remarriage, and Christology (for example, the conflict in England in 1977 over John Hick's *The Myth of God Incarnate*)."[14] It is the last matter that has caused much concern.

The Myth of God Incarnate, edited by John Hick, raised the hackles of many Christians in Great Britain. And rightly so! This well-publicized book had contributions from (along with three others) liberal Anglican scholars including Michael Goulder, Leslie Houlden, Dennis Nineham, and Maurice Wiles—Regius Professor of Divinity, canon of Christ Church, Oxford, and chairman of the Church of England's Doctrine Commission. It maintains that "'orthodoxy' is a myth, which can and often does inhibit the creative thinking which Christianity sorely needs today."[15] What do they mean by the "orthodoxy" that they reject as outmoded? The contributors answer frankly, "[T]he later conception of him [Jesus] as God incarnate, the Second Person of the Holy Trinity living a human life." This they regard as "a mythological or poetic way of expressing his significance for us."[16]

The Myth of God Incarnate disturbed many Christians and quickly precipitated *The Truth of God Incarnate*, edited by Michael Green with contributions from other Evangelical Anglicans. Amazingly, this book was published in the same year as the book it opposed. The preface to this volume does not disguise the reason for its title: "If it seems to you that the title of the present book might owe something to the S.C.M. title *[The Myth of God Incarnate]*, you are quite right."[17] What specifically prompted such an immediate reply on the part of Evangelical Anglicans? The preface answers frankly: "We believe that it is high time for those who do not accept a reductionist Christology to stand up and be counted. We believe that the presuppositions behind the current skepticism are not compelling, and that the implications of it are very far-reaching and corroding. And we believe that a response from a variety of theological and cultural backgrounds such as we represent will sufficiently show that a repudiation of the sort of position most recently evidenced in *The Myth of God Incarnate* is not the concern of a mere conservative backlash, but is broadly based in the Church."[18]

I am grateful for these Evangelical Anglicans courageous enough to enter the fray and defend the faith. But I lament that the false teachers are allowed to continue as ordained ministers and professors in good standing in their Church. Where is church discipline?

Its Role of Bishops

My first problem with Anglicanism is much more important than the second. But I am committed to Presbyterian church government and not a church hierarchy where bishops are over pastors. Now, I do not think that Scripture commands any specific form of church government, but I regard elder rule as most in accord with biblical teaching on the Church and with the general tenor of Scripture (Acts 20:17, 28; 1 Tim. 3:1 – 7; Titus 1:5 – 9). In 1958 the Lambeth Conference, a meeting approximately every ten years of bishops the world over at which the archbishop of Canterbury presides, declared with reference to relations with Presbyterians, "It must be recognized as a fact that Anglicans conscientiously hold that the celebrant of the Eucharist should have been ordained by a bishop standing in historic succession and generally believe it to be their duty to bear witness by receiving Holy Communion only from those who have thus been ordained."[19]

I acknowledge the early references in church history to presiding bishops (for example, in the epistles of Ignatius of Antioch), but in the end Scripture trumps Tradition.

COMMENTS ON LYLE DORSETT'S ESSAY

I was assigned not only to write a freestanding piece on Anglicanism but also to comment specifically on Lyle Dorsett's essay. Before reading his essay, I knew that he had been a professor at Wheaton College and curator of the Marion E. Wade Center that houses the world's largest collection of C. S. Lewis materials. Although I had never met him, I felt as if I almost knew him. This was because in my years at Covenant Seminary, I have taught Wheaton College graduates who studied under him. Uniformly, they spoke highly of his scholarship but even more highly of his godly character.

Lyle and I have more in common than not. We agree attitudinally, concerning the unity of the Christian church, that we are to "welcome one another as Christ has welcomed" us (Rom. 15:7 ESV). Lyle wrote, "It is in a spirit of camaraderie with brothers and sisters of all traditions of God's army who want to fight the good fight and finish the race that I explain and celebrate my own choice of a regiment."

It is not surprising that Lyle agrees with me concerning the strengths of Anglicanism! I am glad that he does not leave out Mary, his wife, but mentions her often as his partner in life and worship. He appreciates the fact that in most Anglican churches, the Nicene Creed is recited each Sunday. His experience of Anglican worship has left him and Mary "more fully tied ... to the ancient creedal tradition for which we longed." He also appreciates the Reformational roots of his new faith tradition (as I do mine): "Now we were fully tethered globally and historically to the great creedal tradition with its deep roots in an ancient church and tradition that included the Protestant Reformation, to be sure, but also the ante-Nicene church." And he specifically mentioned "the Articles of Religion that provide perimeters for our faith."

Lyle and Mary "enjoyed being part of the universal church of international scope." They are thankful to be "part of an extended family of Anglicans in almost every country around the globe."

Perhaps the greatest treasure that the Dorsetts have discovered is in worship. "Like other elements of Anglicanism, the liturgy, vestments, colors, and symbols began to bless me." There is no doubt that Lyle and Mary regard "the highest point of the worship service [as the] celebration of Holy Communion." Indeed, "much of our longing found fulfillment in the 'real presence' of Holy Communion as taught and celebrated by Anglicans."

Like me, Lyle has a deep appreciation for the instruction he received from Evangelical Anglican scholars. His list includes Charles Simeon, G. K. Chesterton, C. S. Lewis, Michael Green (under whose preaching he sat), J. I. Packer, and Dorothy L. Sayers.

It is important to me that Lyle shares my criticism of Anglican toleration of heresy within its ranks, so much so that he joined the international Anglican communion, in the Episcopal Province of Rwanda, rather than the more theologically liberal American Episcopal Church. He was resolved not to serve "under apostate bishops." "But neither of us became fully satisfied until we found Episcopal oversight from conservative, Bible-based Anglican bishops in Rwanda and Singapore." This was a temporary remedy, however, and the "problem of connection and episcopacy was eventually solved when [permanent] oversight ... was provided by the Anglican Province of Rwanda." It needs to be said that the extension of this province to the United States was precipitated by the American Episcopal Church's unprecedented action of ordaining as bishop Gene Robinson, an openly gay man living with another man. I am glad that Lyle's church and mine would not condone such an action.

Even in the matter of church government, where Lyle and I agree to disagree, he shares my opinion that no system of church government is demanded by Scripture. We part ways, however, when it comes to the role of bishops. "The Bible in no way requires episcopal polity for churches, but it clearly presents this as an effective way to keep church order and protect people from heresy and disorder. For my part, as an ordained Anglican priest, I welcome the oversight of a godly bishop." For my part, as an ordained teaching elder in the Presbyterian Church in America, I welcome the oversight and protection of my fathers and brothers in the Missouri Presbytery and our annual general assembly.

I am grateful for this opportunity to be blessed by the testimony of so godly a man and woman. I pray that I might evaluate my own faith tradition with the candor and honesty with which they do theirs: "Anglicanism embraces diversity within the boundaries of historic Evangelical orthodoxy. And this is at once its strength and its weakness. This regiment where Mary and I worship is far from flawless. Like all other regiments, it has factions that are prone to wander from the great tradition, 'the faith that was once for all delivered to the saints' (Jude 3 ESV)."

CHAPTER 12

✣

ANGLICANISM REJOINDER

Lyle W. Dorsett

I like Robert Peterson's charitable spirit. He writes, "I have more to appreciate in the Anglican tradition than I have to critique." Because I similarly acknowledge that my affinity for the Presbyterian tradition is much greater than my disagreements with it, he and I share common ground. It is clear, in the face of growing worldwide attacks on Christians and Christianity in the early twenty-first century, that our enemy is far greater than our differences. Nevertheless, Peterson points out one area of Anglicanism that he finds especially problematic. Although he acknowledges the great merit of the Anglican Book of Common Prayer and the Articles of Religion, he correctly notes that some provinces in the international Anglican communion turn a blind eye toward false teachers among the clergy—even within the ranks of bishops. Peterson rightly criticizes the Episcopal Church in the United States of America (ECUSA) for failing to excommunicate or discipline heretics. While he acknowledges that my province (Rwanda) is doctrinally sound, he bemoans the absence of discipline in some provinces.

While I agree that the ECUSA, the Church of Canada, and several other Anglican provinces tolerate heresy, I fail to see how this differs from the larger tent of Presbyterianism. While Peterson's Presbyterian Church of America (PCA) denomination, like my Rwandan province, is sound, his Reformed tradition under the wider umbrella of Presbyterianism has plenty of biblically errant clergy. In brief, both Peterson and I are comfortable in conservative enclaves of our respective traditions; however, we both are ministering within wider traditions where the corrosive effects of liberalism and modernism are markedly apparent.

It seems appropriate to reflect upon the rapid growth of the PCA and the Anglican Mission in the Americas (AMiA). Both of these regiments of God's army are experiencing rapid growth, while regiments like the Presbyterian Church (U.S.A.) and ECUSA are losing numbers. AMiA and PCA churches are gaining members, and new churches are continually being planted. The causes of these healthy developments are manifold, but some factors are particularly instructive. Some growth in these relatively new manifestations of historic traditions has been inspired by responsible, biblical evangelism. And much expansion is the result of spiritually alert and healthy Christians who choose to live rather than atrophy in necrotic church environments. It needs to be noted that sheep stealing is not what is going on here. On the contrary, healthy sheep are choosing to leave and find healthy folds in their own historic traditions where they can prosper. To the point, the Anglican and Presbyterian communions where Peterson and I serve are attracting all ages of people who have made prayerful and thoughtful decisions to find pastors who are undershepherds of the Great Shepherd — pastors who can be trusted to feed their flocks on Scripture, Holy Communion, and Living Water.

In the final analysis, I pray that both the PCA and the AMiA will remain unyieldingly committed to the authority of the whole counsel of Scripture without becoming prideful and separatistic. The pressures are great to pull us either to the far left or to the far right. We are not called to seek some Aristotelian golden mean, but we must strive to remain in the center of biblical truth. My prayer is that Robert and I can encourage one another to speak, live, and teach biblical truth, but always in love. *Soli Deo gloria.*

CONCLUSION

✣

Robert L. Plummer

W hat if someone reads your book and converts to Catholicism?" my wife asked.

I hesitated to answer. The question touched a raw theological nerve. As originator and editor of the book, I had a duty to make sure all contributors said what they wanted to say as well as they could. On the other hand, as a committed Evangelical theologian, I had personal sympathies in the discussion which were impossible to ignore.

Could my book encourage some readers to embrace a theological tradition that, if given the opportunity, I would personally discourage them from pursuing? The question continued to trouble me. I discussed the matter with a colleague, who noted that Evangelicals are going to either help set the terms of this discussion or simply react to others. Personally, I'd rather help make sure all sides have a fair hearing. Moreover, going back at least to the Reformation, Christians have a long history of publishing academic disputes of this sort. This genre of writing should be understood as in no way implying a contributor's approval of anyone's views except those explicitly expressed by him. Indeed, most contributors to this book see themselves as disagreeing on fundamentally irreconcilable issues. Is the pope the rightful head of the Christian church? Is justification a forensic declaration? Is it appropriate, or even commendable, to use icons in Christian worship? Is special grace communicated to participants in the Lord's Supper, and if so, in what way?

People often find that for which they search. Yet what would I like for readers to take with them from this book? I can think of several things:

1. I hope readers are able to recognize with greater sympathy the complex motivations which influence conversions to other Christian traditions.

2. I want readers who are struggling with the desire to leave their tradition to feel both more understood and, in many cases, more hesitant.

3. I hope that all Christians would find in this volume a model of peaceable ecumenical dialogue. People who claim Jesus as Lord should be able to disagree before a nonbelieving world without denying the love for others we profess marks us as Christians (John 13:34–35).

In closing, it is fitting for me to express gratitude to the writers contributing to this volume. Most of the men who agreed to write for this book are well-known and busy public figures. Yet they saw the value in having this timely public conversation.

And—to the reader—it is my hope that as a result of having read this book, you will treasure more deeply the gospel of our Lord and Savior Jesus Christ.

NOTES

❧

INTRODUCTION

1. Name changed.

2. Evangelicals commonly refer to the Catholic Church as the "Roman Catholic Church," but some Catholics perceive the addition of the adjective *Roman* as pejorative. Out of respect for the Catholic authors in this volume, we will use the terms *Catholic* and *Catholicism*, unless a specific historical situation warrants the addition of *Roman*.

3. According to a study released in February 2008 by the Pew Forum on Religion and Public Life, 7 percent of persons raised as Protestants eventually shift to non-Protestant religious traditions. For certain subgroups, however, the numbers are higher. For example, 10 percent of persons raised as non-denominational Evangelicals eventually adhere to a non-Protestant religious tradition (*U.S. Religious Landscape Survey*, p. 31, *http://religions.pewforum.org*).

4. David W. Bebbington, *Evangelicalism in Modern Britain: A History from the 1730s to the 1980s* (London: Unwin Hyman, 1989), 5–17. These characteristics are sometimes known as the Bebbington quadrilateral. I am grateful that Al Mohler alerted me to this significant study. For a critique of the quadrilateral's sufficiency, see Mohler's chapel address from August 24, 2010, available at *www.sbts.edu/resources*. In *Four Views on the Spectrum of Evangelicalism* (Zondervan, 2011), several prominent conservative Christian leaders debate the proper boundaries and characteristics of Evangelicalism and fundamentalism.

5. See, for example, Robert E. Webber's classic volume *Evangelicals on the Canterbury Trail: Why Evangelicals Are Attracted to the Liturgical Church* (Waco, Tex.: Word, 1985) or, more recently, Todd D. Hunter, *The Accidental Anglican: The Surprising Appeal of the Liturgical Church* (Downers Grove, Ill.: InterVarsity, 2010).

6. "Faith in Flux: Changes in Religious Affiliation in the U.S., April 2009," *http://pewforum.org/Faith-in-Flux.aspx*.

7. See, for example, Dean M. Kelley, *Why Conservative Churches Are Growing: A Study in Sociology of Religion* (New York: Harper & Row, 1977; reprint: Macon, Ga.: Mercer Univ. Press, 1996).

8. Thomas Reese, "The Hidden Exodus: Catholics Becoming Protestants," *National Catholic Reporter* (April 18, 2011), *http://ncronline.org*.

9. See, e.g., Christian Smith, *How to Go from Being a Good Evangelical to a Committed Catholic in Ninety-Five Difficult Steps* (Eugene, Ore.: Cascade, 2011).

10. C. S. Lewis, *An Experiment in Criticism* (Cambridge: Cambridge Univ. Press, 1961), 3. I am grateful for T. David Gordon for pointing me to this quote in his delightful book *Why Johnny Can't Preach* (Phillipsburg, N.J.: P&R, 2009), 50.

11. *U.S. Religious Landscape Survey*, p. 31, *http://religions.pewforum.org.*

12. Ibid.

CHAPTER 2: A RESPONSE TO EASTERN ORTHODOXY

1. See, for example, Kristian Kahrs, "Belgrade Curve: Evangelicals Fear Greater Power of State, Orthodox Church," *Christianity Today* 50.7 (2006): 16; Susan Wunderink, "A Mending in Moscow? Evangelicals Hope New Orthodox Patriarch Will Improve Ecumenical Relations," *Christianity Today* 53.4 (2009): 16–17; Mindy Belz, "Laying Down the Law: Russian Officials Are Taking Seriously a Repressive Law against Religious Minorities, but a Few Are Finding Loopholes," *World* 14.11 (March 20, 1999): 30–31; and Greg Dabel, "Documentary Disinformation Persecution: Russia's Orthodox Church Spearheads a Televised, Nationwide Smear Campaign," *World* 20.34 (September 3, 2005): 20–21.

2. For studies on the Baptist doctrine of the believers' church, see Donald F. Durnbaugh, *The Believer's Church: The History and Character of Radical Protestantism* (New York: Macmillan, 1968); and James Leo Garrett, ed., *The Concept of the Believers' Church: Addresses from the 1967 Louisville Conference* (Scottdale, Pa.: Herald, 1969).

3. Willow Creek's own study of the problem was published by Greg L. Hawkins and Cally Parkinson under the title *Reveal: Where Are You?* (Barrington, Ill.: Willow Creek Resources, 2007). See also Adelle M. Banks, "Willow Creek Finds Limits to Its Model," *Christian Century* 125. 2 (2008): 16; and Mark Branaugh, "Willow Creek's 'Huge Shift': Influential Megachurch Moves Away from Seeker-Sensitive Services," *Christianity Today* 52.6 (2008): 13.

4. Technically, Orthodox theology teaches that the locus of inspiration includes Scripture and the seven ecumenical councils of the Church. However, the last of these councils, Nicaea (787), declared that Tradition is of the Holy Spirit. Consequently, in reality inspiration, in the Orthodox view, extends to the entirety of church tradition.

5. This does not imply any perceivable conflict on the Orthodox side. The rule of Tradition over Scripture would normally preclude conflict. Consequently, it is not surprising that Ellsworth would say, "Contrary to the

thinking of many, there is no conflict or struggle in the Orthodox Church for primacy between Holy Scripture and Tradition."

6. See, for example, Timothy Ware, *The Orthodox Church* (New York: Penguin, 1964), 203–7. Stylianopoulos expresses a common Orthodox view when he says, "The Church is the foundational reality behind both scripture and tradition"; Theodore G. Stylianopoulos, "Scripture and Tradition in the Church" in Mary B. Cunningham and Elizabeth Theokritoff, eds., *The Cambridge Companion to Orthodox Christian Theology* (Cambridge: Cambridge Univ. Press, 2008), 24.

7. The use of Scripture in early Christian writings is a fitting testimony to its recognized authority in the Church. In the early struggle with heresy, reference was made to Scripture and to traditional Church teaching. But the point being made was that Tradition was faithful to Scripture. Irenaeus in his dispute with the Gnostics is an excellent example of this. He argued against any tradition that was secret or substantively different from what can be read openly and plainly in Scripture. The often celebrated passage in *Adversus haereses* 3.1 that speaks of apostolic succession in key churches and the traditional teaching to be found there is arguing a greater point—that the traditional teaching is in fact apostolic instruction as found in, consistent and coherent with, and comprehensively comprised of Scripture. For a brief summary of Irenaeus's view of Scripture, see Eric Osborn, "Defense of Truth and Attack on Heresy" in Angelo D. Berardino and Basil Studer, eds., *History of Theology*, vol. 1, *The Patristic Period*, trans. Matthew J. O'Connell (Collegeville, Minn.: Michael Glazier, 1996), 125–28.

8. Of course, in disputes with heresy, appeals were made to traditions of episcopal teaching. But this was typically a supportive argument to the main point in dispute, which had to do with the teaching of Scripture on the particular issue troubling the Church. The Arian controversy provides an excellent example of this. Athanasius countered Arius's appeal to Tradition by arguing his own continuity with Alexander and the bishops who preceded him. But his primary point was that this episcopal teaching accorded with Scripture, and the focus and primary burden of his argument was to prove from Scripture that the Arian heresy was false. His was a biblical-hermeneutical, not an episcopal-traditional, argument.

9. This is a point which I made in a paper presented to the Society for the Study of Eastern Orthodoxy and Evangelicalism at Wheaton in 1992, "Scripture, Tradition and Authority: An Evangelical Response to Emmanuel Clapsis." The Orthodox seem not to sufficiently appreciate the significance of the Reformation in Western Christianity with respect to the phenomena of Tradition within the Church. The Reformation, as Evangelicals see it,

focused attention on the real possibility that Tradition, through its historical development, could actually come to oppose the gospel! The solution to this problem was to reestablish the primacy of Scripture over Tradition whereby the corrupting developments can be redressed and the gospel restored as the guide to developing Tradition rather than being victimized by it.

10. Arius, *Thalia*, in Athanasius, *Contra Arianos* 1.5. See *St. Athanasius: Select Works and Letters*, trans. J. H. Newman, rev. A. Robertson, Nicene and Post-Nicene Fathers of the Christian Church, series 2, vol. 4 (New York: Christian Literature, 1892; reprint, Grand Rapids, Mich.: Eerdmans, 1975), 308.

11. See Charles Kannengiesser, *Holy Scripture and Hellenistic Hermeneutics in Alexandrian Christology: The Arian Crisis* (Berekley, Calif.: Center for Hermeneutical Studies, 1982).

12. Athanasius, *De decretis* 19; Athanasius, *Ad Afros* 5. See NPNF 2.4, 162–3; 491.

13. For an elaboration of this point, see C. Blaising, "Creedal Formation as Hermeneutical Development: A Reexamination of Nicaea," *Pro Ecclesia* 19 (2010): 371–88.

14. Athanasius, *Ad Afros* 5–6; Athanasius, *De decretis* 21; see NPNF 2.4, 491–92, 164.

15. The classic study is that of Bengt Hägglund, "Die Bedeutung der Regula fidei als Grundlage theologisher Aussagen," *Studia Theologica* 12 (1958): 1–44.

16. This shift in authority is noted in the superb work on patristic theological method referenced above, *History of Theology*, vol. 1, *The Patristic Period*. See especially pp. 416–24.

17. For a brief overview of iconology, including the eighth- and ninth-century conflict with iconoclasm, see Mariamna Fortounatto and Mary B. Cunningham, "Theology of the icon," in *The Cambridge Companion to Orthodox Christian Theology*, 136–49.

18. It is true that arguments were advanced linking iconology to Christology and anthropology. However, this appears to be justification after the fact. The practice developed as a popular tradition with theological reflection at first opposed to and then accommodating the practice. It was not and could not be justified biblically, which was the sole basis for theological justification at the First Council of Nicaea.

19. For the full text and translation of the doctrinal statement of the Seventh Ecumenical Council, see Jeroslav Pelikan and Valerie Hotchkiss, eds., *Creeds and Confessions of Faith in the Christian Tradition*, vol. 1, *Early, Eastern, and Medieval* (New Haven: Yale Univ. Press, 2003), 232–41. The quotation is from Anathema 4 (p. 241).

20. Jaroslav Pelikan has written extensively on the phenomenon of development within theological tradition. See especially his *Historical Theology: Continuity and Change in Christian Doctrine* (London: Hutchinson & Co., 1971).

21. For an overview of Orthodox liturgy and its development, see Alexander Rentel, "Byzantine and Slavic Orthodoxy," in Geoffrey Wainwright and Karen B. Westerfield Tucker, eds., *The Oxford History of Christian Worship* (Oxford: Oxford Univ. Press, 2006), 254–306.

22. Paul's use of priestly language for the gospel ministry can be seen in Romans 15:14–21 and Philippians 2:14–18. See also Romans 12:1–2.

23. See *The Liturgy of Saint John Chrysostom* in Pelikan and Hotchkiss, *Creeds and Confessions*, 1:271–95.

24. Pelikan and Hotchkiss, *Creeds and Confessions*, 1:237–38.

25. See John Calvin, *Institutes of the Christian Religion* 1.12.2–3, in John T. McNeill, ed., *Calvin: Institutes of the Christian Religion*, trans. Ford Lewis Battles, LCC 20–21 (Philadelphia: Westminster, 1960), 118–20.

26. Acts 14:8–18; Revelation 22:8–9.

27. This takes place in the Epiclesis; see Pelikan and Hotchkiss, *Creeds and Confessions*, 1:287.

28. The rich recovery of a number of these works in critical editions and translations has made possible a modern version of the catena genre, as can be seen in Thomas Oden, ed., *The Ancient Christian Commentary on Scripture*, 15 vols. (OT) plus 12 vols. (NT) (Downers Grove, Ill.: InterVarsity, 1998–2010). A similar project, still ongoing, is Robert Louis Wilkin, ed., *The Church's Bible* (Grand Rapids, Mich.: Eerdmans, 2003–).

CHAPTER 3: EASTERN ORTHODOXY REJOINDER

1. Georges Florovsky, *Bible, Church, Tradition: An Eastern Orthodox View*, The Collected Works of Georges Florovsky, vol. 1 (Belmont, Mass.: Nordland, 1972), 19.

2. Bradley Nassif, "Are Eastern Orthodoxy and Evangelicalism Compatible? Yes: The Evangelical Theology of the Eastern Orthodox Church," in Stanley N. Gundry and James Stamoolis, eds., *Three Views on Eastern Orthodoxy and Evangelicalism* (Grand Rapids, Mich.: Zondervan, 2004), 58.

3. John Meyendorff, *A Study of Gregory Palamas* (1998; Crestwood, N.Y.: St. Vladimir's Seminary Press, 2010), 116.

4. John of Damascus, *On Icons*, I.16.

5. Daniel H. Williams, *Retrieving the Tradition and Renewing Evangelicalism: A Primer for Suspicious Protestants* (Grand Rapids, Mich.: Eerdmans, 1999), 13.

CHAPTER 4: A JOURNEY TO CATHOLICISM

1. Loraine Boettner, *Roman Catholicism* (Phillipsburg, N.J.: Presbyterian & Reformed, 1962). I was introduced to Boettner's work in 1980 and 1981 in a series of tracts published by Last Days Ministries, the Catholic Chronicles. Authored by the founder of the ministry, the late Christian musician and composer Keith Green (1953–82), they originally appeared in several issues of the *Last Days Newsletter* to which I had subscribed. Last Days discontinued publishing the tracts soon after Keith's death. They can, however, be found online in several places, including here: *www.theboc.com/freestuff/keithgreen/ catholicchronicles/index.html.*

2. Geisler's philosophical and apologetic work has been deeply influenced by Saint Thomas Aquinas. See, for example, Norman L. Geisler, *Philosophy of Religion* (Grand Rapids, Mich.: Baker, 1974); and Norman L. Geisler, *Thomas Aquinas: An Evangelical Appraisal?*, forward by Ralph McInerny (Grand Rapids, Mich.: Baker, 1991).

3. The Life and Witness of the Christian Community—Marriage and Sex, resolution 15, *www.lambethconference.org/resolutions/1930/1930-15.cfm.*

4. Geisler, for example, argues that artificial birth control and masturbation are not intrinsically wrong and may in some cases be morally permissible and thus are not "unbiblical." (Norman L. Geisler, *Christian Ethics: Options & Issues* [Grand Rapids, Mich.: Zondervan, 1989], 184, 187).

5. Tim Drake, "From the Ark to the Barque: Hadley Arkes Speaks about His Reception into the Catholic Church," *National Catholic Register* (August 24, 2010), *www.ncregister.com/daily-news/from-the-ark-to-the-barque.*

6. John Paul II, *Fides et Ratio: On the Relationship between Faith and Reason* (Toronto: Pauline, 1998).

7. Ibid., 55.

8. Ibid.

9. Ibid.

10. Quoted in H. Leclercq, "The First Council of Nicaea," in *The Catholic Encyclopedia* (New York: Robert Appleton, 1911), *www.newadvent.org/ cathen/11044a.htm.*

11. Council of Chalcedon (AD 451), *www.ewtn.com/faith/teachings/ incac2.htm.*

12. Relying on memory, I recount my answer in Francis J. Beckwith, *Return to Rome: Confessions of an Evangelical Catholic* (Grand Rapids, Mich.: Brazos, 2009), 76–77.

13. *Catechism of the Catholic Church: Revised in Accordance With the Official Latin Text Promulgated by Pope John Paul II*, 2nd ed. (Washington, D.C.: United States Conference of Catholic Bishops, 2000), 1131.

14. See Alister McGrath, *Iustitia Dei: A History of the Christian Doctrine of Justification*, 3rd ed. (New York: Cambridge Univ. Press, 2005), 208.

15. See ibid., 208–92.

16. Ibid., 212–13.

17. Some more careful Evangelical exegetes note that the language of "sanctification" in the New Testament refers primarily to the *initial* setting apart of the believer for salvation (sometimes called "initial sanctification").

18. Portions of this section (III.A.2) are adapted from sections of my *Return to Rome*, 97–106.

19. *Catechism of the Catholic Church*, 1987–89 (notes omitted).

20. See ibid., 1989–99.

21. "With regard to God, there is no strict right to any merit on the part of man. Between God and us there is an immeasurable inequality, for we have received everything from him, our Creator" (Ibid., 2007).

22. Ibid., 2008 (latter emphasis added).

23. Peter J. Kreeft writes something similar: "We do not do good works to get to heaven, but we do good works because heaven has gotten to us" (Peter J. Kreeft, *Catholic Christianity: A Complete Catechism of Catholic Beliefs Based on the* Catechism of the Catholic Church [San Francisco: Ignatius, 2001], 126).

24. "If anyone says that men are justified either by *the sole imputation of the justice of Christ* or by the sole remission of sins, to the exclusion of the grace and the charity which is poured forth in their hearts by the Holy Ghost [Rom. 5:5], and remains in them, or also that the grace by which we are justified is only the good will of God, let him be anathema" (*The Canons and Decrees of the Council of Trent*, trans. Rev. H. J. Schroeder, O.P. [Rockford, Ill.: TAN, 1978], 43, emphasis added).

25. Emphasis added in Scripture quotes in paragraph.

26. Emphasis added in Scripture quotes in paragraph.

27. Emphasis added in Scripture quotes in paragraph.

28. Emphasis added in Scripture quotes in paragraph.

29. *Catechism of the Catholic Church*, 1993, final emphasis added.

30. See McGrath, *Iustitia Dei*, 217.

31. See, for example, Norman L. Geisler, *Systematic Theology*, vol. 3, *Salvation* (Grand Rapids, Mich.: Baker, 2004), 267; R. C. Sproul, "The Battle for Grace Alone," *Tabletalk* (August 1, 2006), available at *http://www.ligonier.org/learn/articles/battle-grace-alone/*; and R. C. Sproul, "The Pelagian Captivity of the Church," *Modern Reformation* 10.3 (May/June 2001): 22–23, 26–29.

32. From the Canons of the Council of Orange: "Canon 1. If anyone denies that it is the whole man, that is, both body and soul, that was 'changed for the worse' through the offense of Adam's sin, but believes that the freedom

of the soul remains unimpaired and that only the body is subject to corruption, he is deceived by the error of Pelagius and contradicts the scripture ..." (*The Council of Orange 529.*, *www.ewtn.com/library/COUNCILS/ORANGE.htm*).

33. From the Canons of the Council of Orange: "Canon 4. If anyone maintains that God awaits our will to be cleansed from sin, but does not confess that even *our will to be cleansed comes to us through the infusion and working of the Holy Spirit,* he resists the Holy Spirit himself who says through Solomon, 'The will is prepared by the Lord' (Prov. 8:35, LXX), and the salutary word of the Apostle, 'For God is at work in you, both to will and to work for his good pleasure' (Phil. 2:13).... Canon 5. If anyone says that not only the increase of faith but also its beginning and the very desire for faith, by which we believe in Him who justifies the ungodly and comes to the *regeneration of holy Baptism—if anyone says that this belongs to us by nature and not by a gift of grace, that is, by the inspiration of the Holy Spirit amending our will and turning it from unbelief to faith and from godlessness to godliness, it is proof that he is opposed to the teaching of the Apostles* ..." (Ibid., emphasis added).

34. Ibid., Canon 13.

35. *The Canons and Decrees of the Council of Trent,* 33.

36. *Catechism of the Catholic Church,* 1987.

37. See *The Council of Orange,* conclusion.

38. Ibid.

39. Ibid., emphasis added.

40. Ibid., Canon 20.

41. Ibid., Canon 9.

42. From chapter V of Trent's sixth session: "It is furthermore declared that in adults the beginning of that justification must proceed from the predisposing grace of God through Jesus Christ, that is, from His vocation, whereby, without any merits on their part, they are called; that they who by sin had been cut off from God, may be disposed through His quickening and helping grace to convert themselves to their own justification *by freely assenting to and cooperating with that grace*; so that, while God touches the heart of man through the illumination of the Holy Ghost, man himself neither does absolutely nothing while receiving that inspiration, since he can also reject it, nor yet is he able by his own free will and without the grace of God to move himself to justice in His sight" (*The Canons and Decrees of the Council of Trent,* 31–32, emphasis added).

43. See note 33.

44. St. Thomas Aquinas, *Summa Theologica* II.I, Q111, art. 2, 2nd and rev., literally translated by Fathers of the English Dominican Province 1920. , online edition, *www.newadvent.org/summa/2111.htm*.

45. Ibid.

46. Ibid.

47. *The Council of Orange*, Canon 24 and conclusion.

48. *The Canons and Decrees of the Council of Trent*, 41 (notes omitted).

49. *Catechism of the Catholic Church*, 1989.

50. *Catechism of the Catholic Church*, 2008 (emphasis in original).

51. "Through the power of the Holy Spirit we take part in Christ's Passion by dying to sin, and in his Resurrection by being born to a new life; we are members of his Body which is the Church, branches grafted onto the vine which is himself [cf. 1 Cor. 12; John 15:1–4]: '[God] gave himself to us through his Spirit. By the participation of the Spirit, we become communicants in the divine nature.... For this reason, those in whom the Spirit dwells are divinized.' [Saint Athanasius, Ep. Serap. 1,24: PG 26,585 and 588]" (*Catechism of the Catholic Church*, 1998).

52. *Catechism of the Catholic Church*, 2009.

53. *Catechism of the Catholic Church*, 1989.

54. See *Catechism of the Catholic Church*, 1399.

55. J. N. D. Kelly, *Early Christian Doctrines*, rev. ed. (New York: Harper Collins, 1978), 440.

56. *Letter to the Romans* 7, as found in Jimmy Akin, ed., *The Fathers Know Best: Your Essential Guide to the Teachings of the Early Church* (San Diego: Catholic Answers, 2010), 293.

57. *Letter to the Smyrnaeans* 6–7, as found in Akin, *The Fathers Know Best*, 293.

58. *First Apology* 66, as found in Akin, *The Fathers Know Best*, 293.

59. *The Lapsed* (Treatise 3) 15–16, as found in Akin, *The Fathers Know Best*, 295.

60. Akin (in *The Fathers Know Best*, 292–98) provides quotes from several other early church writings.

61. *Catechism of the Catholic Church*, 601 (citing Isa. 53:11; cf. 53:12; John 8:34–36; Acts 3:14).

62. Ibid., 1941 (citing Mark 2:7).

63. Ibid., 1430–33.

64. Ibid., 1989.

65. Ibid., 1941 (citing Mark 2:7).

66. Ibid., 1451–53.

67. Ibid., 1455–58.

68. Ibid., 1862–63.

69. Kelly, *Early Christian Doctrines*, 216.

70. Ibid.

71. Ibid., 200–201, 217–19.

72. See the quotes in Akin, *The Fathers Know Best*, 305–11.

73. *Letter to the Philadelphians* 3, 8, as found in Akin, *The Fathers Know Best*, 306.

74. *Letters* 9:2, as found in Akin, *The Fathers Know Best*, 309.

75. *The Priesthood* 3:5, as found in Akin, *The Fathers Know Best*, 310.

76. *Sermons to Catechumens on the Creed*, 15, 16, as found in Akin, *The Fathers Know Best*, 311.

77. See Kelly, *Early Christian Doctrines*, 35–48, 189–93.

78. See St. Irenaeus, *Against Heresies*, 3:3–4, 4:26, 33, available at *www.new advent.org/fathers/0103.htm*.

79. See Tertullian, *Prescription against Heretics*, 20, 21, 27, 28, 32, available at *www.newadvent.org/fathers/0311.htm*.

80. See, for example, Kelly, *Early Christian Doctrines*, 35–48, 189–93; and the works cited in Akin, *The Fathers Know Best*, 182–89.

81. *Epistle to the Corinthians*, 42:4–5; 44:1–2, as found in Akin, *The Fathers Know Best*, 183. Akin dates the letter at AD 70. Others date it later, anywhere from 80 to 98. Regardless of what date, it does provide important information about what the early church believed about ecclesiology.

82. *Letters*, 75:3, as found in Akin, *The Fathers Know Best*, 187–88.

83. *Epistle to St. Cyprian of Carthage*, 74:16, available at *www.newadvent .org/fathers/050674.htm*.

84. *Against the Letter of Mani Called "The Foundation,"* 4:5, as found in Akin, *The Fathers Know Best*, 188.

85. *Letters*, 53:I:2, as found in Akin, *The Fathers Know Best*, 193–94.

86. See, for example, Adrian Fortescue, *The Early Papacy to the Synod of Chalcedon in 451*, 4th ed., ed. Alcuin Reid (San Francisco: Ignatius, 2008; originally published, 1920); and Robert Stackpole, *Saint Peter Lives in Rome*, 2nd ed. (Stockbridge, Mass.: Marian, 2006).

87. See, for example, Olivier Clement, *You Are Peter: An Orthodox Reflection on the Exercise of Papal Primacy,* trans. M. S. Laird (Hyde Park, N.Y.: New City, 2003).

88. See Craig A. Allert, *A High View of Scripture: The Authority of the Bible and the Formation of the New Testament* (Grand Rapids, Mich.: Baker, 2007), 48–66. D. H. Williams writes, "[T]he means by which the biblical books were regarded as inspired and divinely given for Christian doctrine and practice took place in the postapostolic centuries of the early church. This process was a gradual and untidy one that emerged out of the worship and liturgical practices of the early churches" (D. H. Williams, *Evangelicals and Tradition: The Formative Influence of the Early Church* [Grand Rapids, Mich.: Baker, 2005], 55).

89. See *Catechism of the Catholic Church*, 1996–98.

90. Ibid., 166.

91. See *Dei Verbum: Dogmatic Constitution on Divine Revelation* (November 16, 1965), 11, available at *www.vatican.va/archive/hist_councils/ii_vatican_council/documents/vat-ii_const_19651118_dei-verbum_en.html.*

CHAPTER 5: A RESPONSE TO ROMAN CATHOLICISM

1. I intend to set forth this vision and demonstrate how the Evangelical Protestant worldview is more faithful to Scripture, stronger theologically, and better supported by a chastened tradition of church doctrine and practice accumulated over its history than is its Catholic counterpart, in a forthcoming book: Gregg R. Allison, *Intrigue and Critique: An Evangelical Assessment of Roman Catholic Theology and Practice* (Wheaton, Ill.: Crossway, forthcoming).

2. The doctrine of the Trinity, which is at the heart of the doctrine of God, was hammered out and defended during the third and fourth centuries and articulated in the first two general councils — the Council of Nicaea (AD 325) and the Council of Constantinople (AD 381). Catholicism and Protestantism agree with and hold to the Trinitarian doctrine of these councils.

3. On the issue of what constitutes the image of God, and on the specific elements of original sin — guilt, corruption, depravity, inability — Protestantism in its varieties and Catholicism differ.

4. The doctrine of Christ was forged and secured during the fourth and fifth centuries and expressed in the third and fourth general councils — the Council of Ephesus (431) and the Council of Chalcedon (451). Catholicism and Protestantism agree with and hold to the Christology of these councils.

5. Whereas both Protestantism and Catholicism held to a robust doctrine of the inerrancy of Scripture, embracing the legacy of its total truthfulness from the early and medieval church, the modern period has witnessed the demise of this traditional view. Nevertheless, conservatives from both sides affirm biblical inerrancy.

6. The Catholic misinterpretation of this passage sees Jesus as indicating that he would communicate some divine revelation to his disciples, which they in turn would write down in Scripture, but that because of their dullness to understand everything he might possibly wish to communicate to them, he would reveal other divine revelation that would not be written down but would be transmitted orally — Tradition. But Jesus is addressing the plight of the disciples before his death and resurrection, not afterward, and he promises the Holy Spirit (John 16:13; cf. 14:26) so that they would

indeed grasp divine revelation once he left this world. See John Calvin, *Institutes of the Christian Religion*, 4.8.14, in John Baillie, John T. McNeill, and Henry P. Van Dusen, eds., *Library of Christian Classics*, 26 vols. (Philadelphia: Westminster, 1960), 21:1163–64.

7. This objection does not turn a blind eye to the reality that in the early church, the gospel and sound doctrine were transmitted by both spoken word and written letter (for example, 2 Thess. 2:15), but this dual communication should not be seen as consisting of two streams of revelatory content, as the late medieval Catholic Church began to claim.

8. The sufficiency of Scripture means that it contains everything people need to know in order to be saved and to live in a way that fully pleases God (Ps. 19:7–11; 2 Tim. 3:16–17). An implication of the sufficiency of Scripture is that no formulation of church doctrine or practice that comes from outside of Scripture—for example, purgatory, indulgences, transubstantiation, prayers for the dead, penance, the immaculate conception and bodily assumption of Mary—can bind the conscience of Christians as additional beliefs or actions required for salvation and holy living.

9. The necessity of Scripture means that it is needed for sinful human beings to understand the way of salvation, to know God's will, and to acquire wisdom for godly living (Matt. 4:4; 1 Peter 2:1–3). Indeed, without Scripture, the church would not exist or be able to exist. Although the Catholic Church would agree that Scripture is necessary for the *well-being* of the Church, it maintains—because of the existence of its Tradition—that Scripture is not necessary for the *being* of the Church; that is, the Church could still exist if Scripture would cease to be, because it would be guided by Tradition. Protestantism dissents from this view because it contradicts the necessity of Scripture.

10. For example, Tradition claims that Mary was sinless from the moment of her conception to the end of her life, but Scripture affirms that no human being, apart from Jesus, is without sin. Accordingly, Tradition and Scripture conflict, and in this matter Tradition is the more ultimate authority for the Catholic Church.

11. For example, Melito of Sardis, in his list of Old Testament books, included all of the books of the Hebrew Bible except Esther and did not name any apocryphal writings. Origen indicated twenty-two books as belonging to the Old Testament (this number corresponds to the number of books in the Hebrew Bible) and explicitly excluded 1 and 2 Maccabees from his list. Athanasius, while including Baruch and the Letter of Jeremiah as belonging with Jeremiah and Lamentations, listed specific books—Wisdom of Solomon, Ecclesiasticus, Judith, and Tobit (he also included Esther)—

that were not included in canonical Scripture. Most important, Jerome, the translator of the Latin Vulgate, who was well acquainted with the difference between Hebrew Scripture and the Septuagint, indicated the role or purpose of the Apocrypha: "As then the church reads Judith, Tobit, and the books of Maccabees, but does not admit them among the canonical Scriptures, so let it read these two volumes [Wisdom of Solomon and Ecclesiasticus] for the edification of the people, not to give authority to doctrines of the church" (Jerome, *Preface to the Books of Proverbs, Ecclesiastes, and the Song of Songs*, in Alexander Roberts, James Donaldson, Philip Schaff, and Henry Wace, eds., *Nicene- and Post-Nicene Fathers*, 2nd ser., 14 vols. [Peabody, Mass.: Hendrickson, 1994], 6:492). That is, the church could read the apocryphal writings for its growth, but they could not be consulted in the establishment of church doctrine.

12. Augustine championed the inspiration of both the Hebrew Bible and the Septuagint translation—he correctly observed that the New Testament authors cited from the Septuagint, but failed to observe that they never cited from its apocryphal writings—and when he appealed to Jerome to include a Latin translation of those writings in his Vulgate, Jerome capitulated (Augustine, *Letter* 28.2; *Letter* 71, in Alexander Roberts, James Donaldson, Philip Schaff, and Henry Wace, eds., *Nicene- and Post-Nicene Fathers*, 1st ser., 14 vols. [Peabody, Mass.: Hendrickson, 1994], 1:251; 1:326–28; Jerome, *Letter* 105; *Letter* 112, in *NPNF*, 2nd ser., 6:189, 214). The result was that the Old Testament in the Catholic Bible included the apocryphal writings—a reality that would not be seriously challenged until the time of the Reformation.

13. Only regional councils—the Council of Hippo in 393, the Third Council of Carthage in 397, and the Fourth Council of Carthage in 419—approved the canonicity of the longer Old Testament as insisted upon by Augustine. And the claim that the Catholic Church determined the canon of Scripture was a late (fourteenth-century) development that was historically inaccurate, as a closed canon of the Hebrew Bible was inherited from Judaism by the early church.

14. *Canons and Decrees of the Council of Trent*, 4th session (April 8, 1546), *Decree Concerning the Canonical Scriptures*, in Philip Schaff, *Creeds of Christendom*, 3 vols. (New York: Harper, 1877–1905), 2:80.

15. Ibid., 2:83.

16. For several examples, see note 6 and note 30.

17. For further discussion, see Gregg R. Allison, "The Protestant Doctrine of the Perspicuity of Scripture: A Reformulation on the Basis of Biblical Teaching" (PhD diss., Trinity Evangelical Divinity School, 1995).

18. In an encouraging development since Vatican Council II, more and more Catholics are becoming involved in Bible study and familiar with Scripture.

19. Indeed, the doctrine of justification by grace alone through Christ alone by faith alone is referred to as the "material principle" of Protestantism, which insists that it is "the main hinge on which religion turns" (Calvin, *Institutes*, 3.11.1, LCC 20:726). According to the Lutheran *Smalcald Articles*, "Of this article nothing can be yielded or surrendered, even though heaven and earth, and whatever will not abide [all created things], should sink to ruin" (*Smalcald Articles*, 2.1.5, in F. Bente and W. H. T. Dau, trans., *Triglot Concordia: The Symbolical Books of the Evangelical Lutheran Church* [St. Louis: Concordia, 1921], 463).

20. *Canons and Decrees of the Council of Trent*, 6th session (January 13, 1547), *Decree on Justification* 7, in Schaff, 2:94.

21. For the Council of Trent's pronouncements on justification in their entirety, see ibid., Schaff, 2:89–118.

22. I disagree with Beckwith's treatment of justification, particularly his conflation of many passages of Scripture—for example, James 2:21–24; Heb. 11:8; Matt. 25:31–46; Matt. 16:27; Rev. 22:11–12; Matt. 19; Matt. 5; John 14:19–21; Mark 8:34–35; Mark 4:16–17; Rom. 5:19; Gal. 3:26–27; Gal. 5:6; Rom. 2:6–8, 13; Col. 1:22–23; Phil. 2:12–13; Gal. 6:8; 2 Tim. 4:7–8; and many, many more—to blunt the forensic language of what he underscores to be a key biblical passage cited by Protestants in support of their doctrine of justification: Romans 4:1–8. But Protestants are right about this passage as formative for their view: Paul eloquently and forensically speaks of God counting Abraham as righteous (v. 3), counting all who believe in Jesus as righteous (vv. 5–6), justifying the ungodly (v. 5, historically and currently a verse that cannot fit into a Catholic understanding of justification), and not counting sins against those whom he blesses (v. 8). This is the language of imputation within a forensic framework, and this is decisive for a proper view of justification. Marshalling a great number of verses from all over the New Testament, without noting whether they are addressing the work of justification or some other mighty act(s) of God, does not necessarily shed light on Paul's doctrine of justification as set forth in Romans 4:1–8 and certainly cannot be used to blunt what the apostle means in that passage.

23. Beckwith puts his finger on a key question in the debate between Protestantism and Catholicism over the issue of justification when he quotes a statement from the *Catechism of the Catholic Church*: " … God has freely chosen to associate man with the work of his grace." Clearly, to the question,

Is this statement true? Catholicism answers yes, while Protestantism answers no. To the divine declaration pronounced over the ungodly, "You are not guilty but righteous instead" no human cooperation can be attached. And because the declaration brings the future divine judgment into the present and makes it such that the justified will never face the condemnatory sentence of God, no human meriting of eternal life is possible. Is there a human response of repentance and faith to the gospel? Certainly, but this is not human cooperation but the reception of a gift ("justified as a gift" [Rom. 3:24 NASB]). Does the Christian life entail working out one's salvation with fear and trembling (Phil. 2:12) through reading Scripture, prayer, love, participating in the church, service, and the like? Certainly, but this is not human collaboration contributing to one's eventual justification. Here, again, the vast divide between Catholicism and Protestantism on the matter of justification is in evidence.

24. *Ineffabilis Deus* (December 8, 1854), available at *www.papalencyclicals .net/Pius09/p9ineff.htm*.

25. Catholicism denies that Mary engaged in sexual intercourse with Joseph after the birth of Jesus; it holds that Jesus was her only son.

26. *Munificentissimus Deus* (November 1, 1950), available at *www.vatican .va/holy_father/pius_xii/apost_constitutions/documents/hf_p-vii_apc _19501101_munificentissimus-deus_en.html*.

27. *Lumen Gentium*, 62, in Austin Flannery, ed., *Vatican Council II*, vol. 1, *The Conciliar and Post Conciliar Documents*, new rev. ed. (New York: Costello; Dublin, Ireland: Dominican, 1998), 419.

28. *Credo of the People of God*, 15, available at *www.vatican.va/holy _father/paul_vi/motu_proprio/documents/hf_p-vi_motu-proprio_19680630 _credo_en.html*.

29. *Marialis cultus*, 56, available at *www.vatican.va/holy _father/paul_vi/apost_exhortations/documents/hf_p-vi_exh_19740202 _marialis-cultus_en.html*.

30. For example (the following is taken from the biblical theology of Mary as articulated in John Paul II, *Redemptoris Mater* [March 28, 1978; the following biblical citations appear as they are in this encyclical, which is available at *www.vatican.va/holy_father/john_paul_ii/encyclicals/documents/ hf_jp-ii_enc_25031987_redemptoris-mater_en.htm*] and adapted from Gregg R. Allison, book review of Mark A. Noll and Carolyn Nystrom, *Is the Reformation Over? An Evangelical Assessment of Contemporary Roman Catholicism*, in *Journal of the Evangelical Theological Society* 48, no. 4 [December 2005]: 869): In Luke 1:26–38, Mary's response to Gabriel's announcement—"Let it be done to me"—is optative, not imperative as Catholicism interprets;

thus, Mary expresses not her fiat (that is, her authoritative decree) but her wish to obey God's will that has been communicated to her by the final angelic words, "Nothing will be impossible with God." Accordingly, this text is not about Mary; it is about the power of God to effect the incarnation of his Son. Moreover, nothing that Mary does—not her faith, her obedience, her courage, or anything else—contributes decisively to this miracle. A second example is similar: At the wedding in Cana (John 2:1–11), Jesus' courteous reproach of his mother ("O woman, what have you to do with me? My hour has not yet come"), followed by Mary's order to the servants ("Do whatever he tells you"), can in no way be taken as Mary acting as intercessor and mediatrix between human needs and the power of her Son. A third example underscores a problem of allowing a historical development of doctrine and practice to become unmoored from a solid biblical anchor: Following the New Testament parallelism between Adam and Christ, the second Adam who undoes the disobedience of the first Adam (for example, Rom. 5:12–19), the early church constructed a parallelism between Eve and Mary, a "second Eve" who reverses the disobedience of the first Eve. Of course, unlike the first parallelism, this second parallelism is without biblical support, yet the church permitted it to expand until the doctrine of Mary is what it is today. And the development has come at the expense of clear biblical affirmations that the church does not stand in need of a helping mediator between human beings and a predominately divine *God*-man, as Hebrews 2:14–18 and 4:15–16 affirm.

31. The following is adapted from Allison book review, *Journal of the Evangelical Theological Society*, 868–69.

32. Looking back at this development, Jerome underscored the reactive nature of the elevation of the office of bishop: "When subsequently one presbyter was chosen to preside over the rest, this was done to remedy schism and to prevent each individual from rending the church of Christ by drawing it to himself" (Jerome, *Letter 146, to Evangelus*, 1, in *NPNF*, 2nd ser., 6:288). Elsewhere, Jerome was not so deferential to historical factors as the explanation for this development: "A presbyter ... is the same as a bishop, and before dissensions were introduced into religion by the instigation of the devil and it was said among the peoples, 'I am of Paul, I am of Apollos, and I of Cephas' [1 Cor. 1:12; cf. 3:4], churches were governed by a common council of the presbyters acting together; afterwards, when everyone thought that those whom he had baptized were his own, and not Christ's, it was decreed in the whole world that one chosen out of the presbyters should be placed over the rest, and to whom all care of the church should belong, that the seeds of schism might be plucked up [removed]" (*Commentary on Titus*,

1.6–7, in John Harrison, *Whose Are the Fathers?* [London: Longmans, Green and Co., 1867], 488). Accordingly, Jerome emphasized that the development of the office of bishop was at odds with both Scripture and the leadership structure of the earliest churches. Given Jerome's complaint, I don't understand Beckwith's contention that none of the early Christians, including respected church fathers, objected to the development of episcopalian church government.

33. Titus 1:5–9 and Acts 20:17, 28 use the terms *elder* and *bishop* (*overseer* in the NIV) interchangeably. The existence of two offices, not three, in the early church is evidenced in the *Didache*, 15, in Alexander Roberts, James Donaldson, Philip Schaff, and Henry Wace, eds., *Ante-Nicene Fathers*, 10 vols. (Peabody, Mass.: Hendrickson, 1994), 7:381; cf. Polycarp, *Letter to the Philippians*, 5 (*ANF*, 1:34). It was Ignatius who called for a threefold office, making a distinction between bishop and elder by elevating the former over the latter (Ignatius, *Letter to the Philadelphians*, 4 [*ANF*, 1:81]; *Letter to the Magnesians*, 6, 13 [*ANF*, 1:61, 64]).

34. For example, according to Martin Luther, "It is not water … that does it, but the Word of God which is with and in the water, and faith, which trusts in the Word of God in the water. For without the Word of God the water is nothing but water, and no baptism; but with the Word of God it is a baptism" (Martin Luther, *Small Catechism*, 4.3, in Schaff, 3:86). With regard to the element of faith, Luther explained, "Faith clings to the water, and believes that it is baptism, in which there is pure salvation and life; not [salvation] through the water … but through the fact that it is embodied in the Word and institution of God, and the name of God inheres in it" (Luther, "Of Infant Baptism," *Large Catechism*, 4.28, in *Triglot Concordia*, 739). Huldrych Zwingli warranted the practice on the basis of an analogy between the old covenant practice of circumcision and the new covenant practice of infant baptism. Israel had two signs of their covenant with God, circumcision and the Passover; similarly, the Church has baptism and the Lord's Supper, and baptism, like circumcision, is administered to infants (Huldrych Zwingli, *Of Baptism*, in Geoffrey W. Bromiley, ed., *Zwingli and Bullinger*, LCC 24:153). Calvin concurred: "Apart from the difference in the visible ceremony, whatever belongs to circumcision pertains likewise to baptism..... By this it appears incontrovertible that baptism has taken the place of circumcision to fulfill the same office among us" (Calvin, *Institutes*, 4.16.4, LCC 21:1327). He saw a great benefit of baptism for the parents of children who are baptized, as they see God's covenant of mercy being extended to their children (Ibid., 4.16.9, LCC 21:1332). As for the benefit accruing to the children themselves, Calvin offered, "Being engrafted

into the body of the church, they are somewhat more commended to the other members. Then, when they have grown up, they are greatly spurred to an earnest zeal for worshipping God, by whom they were received as children through a solemn symbol of adoption before they were old enough to recognize him as Father" (Ibid.). Thus, "infants are baptized into future repentance and faith" (Ibid., 4.16.20, LCC 21:1343). The Anabaptists and the Baptists broke from the centuries-old tradition of infant baptism, finding biblical support for the immersion of those who have heard the gospel, repented of their sins, believed in Christ, and offered a credible profession of faith, and finding no biblical warrant for infant baptism. Baptism of believers thus vividly portrays their identification in the death, burial, and resurrection of Christ (Rom. 6:3–6), their cleansing from sin (Acts 22:16), their escape from divine judgment (1 Peter 3:21), and their obedience to the Lord's command (Matt. 28:18–20) (*Schleitheim Confession*, art. 1, in William L. Lumpkin, *Baptist Confessions of Faith*, rev. ed. [Valley Forge: Judson, 1969]), 25; *London Confession of Faith*, 39, 40, in Lumpkin, 167; *Second London Confession of Faith*, 29, in Lumpkin, 291).

35. Martin Luther, *The Babylonian Captivity of the Church*, in Jaroslav Pelikan, Hilton C. Oswald, and Helmut T. Lehmann, eds., *Luther's Works*, 55 vols. (St. Louis: Concordia, 1955–1986), 36:23–31; Huldrych Zwingli, *An Exposition of the Faith*, in Bromiley, *Zwingli and Bullinger*, LCC 24: 254—55; John Calvin, *Institutes*, 4.17.12, LCC 21:1372–73.

36. *Catechism of the Catholic Church*, 1030, available at *www.usccb.org/catechism/text*.

37. Gregg R. Allison, "The Bible in Christianity: Roman Catholicism," *English Standard Version Study Bible* (Wheaton, Ill.: Crossway, 2008), 2615.

38. The following discussion is prompted by the excellent article by Scot McKnight titled "From Wheaton to Rome: Why Evangelicals Become Roman Catholic," *Journal of the Evangelical Theological Society* 45/3 (September 2002): 451–72.

39. Recall that Catholicism denies that Christians may possess the assurance of their salvation, because they may forfeit divine grace.

40. Catholicism does this sifting as well, only not to the extent that is demanded. For example, though the early and medieval church emphasized that the death of Jesus Christ was a ransom paid to Satan, later-developed Catholicism moved away from this model of the atonement because of its lack of biblical support.

41. For Catholicism's denial that Protestant "ecclesial communities" constitute true churches, because of their failure to embrace apostolic succession, see the *motu proprio* of Pope Benedict XVI, "Responses to Some Questions

Regarding Certain Aspects of the Doctrine of the Church" (July 10, 2007), available at *www.vatican.va/roman_curia/congregations/cfaith/documents/ rc_con_cfaith_doc_20070629_responsa-quaestiones_en.html.*

CHAPTER 6: CATHOLICISM REJOINDER

1. For a contrary point of view, see J. N. D. Kelly, *Early Christian Doctrines*, rev. ed. (San Francisco: HarperOne, 1978), 52–56. Kelly writes, "The West, as a whole, was inclined to form a much more favourable estimate of the Apocrypha. Churchmen with Eastern contacts, as was to be expected, might be disposed to push them in the background.... [L]ater [Jerome] grudgingly conceded that the Church read some of these books for edification, but not to support doctrine. For the great majority, however, the deutero-canonical writings ranked as Scripture in the fullest sense" (Ibid., 55).

2. This latter rejected tradition includes, as Allison concedes, Saint Augustine as well as the Council of Hippo (AD 393), the Third Council of Carthage (AD 397), and the Fourth Council of Carthage (AD 419). Nevertheless, as I indicate in the prior note, Kelly maintains that this tradition represented "the great majority" in the Western Church.

3. See *www.dennyburk.com/AmendETS/?page_id=3.*

4. Ted Olsen, "Evangelical Theological Society Votes Not to Amend" (November 21, 2008), *http://blog.christianitytoday.com/ctliveblog/ archives/2008/11/evangelical_the.html.*

5. See Craig A. Allert, *A High View of Scripture: The Authority of the Bible and the Formation of the New Testament* (Grand Rapids, Mich.: Baker Academic, 2007), 48–66. D. H. Williams writes, "[T]he means by which the biblical books were regarded as inspired and divinely given for Christian doctrine and practice took place in the postapostolic centuries of the early church. This process was a gradual and untidy one that emerged out of the worship and liturgical practices of the early churches" (D. H. Williams, *Evangelicals and Tradition: The Formative Influence of the Early Church* [Grand Rapids, Mich.: Baker Academic, 2005], 55).

6. See Allert, *A High View of Scripture*, 48–66; and Williams, *Evangelicals and Tradition*, 47–84.

CHAPTER 7: A JOURNEY TO EVANGELICALISM

1. A recent survey by the Pew Forum concluded that there are currently fifteen million former Catholics now attending Protestant churches in America (The Pew Forum on Religion and Public Life, "Faith in Flux: Changes in Religious Affiliation in the U.S." [Executive Summary, April 2009], *Pew Research Center, http://pewforum.org/Faith-in-Flux.aspx*).

2. Mark Christensen, "Coming to Grips with Losses: The Migration of Catholics into Conservative Protestantism," *America* (January 26, 1991), 58–59.

3. Ibid.

4. Peter Kreeft, "Ecumenical Jihad," in James S. Cutsinger, ed., *Reclaiming the Great Tradition* (Downers Grove, Ill.: InterVarsity, 1997), 27.

5. The conscious violation of a precept is considered to be a mortal sin (*Catechism of the Catholic Church*, par. 2041–43, 2nd ed. [Citta del Vatticano: Libreria Editrice Vaticana, 1997]).

6. Notwithstanding the so-called Old Testament Apocrypha or, in Catholic terms, the "deuterocanonicals." These are a collection of writings found in the Catholic Old Testament from the intertestamental period (the four hundred years between the Old and New Testaments), comprising seven books: Tobit, Judith, 1 Maccabees, 2 Maccabees, Wisdom of Solomon, Sirach (also called Ecclesiasticus), and Baruch. In addition, there are also passages of text: The Letter to Jeremiah (which became Baruch ch. 6), The Prayer of Azariah (which became Daniel 3:24–90), an additional 107 verses in the Book of Esther, Susanna (which became Daniel 13), and Bel and the Dragon (which became Daniel 14). These books were made an official part of the Catholic Old Testament at the Council of Trent (1545–63).

7. *Catechism of the Catholic Church*, par. 779.

8. *Catechism of the Catholic Church*, par. 780.

9. Sebastian Tromp, S.J., *Corpus Christi Quaod Est Ecclesia*, trans. Ann Condit (New York: Vantage, 1960), 194.

10. Pope Benedict XVI, *Joseph Ratzinger in* Communio, vol. 1, *The Unity of the Church* (Grand Rapids, Mich.: Eerdmans, 2010), 73–74. Since Vatican II, the language of "Continuous Incarnation" has been eclipsed by the council's emphasis on "The Pilgrim People of God." Nevertheless, the incarnation concept is so fundamental that it is still helpful for understanding how Catholic authority operates.

11. Hans Urs von Balthasar, *Theo-Drama: Theological Dramatic Theory*, vol. 4 (San Francisco: Ignatius, 1988), 131.

12. Yves Congar, O.P., *Jesus Christ,* trans. Luke O'Neill (New York: Herder and Herder, 1965), 156–57.

13. Émilien Lamirande, *The Communion of Saints,* trans. A. Manson (New York: Hawthorn, 1963), 73.

14. *Catechism of the Catholic Church*, par. 795.

15. Joseph Cardinal Ratzinger, *Principles of Catholic Theology: Building Stones for Fundamental Theology,* trans. Sr. Mary Frances McCarthy, S.N.D. (San Francisco: Ignatius, 1987), 44–47, 245. Some works that draw on this theme are Henri de Lubac, S.J., *Catholicism: A Study of Dogma in Relation*

to the Corporate Destiny of Mankind, trans. Lancelot C. Sheppard (London: Burns, Oates & Washbourne, 1950); David Tracy, *The Analogical Imagination: Christian Theology and the Culture of Pluralism* (New York: Basic, 1977); and Sebastian Tromp, S.J., *Corpus Christi Quaod Est Ecclesia*, trans. Ann Condit (New York: Vantage, 1960).

16. The language of "institution" must not undermine our appreciation for the fact that at its core the Church is a living being, as Pope Benedict XVI reminds (Pope Benedict XVI, *Joseph Ratzinger in* Communio, vol. 1, *The Unity of the Church* [Grand Rapids, Mich.: Eerdmans, 2010], 63).

17. *Catechism of the Catholic Church*, par. 96.

18. Dei Verbum 10; *Catechism of the Catholic Church*, par. 97.

19. *Catechism of the Catholic Church*, par. 85–86.

20. Lumen Gentium 11; *Catechism of the Catholic Church*, par. 1324.

21. The Church obliges the faithful to take part in the Eucharist on Sundays and feast days and, prepared by the sacrament of reconciliation, to receive it at least once a year, if possible during the Easter season. The Church also strongly encourages the faithful to receive the Holy Eucharist on every Sunday and on feast days, or more often still, even daily (*Catechism of the Catholic Church*, par. 1389).

22. From a joint online survey with Frank Beckwith, *www.chriscastaldo .com*, June 1, 2010.

23. One finds, for instance, a remarkable similarity between the views of John Calvin and those of the Catholic theologian Edward Schillebeeckx on the Spirit-empowered outworking of our union with Christ (*Institutes* 3.1.2., Edward Schillebeeckx, O.P., *Christ the Sacrament of the Encounter with God* [New York: Sheed and Ward, 1963], 15).

24. Evangelicals make this case in a variety of ways. For instance, Mark Saucy uses the *munus triplex Christi* (the threefold office of Christ as prophet, priest, and king) to suggest that the grounding of sacramental ecclesiology and soteriology is a misappropriation of incarnational theology ("Evangelicals, Catholics, and Orthodox Together: Is the Church the Extension of the Incarnation?" *Journal of the Evangelical Theological Society* 43 2000. : 193–212). In the vein of biblical theology is the work of Leonardo De Chirico, who compares the biblical adverbs *hapax* (a punctiliar event) and *mallon* (a continuous process) in light of Jesus' ascension, to suggest that the Catholic emphasis on Christological continuation confuses redemptive historical time distinctions ("The Blurring of Time Distinctions in Roman Catholicism," *Themelios* 29 2004. : 40–46). Similar to this is Herman Ridderbos's evaluation of Paul's "head" and "body" metaphors, the discontinuity of which, he argues, militates against the Catholic position

(Herman Ridderbos, *Paul: An Outline of His Theology*, trans. John Richard De Witt [Grand Rapids, Mich.: Eerdmans, 1975], 362–93). Kevin Vanhoozer's canonical linguistic approach is also illuminating, particularly as it differentiates the canonical script from the faith community (Kevin J. Vanhoozer, *The Drama of Doctrine: A Canonical Linguistic Approach to Christian Theology* [Louisville: Westminster John Knox, 2005]). For a classic Reformed defense of *sola scriptura* against the backdrop of Catholicism, see Herman Bavinck, *Reformed Dogmatics: Prolegomena*, vol. 1, ed. John Bolt, trans. John Vriend (Grand Rapids, Mich.: Baker, 2003), 457ff.

25. The words *supreme* and *ultimate* here are not to suggest that Scripture is superior to the person of Jesus. Rather Scripture reveals the truth of Jesus in written form and thus bears witness to his supremacy. One of the more readable and insightful explanations of the doctrine of Scripture alone is Keith A. Mathison's *The Shape of Sola Scriptura* (Moscow, Ida.: Canon, 2001).

26. Jesus is described as God's Word, for instance, in John's gospel: "In the beginning was the Word, and the Word was with God, and the Word was God" (John 1:1; cf. 1 Peter 1:23–25; 1 John 1:1; Rev. 19:13).

27. Through Scripture, God grants new life (John 5:24; Rom. 10:8–10; Eph. 1:13; James 1:18; cf. Heb. 4:12), reveals his will (Matt. 4:4; 7:21; 1 Tim. 3:6–16; 2 Tim. 2:15; 3:16–17; Heb. 1:2), and rules over his people (John 17:17, 1 Cor. 14:37; Phil. 2:16; 1 Tim. 5:17).

28. Alister McGrath, *Christianity's Dangerous Idea: The Protestant Revolution—A History from the Sixteenth Century to the Twenty-First* (New York: Harper Collins, 2007), 201.

29. R. C. Sproul, *Scripture Alone: The Evangelical Doctrine* (Phillipsburg, Pa.: P&R Publishing, 2005), 177.

30. Ibid., 180.

31. *Catechism of the Catholic Church*, par. 888–92.

32. Sproul, *Scripture Alone*, 189–90.

33. Literally "nude Scripture," also referred to as *nulla traditio*, "no tradition."

34. A. N. S. Lane, "Sola Scriptura? Making Sense of a Post-Reformation Slogan," in D. F. Wright and Philip Satterthwaite, eds., *A Pathway into the Holy Scriptures* (Grand Rapids, Mich.: Eerdmans, 1994), 324.

35. Harold O. J. Brown, *Reclaiming the Great Tradition*, ed. James S. Cutsinger (Downers Grove, Ill.: InterVarsity, 1997), 77.

36. The typical Catholic argument against the doctrine of *sola scriptura*, which asserts that it is self-refuting, trades on a misunderstanding of what the doctrine teaches. Scripture alone does not assert that the Bible is the only source of truth; it asserts that it is the only inspired, inerrant form of truth to which we have access today.

37. Ibid., 85.

38. Peter Feuerherd, *Holyland USA: A Catholic Ride through America's Evangelical Landscape* (New York: Crossroad, 2006), 72.

39. Some candid disclosure on this diversity, written by bishops of the Catholic Church, may be found in John Heaps, *A Love That Dares to Question: A Bishop Challenges His Church* (Grand Rapids, Mich.: Eerdmans, 1998); and Father Charles E. Coughlin, *Bishops versus the Pope* (Bloomfield Hills, Mich.: Helmet and Sword, 1969).

40. Avery Cardinal Dulles, S.J., *Magisterium: Teacher and Guardian of the Faith* (Naples: Sapientia, 2007), 10, emphasis added.

41. Augustine, *Grace and Free Choice* 6:15, quoted in Tony Lane, *Justification by Faith in Catholic-Protestant Dialogue: An Evangelical Assessment* (London: T & T Clark, 2002), 199.

42. For more on the relationship between faith and reason, see the encyclical of John Paul II titled *Fides et Ratio*, promulgated on September 14, 1998. To gain an understanding of the various ways that Catholics correlate faith and reason, see Father Thomas P. Rausch's helpful book *Reconciling Faith and Reason: Apologists, Evangelists, and Theologians in a Divided Church* (Collegeville, Minn.: Liturgical Press, 2000).

43. Scott W. Hahn, *Covenant and Communion: The Biblical Theology of Pope Benedict XVI* (Grand Rapids, Mich.: Brazos, 2009), 38.

44. If brilliant biblical theologians such as Benedict and Hahn make this exegetical move, what does it say about the many Catholics who rely on philosophical systems without a firm commitment to Scripture? By the way, Evangelicals should realize that we are not immune to this problem of imposing systematic formulations. We have our own scholastic traditions which can predetermine our conclusions.

45. The conceptual foundations of redemptive history operated according to a Hebraic matrix for many centuries, apart from Hellenistic categories. It is partly anachronistic to insist that such categories are now necessary in order for God's people to rightly understand divine revelation.

46. James R. Payton, *Getting the Reformation Wrong: Correcting Some Misunderstandings* (Downers Grove, Ill.: InterVarsity, 2010), 159.

47. Ibid., 156–57.

48. This is true, for instance, in the Church's position on the seven sacraments established by the Fourth Lateran Council in 1215, purgatory at the Council of Ferrara-Florence in 1438–39, the Immaculate Conception of Mary in *Ineffabilis Deus*, 1854, or her assumption in *Munificentissimus Deus*, 1950.

49. Martin Marty, *Martin Luther* (New York: Viking Penguin, 2004), xii.

50. Roland H. Bainton, *Here I Stand: A Life of Martin Luther* (Nashville: Abingdon, 1978), 49–50.

51. The Lutheran World Federation and the Roman Catholic Church, *The Joint Declaration on the Doctrine of Justification*, English-language ed. (Grand Rapids, Mich.: Eerdmans, 2000); Pope Benedict XVI, *Saint Paul* (San Francisco: Ignatius, 2009).

52. See the Vatican II document titled *Constitution on the Sacred Liturgy*. The word *perpetuated* is used in paragraph 47 (continue to 58 for the entire section). You'll also find the concept of eucharistic sacrifice in paragraphs 7, 8, and 83 (Walter M. Abbott, S.J., ed., *The Documents of Vatican II* [New York: Herder and Herder, 1966]). The current *Catechism of the Catholic Church* also conveys the idea in paragraphs 1371, 1372, 1410, and 1419. The eucharistic sacrifice is also applied to those who are in purgatory (par. 1371).

53. Hence the term *host* to describe the consecrated bread; it is the Latin word for "victim."

54. *Catechism of the Catholic Church*, par. 1367 (see also pars. 1407–10); *Constitution on the Sacred Liturgy*, par. 48ff. A particularly clear explanation is found in Ralph Martin's *The Catholic Church at the End of an Age, What Is the Spirit Saying?* (San Francisco: Ignatius, 1994), 167–72.

55. *Catechism of the Catholic Church*, pars. 1366, 1367, 1383. You can say that the Mass is a repetition of the Lord's Supper, but not a repetition of the death of Christ.

56. Now, years later, I have learned that provocation is not a virtue, especially in a pastor.

57. Please don't read into this analogy anything beyond the simple point that we may love those with whom we disagree. Nothing else correlates, except perhaps Frank Beckwith's affection for Bob Dylan.

CHAPTER 8: A RESPONSE TO EVANGELICALISM

1. See Mark A. Noll and Carolyn Nystrom, *Is the Reformation Over? An Evangelical Assessment of Contemporary Roman Catholicism* (Grand Rapids, Mich.: Baker, 2005).

2. This is a major theme in my book *The Unintended Reformation: How a Religious Revolution Secularized Society* (Belknap Press of Harvard Univ. Press, 2012).

3. For a useful introductory overview of this point, see Peter M. J. Stravinskas, *The Catholic Church and the Bible*, rev. ed. (San Francisco: Ignatius, 1987), esp. 57–106.

4. For an overview of the many complex issues involved in the historical formation of the Old and New Testaments from stories to Scripture to

canon, see Lee Martin McDonald, *The Biblical Canon: Its Origin, Transmission, and Authority* (Peabody, Mass.: Hendrickson, 2007); for the textual formation and transmission of the New Testament, including the Greek text as well as Syriac, Latin, and Coptic translations from the late second century, see Kurt Aland and Barbara Aland, *The Text of the New Testament: An Introduction to the Critical Editions and to the Theory and Practice of Modern Textual Criticism*, 2nd ed., trans. Erroll F. Rhodes (Grand Rapids, Mich.: Eerdmans, 1989), 14, 48–71 (with the phrase "living text" at 14, 69); and on the substantively inextricable and complex relationships between the content of the texts of the New Testament and their reception as canonical, see Brevard S. Childs, *The New Testament as Canon: An Introduction* (1984; Valley Forge, Pa.: Trinity Press International, 1994), in which Childs notes that because of the dearth of surviving evidence, the awareness had grown among New Testament biblical scholars by the end of the twentieth century "of the difficulty, if not impossibility, of reconstructing an adequate history of the New Testament's textual transmission in the period before AD 200" (p. 525). A brief overview of issues pertaining to canonical formation of the Old and New Testaments is Raymond Brown and Raymond F. Collins, "Canonicity," in *The New Jerome Biblical Commentary*, ed. Brown, Joseph A. Fitzmyer, and Roland E. Murphy (Upper Saddle River, N.J.: Prentice Hall, 1990), 1034–54, with mention of the Council of Hippo (AD 393) and the third and fourth Councils of Carthage (AD 397, 419) at pp. 1036, 1051.

For the entire tradition of patristic and medieval exegesis, nothing has surpassed the monumental study by Henri de Lubac, *Exégèse médiévale: les quatre sens de l'écriture*, 4 vols. (Paris: Aubier, 1959–64); on medieval preaching in particular, see Hughes Oliphant Old, *The Reading and Preaching of the Scriptures in the Worship of the Christian Church*, vol. 3, *The Medieval Church* (Grand Rapids, Mich.: Eerdmans, 1999); on the centrality of Scripture to Benedictine monasticism, see the classic work by Jean Leclercq, *The Love of Learning and the Desire for God: A Study of Monastic Culture*, trans. Catherine Misrahi (New York: Fordham Univ. Press, 1982); for early sixteenth-century scholarship among northern humanists, see the articles in *Biblical Humanism and Scholasticism in the Age of Erasmus*, ed. Erika Rummel (Leiden: E. J. Brill, 2008); on the abiding vitality of Catholic biblical exegesis before and after the Council of Trent in the sixteenth century, notwithstanding the constrictions that followed the Reformation, see Guy Bedouelle, "La Réforme catholique," in *Le temps des Réformes et la Bible*, ed. Bedouelle and Bernard Roussel (Paris: Beauchesne, 1989), 327–68; and for post-Tridentine preaching in particular, especially among the Jesuits, see the magisterial study by Marc Fumaroli, *L'Âge de l'éloquence: rhétorique et "res literaria" de la Renaissance au seuil de l'époque classique* (Geneva: Droz; Paris: Champion, 1980). The work of Raymond Brown can be sampled in his contributions to the *New Jerome Biblical Commentary*; see also Brown, *Introduction to the New Testament* (New York: Doubleday, 1997), and *The Death of the Messiah*, vol. 1 (New York: Doubleday, 1994); John Meier's monumental and ongoing study is *A Marginal Jew: Rethinking the Historical Jesus*, 4 vols. (New York: Doubleday, 1991–94; New Haven and London: Yale Univ. Press, 2001–9). A sense of Benedict XVI's depth and breadth as a biblical theologian is apparent throughout his oeuvre, including Joseph Ratzinger, *Introduction to Christianity*, trans. J. R. Foster (1969; San Francisco: Ignatius, 2004); and Ratzinger, *The Spirit of the Liturgy*, trans. John Saward (San Francisco: Ignatius, 2000).

5. Augustine, *De doctrina Christiana*, 1.43, in ibid., *Corpus Augustinianum Gissense*, ed. Cornelius Mayer, electronic ed., part 2 (Charlottesville, Va.: Intelex, 2000): "Homo itaque fide et spe et caritate subnixus eaque inconcusse retinens non indiget scripturis nisi ad alios instruendos."

6. On this point see especially the recent book by the distinguished sociologist of religion (and recent convert to Catholicism from Evangelical Protestantism) Christian Smith, *The Bible Made Impossible: Why Biblicism Is Not a Truly Evangelical Reading of Scripture* (Grand Rapids, Mich.: Brazos, 2011). I thank Chris for his comments on an earlier version of this essay and for many conversations about religion, theology, history, and sociology.

7. Martin Luther, *Disputatio excellentium ... Iohannis Eccii et D. Martini Lutheri Augustiniani* 1519. , in D. Martin Luther's *Werke. Kritische Gesamtausgabe* [hereafter WA], vol. 2 (Weimar: Hermann Böhlau, 1884), 279, lines 23–26.

8. Luther, *Tractatus de libertate Christiana* 1520. , in *WA*, vol. 7 (Weimar: Hermann Böhlaus Nachfolger, 1897), 51, lines 12–13: "Quaeres autem, 'Quod nam est verbum hoc, aut qua arte utendum est eo, cum tam multa sint verba dei?' " Luther translated his Latin into German differently, avoiding any reference to "so many words of God" for a wider audience: "Fragistu aber 'wilchs ist denn das wort, das solch grosse gnad gibt, Und wie sol ichs gebrauchen?' " (Luther, *Von der Freiheit eines Christenmenschen* 1520, in ibid., 22, lines 23–24).

9. For the Old Testament, eucharistic practices, and oral confession, see Ronald J. Sider, *Andreas Bodenstein von Karlstadt: The Development of His Thought, 1517–1525* (Leiden: E. J. Brill, 1974), 108–12, 143–46; for images, see Karlstadt, *Von abtuhung der Bylder, Vnd das keyn Betdler vnther den Christen seyn soll* 1522. , repr. in *Flugschriften der frühen Reformationsbewegung (1518–1524)*, vol. 1, ed. Adolf Laube et al. (Verduz: Topos Verlag, 1983), 105–27. Karlstadt refused to change his views, so his preaching was

restricted and a treatise that he had written (in a veiled manner) against Luther was confiscated and destroyed. See James S. Preus, *Carlstadt's Ordinaciones and Luther's Liberty: A Study of the Wittenberg Movement 1521–22* (Cambridge, Mass.: Harvard Univ. Press, 1974), 73–77.

10. For a list of no fewer than twenty-eight treatises by nine different opponents of Luther's view on the Lord's Supper, in Latin as well as German, published from 1525 through 1527, see *Luther's Works*, vol. 37, ed. Robert H. Fischer (Philadelphia: Fortress Press, 1961), 8–11; see also G. R. Potter, *Zwingli* (Cambridge: Cambridge Univ. Press, 1976), 296. The classic, magisterial work on the theological controversy is Walther Köhler, *Zwingli und Luther: Ihr Streit über das Abendmahl nach seinen politischen und religiösen Beziehungen*, 2 vols. (1924, 1953; New York and London: Johnson, 1971). For an overview of the early conflict between Luther and Zwingli, and its consequences, see Philip Benedict, *Christ's Churches Purely Reformed: A Social History of Calvinism* (New Haven and London: Yale Univ. Press, 2002), 15–48. That the theologians at Marburg agreed on fourteen of fifteen disputed points only underscores how important was the disagreement about this one issue, which, through centuries of variegated relations between Lutherans and Reformed Protestants, has had enormous political and social consequences down to the present.

11. On Zwingli and the earliest Swiss Anabaptists, see Potter, *Zwingli*, 160–97; for a recent, thorough overview of the origins of Swiss Anabaptism, see C. Arnold Snyder, "Swiss Anabaptism: The Beginnings, 1523–1525," in *A Companion to Anabaptism and Spiritualism, 1521–1700*, ed. John D. Roth and James M. Stayer (Leiden: E. J. Brill, 2007), 45–81. For the Zurich city council's mandate of March 7, 1526, sentencing obstinate Anabaptists to death by drowning, see *Quellen zur Geschichte der Täufer in der Schweiz*, vol. 1, ed. Leonhard von Muralt and Walter Schmid (Zurich: S. Hirzel-Verlag, 1952), 180–81; see also Snyder, *Anabaptist History and Theology: An Introduction* (Kitchener, Ont.: Pandora, 1995), 60.

12. On the Peasants' War, see Peter Blickle, *The Revolution of 1525: The German Peasants' War from a New Perspective*, trans. Thomas A. Brady Jr. and H. C. Erik Midelfort (Baltimore and London: Johns Hopkins Univ. Press, 1981), as well as Tom Scott, "Hubmaier, Schappeler, and Hergot on Social Revolution," in *The Impact of the Reformation: Princes, Clergy, and People*, ed. Bridget Heal and Ole Peter Grell (Aldershot, U.K., and Burlington, Vt.: Ashgate, 2008), 15–36; on Thomas Müntzer, see Hans-Jürgen Goertz, *Thomas Müntzer: Apocalyptic, Mystic, and Revolutionary*, trans. Jocelyn Jaquiery, ed. Peter Matheson (Edinburgh: T. & T. Clark, 1993), and Abraham Friesen, *Thomas Muentzer, a Destroyer of the Godless: The Making*

of a Sixteenth-Century Religious Revolutionary (Berkeley and Los Angeles: Univ. of California Press, 1990). For Hans Hergot and Michael Gaismair, see "Michael Gaismairs Tiroler Landesordnung" 1526. , and Hans Hergot, *Von der neuen Wandlung eines christlichen Lebens* 1527. , in *Flugschriften der Bauernkriegszeit*, ed. Adolf Laube and Hans Werner Seiffert (Berlin: Akademie-Verlag, 1978), 139–43, 547–57; Blickle, *Revolution of 1525*, pp. 145–54; Scott, "Hubmaier," in *Impact*, ed. Heal and Grell, pp. 32–36; and Walter Klaassen, *Michael Gaismair: Revolutionary and Reformer* (Leiden: E. J. Brill, 1978).

13. For two examples, see Mark U. Edwards Jr., *Luther and the False Brethren* (Stanford: Stanford Univ. Press, 1975), 197, and Elsie Anne McKee, *Katharina Schütz Zell*, vol. 1 (Leiden: E. J. Brill, 1999), 265, 273. Edwards distinguishes between "central reformation principles" and "issues such as acceptable ceremonial practice, the real presence in the Lord's Supper, the separation of secular and spiritual authority, and the relation between law and gospel" (197), and McKee contrasts "the Reformation basics" with "the secondary issues which were debated among Protestants," relegating to the latter category the boundaries between different groups, the toleration of those with different views, the Lord's Supper, baptism, and church order (vol. 1, 265). The problem of minimizing the differences that in fact concretely (and often with hostility) divided Christians among themselves characterizes the entire conceptualization of the Reformation era in Scott Hendrix, *Recultivating the Vineyard: The Reformation Agendas of Christianization* (Louisville and London: Westminster John Knox, 2004).

14. See Brad S. Gregory, *Salvation at Stake: Christian Martyrdom in Early Modern Europe* (Cambridge, Mass., and London: Harvard Univ. Press, 1999); Gregory, "Anabaptist Martyrdom: Imperatives, Experience, and Memorialization," in *A Companion to Anabaptism and Spiritualism, 1521–1700*, ed. John D. Roth and James M. Stayer (Leiden and Boston: E. J. Brill, 2007), 467–506.

15. Huldrych Zwingli, *Von Clarheit vnnd gewüsse oder vnbetrogliche des worts gottes* 1522. , in *Huldreich Zwinglis Sämtliche Werke*, vol. 1, ed. Emil Egli and Georg Finsler, in *Corpus Reformatorum*, vol. 88 (Leipzig: M. Heinsius, 1905), 379, lines 18–19.

16. Luther, *Vom Abendmahl Christi, Bekenntnis* 1528. , in *WA*, vol. 26 (Weimar: Hermann Böhlaus Nachfolger, 1909), 317, lines 20–22.

17. For a concise overview, see Richard C. Gamble, "Calvin's Controversies," in *The Cambridge Companion to John Calvin*, ed. Donald K. McKim (Cambridge: Cambridge Univ. Press, 2004), 188–203; see also Jean-François Gilmont, *John Calvin and the Printed Book*, trans. Karin Maag (Kirksville,

Mo.: Truman State Univ. Press, 2005), 69–73, 93–107. On Luther's doctrinal conflicts with magisterial and radical Protestants, see Edwards, *Luther and the False Brethren*.

18. For the division between Gnesio-Lutherans and Philippists prior to the Formula of Concord, see Irene Dingel, "The Culture of Conflict in the Controversies Leading to the Formula of Concord (1548–1580)," in *Lutheran Ecclesiastical Culture, 1550–1675*, ed. Robert Kolb (Leiden: E. J. Brill, 2008), 15–64; on conflicts between Calvinists and Arminians in the Dutch Republic and England, see Benedict, *Christ's Churches*, 305–16.

19. William Chillingworth, *The Religion of Protestants a Safe Way to Salvation* ... (Oxford: Leonard Lichfield, 1638), 375. On radical Protestantism during the English Revolution, see Christopher Hill, *The World Turned Upside Down: Radical Ideas during the English Revolution* (Harmondsworth, U.K.: Penguin, 1972); *Radical Religion in the English Revolution*, ed. J. F. McGregor and Barry Reay (London and New York: Oxford Univ. Press, 1984); Nicholas McDowell, *The English Radical Imagination: Culture, Religion, and Revolution, 1630–1660* (Oxford: Clarendon Press, 2003); and Ann Hughes, *Gangraena and the Struggle for the English Revolution* (Oxford: Oxford Univ. Press, 2004).

20. On religious diversity in the Dutch Republic, see *The Emergence of Tolerance in the Dutch Republic*, ed. C. Berkvens-Stevelinck, J. Israel, and G. H. M. Posthumus Meyjes (Leiden: E. J. Brill, 1997); *Calvinism and Religious Toleration in the Dutch Golden Age*, ed. R. Po-chia Hsia and H. F. K. van Nierop (Cambridge: Cambridge Univ. Press, 2002); S. Zijlstra, *Om de ware gemeente en de oude gronden: Geschiedenis van de dopersen in de Nederlanden, 1531–1675* (Hilversum: Uitgeverij Verloren, and Leeuwarden: Fryske Akademy, 2000); Benjamin J. Kaplan, *Divided by Faith: Religious Conflict and the Practice of Toleration in Early Modern Europe* (Cambridge, Mass., and London: Belknap Press of Harvard Univ. Press, 2007), 172–76, 237–39, 241–43, 321–24.

21. Colonial North America pullulated with all sorts of divergent Protestant truth claims and correlative established churches, dissenter denominations, millenarian expectations, and prophetic assertions. See, for example, David D. Hall, *Worlds of Wonder, Days of Judgment: Popular Religious Belief in Early New England* (New York: Knopf, 1989); Jon Butler, *Awash in a Sea of Faith: Christianizing the American People* (Cambridge, Mass., and London: Harvard Univ. Press, 1990); and Erik R. Seeman, *Pious Persuasions: Laity and Clergy in Eighteenth-Century New England* (Baltimore and London: Johns Hopkins Univ. Press, 1999), in which Seeman notes (p. 204) that "[i]n the last decades of the eighteenth century New England's religious culture consisted

of a bounteous and almost bewildering variety of beliefs and practices," apart from the even greater variety when the mid-Atlantic and southern states are considered. The "democratization" of American Protestantism in the first third of the nineteenth century "produced not just pluralism but also striking diversity. The flexibility and innovation of religious organizations made it possible for an American to find an amenable group no matter what his or her preference in belief, practice, or institutional structure" (Nathan O. Hatch, *The Democratization of American Christianity* [New Haven and London: Yale Univ. Press, 1989], 65). The same American Protestant pluralism is confirmed more broadly in the work of scholars such as George Marsden and Mark Noll, the latter of whom notes that in the U.S., "[b]y one recent count, there are now nineteen separate Presbyterian denominations, thirty-two Lutheran, thirty-six Methodist, thirty-seven Episcopal or Anglican, sixty Baptist, and 241 Pentecostal" (Mark A. Noll, *The Work We Have to Do: A History of Protestants in America* [Oxford: Oxford Univ. Press, 2000], 124).

22. Desiderius Erasmus, *De libero arbitrio diatribe, sive collatio* (Basel: Johannes Froben, 1524), sig. b1. On the inextricability of rival claims about the testimony of the Holy Spirit from Reformation-era exegetical disputes, see the recent work by Susan E. Schreiner, *Are You Alone Wise? The Search for Certainty in the Early Modern Era* (Oxford and New York: Oxford Univ. Press, 2011).

23. "Wer des glaubens gefeilet hat, der mag darnach glewben was er wil, gilt eben gleich" (Luther, *Sermon Von dem Sacrament des leibs vnd bluts Christi, widder die Schwarmgeister* 1526. , in *WA*, vol. 19 [Weimar: Hermann Böhlaus Nachfolger, 1897], 484, lines 19–20).

24. J[ohn] M[ilton], *A Treatise of Civil power in Ecclesiastical causes Shewing That it is not lawfull for any power on earth to compell in matters of religion* (London: Tho[mas] Newcomb, 1659), 7–8, 9.

Chapter 9: Evangelicalism Rejoinder

1. Augustine, *De Doctrina Christiana*, 2.6.7. Augustine explores challenges of interpreting obscure passages in several chapters of Book II and into Book III.

Chapter 10: A Journey to Anglicanism

1. C. S. Lewis, *Mere Christianity* (New York: Macmillan, 1952), 36.

2. Ibid., xi.

3. Scholars by no means agree on the meaning of "the breaking of bread" in Acts 2:42. Some see verse 42 referring to Holy Communion, while verse 46 refers to ordinary meals. This is because of the definite article rendered

in some translations, "the breaking of the loaf." It is my contention that this is referring to Holy Communion. See Ajith Fernando, *The NIV Application Commentary, Acts* (Grand Rapids, Mich.: Zondervan, 1998), 120 and n. 5 for a discussion. In a sermon at Christ the King Anglican Church, Professor Frank Thielman made it clear that verse 42 is stronger than merely eating together (November 16, 2008).

4. The early inauguration of Holy Communion is discussed in Kenneth E. Kirk, *The Apostolic Ministry* (New York: Morehouse-Gorham, 1946), 247–49.

5. Alister McGrath, *J. I. Packer: A Biography* (Grand Rapids, Mich.: Baker, 1997), 17.

6. Lyle W. Dorsett, *And God Came In: The Extraordinary Story of Joy Davidman, Her Life and Marriage to C. S. Lewis.* Published originally by Macmillan in 1983, it has continually remained in print. Most recently, a new edition with a new foreword and afterword came out in 2010 as part of the Hendrickson Classic Christian Biography Series.

7. Lyle W. Dorsett, *Seeking the Secret Place: The Spiritual Formation of C. S. Lewis* (Grand Rapids, Mich.: Brazos, 2004).

8. See C. S. Lewis, *English Literature in the Sixteenth Century, Excluding Drama* (London: Oxford Univ. Press, 1954), which became the academic fruit of his years of study of this period.

9. C. S. Lewis, *Letters to Malcolm: Chiefly on Prayer* (London: Bless, 1964), 133.

10. An excellent book on this subject of real presence is John Jefferson Davis, *Worship and the Reality of God: An Evangelical Theology of Real Presence* (Downers Grove, Ill.: InterVarsity, 2010).

11. See Dorsett, *Seeking the Secret Place*, 82 and n. 24.

12. See Thaddeus Barnum, *Never Silent: How the Third World Missionaries Are Now Bringing the Gospel to Us* (Colorado Springs: Eleison, 2008).

13. Peter C. Moore, *A Church to Believe In* (Solon, Ohio: Latimer, 1994), 157.

14. Ibid.

Chapter 11: A Response to Anglicanism

1. I gladly thank Steve Jamieson, reference and systems librarian, and James Pakala, library director, both of the J. Oliver Buswell Jr. Library at Covenant Theological Seminary, for reference help.

2. Robert A. Peterson, *Election and Free Will: God's Gracious Choice and Our Responsibility* (Phillipsburg, N.J.: P&R, 2007), 133.

3. *Evangelical Dictionary of Theology*, ed. Walter A. Elwell, 2nd ed. (Grand Rapids, Mich.: Baker Academic, 2001), s.v. "Anglican Communion," 62.

4. *Encyclopedia of Christianity*, ed. John Bowden (Oxford: Oxford Univ. Press, 2005), s.v. "Anglicanism," 46.

5. *The Oxford Dictionary of the Christian Church* (Oxford: Oxford Univ. Press, 2005), s.v. "Anglicanism," 67.

6. *Sacramentum Mundi*, ed. Karl Rahner et al. (Basle-Montreal: Hermann-Herder-Foundation, 1968), s.v. "Anglican Communion," 36.

7. Gerald Bray, "Why I Am an Anglican," in *Why We Belong: Stories of Evangelical Unity and Denominational Diversity*, ed. Anthony Chute, Christopher W. Morgan, and Robert A. Peterson (Wheaton, Ill.: Crossway, forthcoming in 2012), 1.

8. Ibid., 5.

9. *Encyclopedia of Christianity*, ed. John Bowden, s.v. "Anglicanism," 45.

10. Ibid.

11. Bray, "Why I Am an Anglican," 8–9.

12. Ibid., 7.

13. Ibid., 15.

14. *The Encyclopedia of Christianity*, ed. Erwin Fahlbusch et al. (Grand Rapids, Mich.: Eerdmans, 1999), s.v. "Anglican Communion," 58.

15. John Hick, ed., *The Myth of God Incarnate* (Philadelphia: Westminster, 1977; copyright SCM Press, 1977), x.

16. Ibid., ix.

17. Michael Green, ed., *The Truth of God Incarnate* (Grand Rapids, Mich.: Eerdmans, 1977), 13.

18. Ibid., 14.

19. *Report*, 2, London (1958), 44, as cited in *Sacramentum Mundi*, s.v. "Anglican Communion," 36–37.